A HISTORY OF EDUCATIONAL THOUGHT

History of the generations

On this date of which I used this book . . .

9/25/01 → Our nation is still feeling the damage from the World Trade Center terrorist attack. It will be strange and unsettling to go home and not see the Twin Towers standing as I fly over New York City. The economy is in recession

A HISTORY OF EDUCATIONAL THOUGHT

BY

PERCIVAL R. COLE

M.A. (Sydney)

Teacher's Diploma (London), Ph.D. (Columbia); F.C.P., Vice-Principal, Sydney Teachers' College, and Lecturer in Education, University of Sydney; sometime Instructor in the History of Education, Teachers' College of Columbia University; Visiting Carnegie Professor of International Relations at the Universities of Hawaii and Washington, 1929

GREENWOOD PRESS, PUBLISHERS

WESTPORT, CONNECTICUT

The Library of Congress has catalogued this publication as follows:

Library of Congress Cataloging in Publication Data

Cole, Percival Richard, 1879-1948.
A history of educational thought.

Reprint of the 1931 ed.
Includes bibliographies.
1. Education--History. 2. Education--Philosophy. 3. Educators. I. Title.
LA21.C66 1972 370'.9 74-138214
ISBN 0-8371-5569-X

Originally published in 1931
by Oxford University Press, London

Reprinted with the permission
of Oxford University Press

First Greenwood Reprinting 1972

Library of Congress Catalogue Card Number 74-138214

ISBN 0-8371-5569-X

Printed in the United States of America

CONTENTS

BOOK III. EDUCATIONAL THOUGHT IN THE MIDDLE AGES

BOOK IV. RENAISSANCE EDUCATIONAL THOUGHT

BOOK V. SOME ASPECTS OF MODERN EDUCATIONAL THOUGHT

INTRODUCTION

WHAT is the history of education? It is, in the first place, the outcome of an application of the historical method to education, whatever that may be. As to the historical method, its canons are fairly well known. It is scientific. It does not treat all authorities as of equal value. It is not content with secondary authorities, when primary sources may be consulted. It recognizes the possibility that even primary source-material may be vitiated by the corruption of texts, as well as by the ignorance or bias of the authors. It avoids generalizations which are not founded upon the adequate examination of facts; in short, it has an inductive character. Yet, if these canons of method be granted, there remains the further question—What is education?

Clearly, the scope and limits of the history of education depend entirely upon the definition of education itself. There is, unfortunately, no accepted definition of education; or rather, there are so many definitions that the offer of another is inevitable. What is sought at present is the most useful definition for the purposes of the historical investigator. For the present purpose, indeed, some definitions, although good enough in themselves, are of little value. For example, education has been defined as a process aiming at the harmonious development of the faculties; but a history of this process would be inadequate as a history of education. For historical purposes, the definition should refer to society as well as to the individual. When any given field is viewed by the historian of education, he perceives that the people are divided into two main classes, those of mature mind, and those whose mind is in process of development towards maturity. Accordingly, the reader of these pages will understand that their scope and limits are determined by the following definition: education is the process by which the more mature members of a community train and instruct the less mature, in order that the latter may conform to certain standards, and inherit certain social acquisitions.

If the definition offered be accepted, it follows that the history of education involves not a simple, but a twofold investigation. Something must be known of the aims, the standards, and the general civilization of a community, before the means of education which it adopts become intelligible. This is particularly true of the old Greek period, because of the radical contrast of many of the intellectual, moral, aesthetic, religious, and economic ideas of the ancient Greeks with our own. The old Greek civilization is the key to the old Greek education. In these pages, accordingly, the discussion of the means of education is regarded as secondary to the analysis of the ideals and standards of civilization.

There still remains the question, why should the history of education be studied? Essentially, no doubt, in order that the aims, methods, and existing institutions of education may be better understood. The present is essentially the age of the historical method. The historical mode of approach is universally adopted in the study of law, politics, ethics, and philosophy. For like reasons it should be utilized in the study of education. The past illumines the present. Without history, one may learn what a thing is; but not whence it is, nor why it is, nor what it is on the way to become. History alone reveals not merely structure, but life. The history of education is an account of the living growth of educational aims, methods, curricula, and institutions, without which they would appear merely as empirical, static, inanimate.

Along with the revelation of education as a living growth through the ages, the history of education has certain secondary uses which are themselves of the greatest importance. In the first place it presents an opportunity of pioneer work. There are few subjects in which there remains so much virgin ground, still untrodden by the investigator. For example, nobody has done justice to the educational ideas of Roger Bacon. Hence, to the scientific mind, the history of education offers abundant opportunity for the patient extrication and elucidation of facts. It is a quarry from which the truth is still to be hewn.

Secondly, the history of education may be converted into an instrument of culture. It has been argued above that the subject consists, in part, of an analysis of standards of civilization. Can the growth of the higher mental powers be stimulated better than by undertaking such a task? Is there a more cultural occupation, for example, than the analysis of ancient Greek ideals? Surely the progressive examination of social standards throughout the ages is worthy of the widest and deepest learning. Indeed, the historian of education is constantly confounded by a sense of the utter impossibility of doing full justice to his work. Moreover, there is a second way in which his subject exercises a cultural influence. It is more than a coincidence that the list of writers of primary works upon education should include the world's greatest intellects, Plato, Aristotle, Quintilian, Milton, Locke,

Rousseau, and Kant. To the works of these, and such as these, the student is referred for his material. How many would have failed of contact with the greatest thinkers of the past, were it not for their study of the history of education?

Lastly, the history of education has a distinct professional value to the teacher. He need not think himself above profiting from Plato's discussion of school literature, from Aristotle's examination of educational values, or even from Quintilian's suggestions about method. He may learn even from the mistakes in the psychology of Locke, or in the sociology of Rousseau. In short, he can scarcely study the history of education, without becoming a better teacher.

The work of writing the following History of Educational Thought has extended over a period of more than twenty years. Certain chapters are founded entirely upon the author's study of the Latin texts of Ausonius, Capella, the Theodosian Code, and Alsted. In large part the remainder of the book is the result of a direct study of the source-material available in various languages. A fuller treatment of two of the chapters may be had in the author's monograph, *Herbart and Froebel, an Attempt at Synthesis*. In this and in a second monograph, *Social Foundations of Greek Education*, may be found references to numerous sources of information. For the convenience of students, small sectional bibliographies of British and American works have been inserted in the present volume, which it has not been thought advisable to burden with detailed references. A portion of the book has appeared previously in printed form in *Studies in the History of Education*, in *Schooling*, or in *The Sydney Morning Herald*. To the last-mentioned journal the author is indebted for permission to republish the final chapter, British and American Paths to Culture.

A SELECT BIBLIOGRAPHY

A

Adams: *Evolution of Educational Theory.*
Adamson: *Guide to the History of Education.*
—— *Short History of Education.*
Boyd: *History of Western Education.*
Compayré: *History of Pedagogy* (translated Payne).
Graves: *A Student's History of Education.*
Monroe, P. (edited): *Cyclopedia of Education.*
—— *Source Book of Greek and Roman Education.*
—— *Text Book in the History of Education.*
Watson (edited): *The Encyclopaedia and Dictionary of Education.*

B

Aspinwell: *Outlines of the History of Education.*
Beatty: *Brief History of Education.*
Boyer: *History of Education.*
Chrisman: *The Historical Child.*
Clough: *Short History of Education.*
Cubberley: *History of Education.*
—— *Readings in the History of Education.*
Davidson: *History of Education.*
Emerson: *Evolution of the Educational Ideal.*
Monroe, P.: *Brief Course in the History of Education.*
Painter: *History of Education.*
Seeley: *History of Education.*
Taylor: *Syllabus of History of Education.*
Wodehouse: *A Survey of the History of Education.*

See also:

Burnham and Suzzallo: *History of Education as a Professional Subject.*
Cubberley: *Syllabus in the History of Education.*
Monroe, W. S.: *A Bibliography of Education.*
Norton: *Scope and Aims of History of Education.*

BOOK I

GREEK EDUCATIONAL THOUGHT

I

ETHICAL PRINCIPLES UNDERLYING GREEK EDUCATION

ONE of the chief functions of education, if not the chief of all its functions, is the making of character. This generalization, however, does not imply the existence of any great uniformity among historical systems of education. It is, indeed, known that ideals of character may be very differently conceived at different times and within different social groups. The good Spartan, if such were the will of the Council of Elders, exposed his infant child on the slopes of Mount Taygetus. Yet it is safe to predict that the moral ideals of any community must necessarily form an integral part of its educational theory. People have always educated their children according to some conception of goodness, whether the good life be held to lie in conformity to custom or in progress, in citizenship, or in individual perfection. It is possible, doubtless, to study the practice of education apart from its theory; but such a procedure is inadvisable, since a theory of education is simply an account of what is considered to be the best educational practice.

The ethical principles of ancient Hellas were closely bound up with the idea of the State. The modern view of the State tends to hypostatize it either as a meddlesome institution which tends to encroach upon the rights of the individual, or as a piece of machinery for social betterment, the possibilities of which might be very well utilized to an increasing extent. In either case the State is regarded as a social organ only; not as equivalent to society itself. The Greek state, however, was a true organism rather than a mere organization. Apart from the State a man had no rational existence—he had *mere* life, not *good* life. As Aristotle pointed out, whereas the older life of the Greek people in village communities had provided them with what is necessary for existence, the organization of the polis or city-state enabled them to seek not only what is necessary, but what is good.

The Greek was the first to reconcile in a satisfactory way the antinomy of freedom and necessity. To him at his best the laws were not tyrants, but, in the phrase of Aristotle, 'reason without passion'. Plato describes them as the friends of Socrates; and as no tyrants.

Aristotle calls them no taskmasters, but saviours. The service of the laws was the service of the gods. Greek law has been described as less abstract than Roman, less rigid than Hebrew, a living voice ranging through sympathetic admonition to stern command. To Plato and Aristotle the State signified the centre of the spiritual life. The goodness of the State seemed preferable even to its wealth and power; its greatness lay not in its bigness. The State was the people.

Ideals of the good life, then, were primarily political and social. They were equivalent, in fact, to concepts of the rights and duties of citizens. By such philosophers as Plato and Aristotle, ethical ideals were subsumed under the notion of justice. In the words of Aristotle: 'Justice, we say, is a social virtue, and all others must yield her the precedence'. Justice, according to Plato, is not merely to tell truth and pay one's debts, nor is it the interest of the stronger, nor a sort of honour among thieves. Rather is it the excellence of the soul, a sublime simplicity, a moderation, a harmony, identical with wisdom and virtue, a highest good, a confluence of wisdom, courage, and temperance, a bearing of one another's burdens. Education was considered to be the means of attaining this principle of justice within the limits of the polis.

It must not be supposed that the entire subordination of the individual to the State commended itself to the Athenian as it did to the Spartan mind. In the Platonic ethics, the individual good of a man was identical with his good as a citizen. Hellenic virtue had its individual as well as its social aspect. It was a health of the soul, a good habit, a love of true beauty and order, a harmony and temperance, apt to be impeded either by riches or by poverty, a just and perfect unity of the manifold elements of the soul. The Greek conception of the relation of ethics to education may be gathered from two sentences of Aristotle (*Pol.* iii. 13; and iv. 17). 'Virtue and education may most justly dispute the right of being considered as the necessary means of enabling the citizens to live well.' 'It will be found to be education and morals that are almost the whole which go to make up a good man, and that the same qualities will make a good citizen or a good king.'

Not only did the Greeks identify the good man with the good citizen; they came near the identification of the good with the beautiful. Greek morality, on the whole, was a kind of beauty, ethics a kind of aesthetics, God the great artist. Education in art was held to be, in a peculiar sense, education of character. Hence Plato suggests a censorship not only of words, but of rhythms, melodies, and all sights and sounds by which boys are environed. A beautiful simplicity is to characterize all educational music and gymnastic. On the other hand, the Greek mind showed little realization of the Hebraic sense of sublimity and holiness, the Puritan conviction of sin, or the Kantian conception of duty as a categorical imperative. In fact, a general repugnance to extremes was characteristic of Hellenic thought. It was held that education ought to preserve individuals from effeminacy by an early severity of discipline, and from brutalization by an atmosphere of beauty and grace. The relation of the aesthetic to the ethical is beautifully depicted in the words of Plato (*Rep.* iii. 401, trans. Jowett): 'Let our artists rather be those who are gifted to discern the true nature of the beautiful and graceful; then will our youth dwell in a land of health, amid fair sights and sounds, and receive the good in everything; and beauty, the effluence of fair works, shall flow into the eye and ear, like a health-giving breeze from a purer region; and insensibly draw the soul from earliest years into likeness and sympathy with the beauty of reason.'

Such were the ethical principles which, in a measure, governed the education of the ancient Greeks; but the question remains by what sanctions were such principles safeguarded. Philosophical ideals have little influence upon the conduct of the many who fail to guide their lives by reason. In modern times, the religious sanction is probably more effective than any other as a regulative influence upon life; but the ancient Greek religion had little connexion with either morality or creed. The young Greek might be induced to regulate his life according to the precepts of philosophy; but hardly according to the commands of the gods, whose example was obviously defective, or with a view to a future life, of which he had but a vague and shadowy notion.

The principal safeguards of conduct were in fact law and custom, patriotism, the conception of moral nobility as internal, the idea that pleasure accompanies the good life, a popular belief in Fate and the Furies, moral teaching based upon Homer and the theogeny of Hesiod, a conception of family honour, a desire for fame after death, and a close supervision of the whole period of boyhood by trusted slaves called pedagogues. It cannot be argued that these safeguards of conduct proved generally adequate to maintain a high standard of moral action. Greek life seems to have been purest before the philosophers had destroyed the simple though illogical faith of the people in their old gods. The somewhat exaggerated antithesis drawn in the *Clouds* of Aristophanes between the modesty and propriety of boyhood in earlier Athens and the immoral reaction of a more sophisticated period is in part the perennial plaint of age against youth, but probably in part just. The Athenians understood morality better than they practised it; their sublime philosophy cohabited with degrading vice.

II

THE INFLUENCE OF GREEK RELIGION ON EDUCATION

THE primitive mind tends to invest inanimate objects with its own characteristics and powers. If a savage be injured by the falling of a tree, or be swept away by a current, it is clear to him and to his tribe that the tree or the stream has sought to do him an injury. The tribe may indeed have reached the point of distinguishing between the stream or the tree and the spirit which inhabits or which patronizes it. In any case there is a universal tendency among primitive communities to presuppose that each grove, pond, hill, stream, or cavern is the special concern of some spirit or demon. The general name given to this tendency is animism.

It has frequently been observed that young children tend to treat inanimate objects as if they were sentient. Even an adult who stubs his foot accidentally may become incensed with the stone which has been the innocent cause of his undoing. He may conceivably attempt to punish the stone by throwing it roughly against a larger stone, or by hurling it into the depths of a pond. Thus animism may be regarded as a natural and almost instinctive form of belief. It is the simplest and least reflective form of religion.

Primitive animism invariably exercises a cruel and depressing influence upon education. Not content with bestowing mysterious powers upon natural or imaginary objects, it further assumes that the disposition of the spirit world towards man is baleful and malevolent. Evidently, when times are good the savage pays little attention to the supernatural, but in times of crisis or catastrophe he remembers his ju-ju, threatens or beseeches his medicine-man, and sacrifices a chicken or goat in order to appease the demon whose anger he deems himself to have aroused. Nor is this to be wondered at; for it was in times of trial that the ancient Hebrews remembered Jehovah, and it is in time of war that the churches are most filled to-day. If it be granted that the savage neglects the spirit world in time of prosperity, but endeavours to propitiate it in time of adversity, then the gloom and cruelty of his beliefs is readily understood. His religion becomes fetish-worship. He feels himself to be surrounded by devils who are easily offended, and who can only be placated by sacrifice and suffering.

What, then, of the Greek religion? In its plethora of local nymphs and satyrs, its dryads and hamadryads, its dark tales of Hades, its misty legends of the Titans and thundering Zeus, the Greek religion may be likened to primitive animism and terrorism. Yet terrorism was by no means the salient characteristic of the Greek religion, which was redeemed, firstly, by the charm of beauty. The poetry of Homer had surrounded the field of the supernatural by an ocean of fantasy. Hellenic religion became a great aesthetic influence, a means of training the young in the appreciation of ideas of nobility and fairness, a beautiful aura clinging to the orbit of the soul. A second advantage of the Greek religion lay in the establishment of conventional modes of communication with material and spiritual forces. In a storm the Greek crew might appeal to Poseidon, that he should allay the waters, so that the ship might come safely to port. Similarly, the husbandman by paying due observance to Demeter might secure for himself a good harvest. The whole environment of the Greek was transmuted into 'a pantheon of fair and concrete personalities'. The sun became Helios or Apollo; the uncontrollable and capricious heavens, Zeus; the seas, Poseidon; the earth, Demeter. Thus, by assimilating nature to himself, the Greek made himself at one with nature. In this way his religion prevented him from regarding nature after the manner of primitive man, as merely inimical and catastrophic.

The Greek religion, then, linked the young with poetry and nature; but more than this, unlike modern churches, it educated the citizen as such. In Homeric times, it was closely associated with the institution of royalty. In the polis or city-state it formed a bond of unity, and habitually symbolized state activities. The absence of a fixed creed, and the comparative indifference to moral commandments, left religion free to concentrate upon ceremonies, which were frequently held in connexion with political affairs. For example, at Athens, the enrolment of youths in the Ephebic corps for military training became an occasion of impressive ceremonies in the temples. The state, rather than the individual soul, was the special care of the gods.

It cannot be argued, however, that religion influenced the private morality of the Greek to the same extent as it affected his love of beauty, his appreciation of nature, and his sense of civic obligation. No doubt his character must have been influenced by the solemn processions in which he joined, by the choral dances in which he took part, and by the sacrifices and acts of veneration at which his assistance was required. On the other hand, his religion provided few of the sanctions which enforce morality. The example of the gods was bad, nor did Plato underestimate the danger to the young who were accustomed to read in the school copy of Homer that God is the author of evil, false, subject to change, and swayed by evil passions. Nor was the Greek youth restrained by the hope of happiness, or by the fear of punishment in a future life. His hell was without terror, his heaven without ecstasy. He was bound by no rigid decalogue. Unlike the Hebrew, he failed to apprehend either the vileness of sin or the beauty of holiness. He was trained to reverence and to moderation, but not to fixity of principle or to a realization of his own unworthiness before God.

It is now apparent that the Greek religion, as an educational influence, was effective in training for citizenship, and in promoting a taste for the beautiful both in art and in nature; but that it failed to establish firm moral principles, fixed beliefs, or inexorable habits. It remains to be observed that the more thoughtful and critical among the Greeks themselves perceived the errors and contradictions in which the ancient stories of the gods abounded. Plato and others attempted with some success to construct a more reasonable theology than that which was founded upon Homer and tradition. The latter was found wanting by Socrates, and was rendered unrecognizable by Plato. Henceforth, the more thoughtful and better educated among the Greeks, those who attended the philosophical schools, began to seek in philosophy a substitute for religion. Philosophers were sometimes employed even for the consolation of the aged, the sick, or the dying. They founded semi-religious sects, opened schools, and made converts. Plato, the greatest of all philosophers, had pointed out that the right and the good are autonomous; and that an act is not right because the gods do it, but rather the gods do it because it is right. Religious speculation was transformed and elevated by Plato's theory that God does only what is good. Henceforth a new avenue of religious thought was open to the philosophic Greek. The majority of men, however, are not philosophically inclined; and many Greeks, dissatisfied with the naïve religious assumptions of the past, yet demanding a less abstract religion than that of the philosophers, turned their feet into the paths of mysticism, a type of religious life which culminated at length in the Neo-Platonism of Alexandria.

In conclusion, the influence of the Greek religion upon the young was not terroristic, but rather aesthetic. It was exerted through a series of ceremonies, dances, games, dramas, public and private functions, sacrifices, and libations. Its educational appeal was ceremonial and mediatory; not doctrinal, dedicatory, nor moral. Its ethical principles and its system of rewards and punishments were alike inadequate, with the result that in the end the allegiance of seekers after religious truth was transferred either to philosophy or to mysticism.

III

GREEK EDUCATION AND THE STATE

THE fundamental question concerning education is: How is the individual related to society? Upon the answer given to this question the character of the education of the young depends. Children are individuals not yet completely socialized. If the individual is subservient to the community, his education must be through discipline. Such was the view maintained in ancient Sparta. If society exists for the sake of individuals, then intellectual culture becomes its end. Such a conception of education dominated cosmopolitan Greek education from the time of Alexander the Great. If the relation between the individual and society is reciprocal and organic, then education is a process of development, through which the individual grows into a larger life. This theory dominated Greek education in general during its healthiest and greatest period.

The first fact which calls for attention is that in ancient Greece, to a far greater extent than in modern Europe, the State was society. Even in modern times the State occupies a position of some preeminence among institutions, although it remains, on the whole, merely one among a number of others. In ancient Greece it included them all. No question, not even that of a religious ceremony, or of a family obligation, lay outside its sphere. Yet the State was not in general tyrannical. The Greek, in contrast to the Persian or the Egyptian, felt himself to be a free man. His State, in fact, resembled an enlarged family. Its small size contributed to this effect. Where there were only a few thousand citizens, the more prominent were known to all, at least by sight, if not more intimately. Thus the Greek lived in a closer and more personal relation with his State than is possible under modern conditions. His education was a State concern, in much the same manner as it was a family concern.

In this connexion, the historical development of the polis or city-state is important. The Greeks originally settled down in small village communities, bound by ties of kinship, and governed, like other such settlements in various parts of the world, by a headman with the advice of a council. By conquest a number of such communities was united under a monarchy, which was the earliest form of government of the polis. Whenever a monarch was overthrown by his nobles, either another monarchy might be substituted, or else an aristocratic or oligarchic form of government. Occasionally, the people took the government into its own hands, with the result that Athens and other states became democracies. In Homeric times monarchy prevailed, and the monarch's court commonly included a form of school. One has only to recall the account of the instruction of the heroes by Cheiron the centaur, in order to realize that, even at a very early period, well-born youths received systematic teaching. Nor did the State ever relax its interest in education. Solon, the ancient Athenian law-giver, passed laws concerning schools. Lycurgus, the legendary founder of Sparta, made education his chief concern. Even the Demes, the survival of village communities in Attica, submitted candidates for the Ephebic college to some sort of examination. Democracy was particularly favourable to general education. The sausage-seller in the comedy of Aristophanes, satirized as the most ignorant person in Athens, can at least read 'in a kind of way'.

The extent of State intervention in Greek education is an interesting if somewhat obscure topic. It was clearly the custom of the polis to take an active interest in educational matters. According to the political theory of Aristotle, while village communities made mere living possible, the polis existed for the sake of living well, and living well meant, above all, education. In Sparta the State took complete charge of the education of boys from the age of seven years. It even determined whether an infant were to be reared or exposed to death. In Athens, however, the State was mainly content to supervise the teachers, and to leave the actual support of schools to private enterprise. Since Athens became, in the words which Thucydides put into the mouth of Pericles, the school of Hellas, it is certain that the Athenian system was the more typical. Yet, even in Athens, one part of the education of a well-born youth was undertaken entirely by the State. Youths of about eighteen were trained for two years in the Ephebic corps, the principal object of which was the cultivation of military efficiency. Moreover, the State sometimes educated destitute children. At a later date the Greek historian, Polybius, himself an ardent admirer of Roman customs, expressed surprise that Rome should be content to entrust so important a function as education to the capricious judgement of private individuals.

In the great days of Greece, good citizenship was the chief end of education. It is not surprising, however, that in those days of almost incessant war the ideal of good citizenship was essentially military.

The soldier rather than the producer fulfilled the Greek ideal. Hence, perhaps, arose much of the factiousness which characterized many cities. The Spartans merely carried to extremes a military practice which was in some sort universal. A military education *per se* is somewhat barren and formal; but Athens showed how it might be combined with a rich content of intellectual and aesthetic culture.

The civic character of Greek education was sapped ultimately by the loss of political freedom. It may be doubtful, indeed, whether the political genius of the Greeks was equal to that of the Romans. All attempts to found a Greek Empire ended in early failure. Systems of justice were cumbrous, and laws badly administered. Political life became increasingly corrupt. The loss of Athenian independence, followed by the hegemony of Philip and Alexander, led to the gradual elimination of local and national influences from education. So long as the life of the Greek city-state was vigorous, integral, and independent, so long the ideal of education continued to be social; afterwards it became individual. Thus, in its later or cosmopolitan period, Greek culture was influenced but little by the State. Governments still maintained an interest in education, but they could not restore its originality and creative power. The history of ancient Greece ends in a story of decline. The individual ideal, as held by the Stoics, may, indeed, have been nobler than any conception primarily social; but it was divided from practical life by a great gulf, so that the individual philosopher sought to realize within himself alone those values and satisfactions that, unless shared, are an empty name.

IV

THE ECONOMIC THEORY UNDERLYING GREEK EDUCATION

'TO be always seeking after the useful', wrote Aristotle, 'does not become free and exalted souls.' The highest Greek thought, aiming as it did at things which were good in themselves, had little appreciation of economic pursuits, which exist only for the sake of something else. Food is not produced or used for the food's sake, nor a house for the house's sake, nor clothing for the clothing's sake; but food, shelter, and clothing exist that a man may live, which is the first pre-requisite to living well. On the other hand, music is studied for its own sake, not for some external end; and the same may be said of philosophy, history, and other pursuits which were held to be part of a rational and good life, as opposed to mere existence.

In Aristotle's time the traditional Greek curriculum consisted of four subjects—music (including literature), gymnastics, the arts of reading and writing, and sometimes drawing. The two latter are summarily dismissed from his analysis as being utilitarian or illiberal. Drawing had been introduced into the schools at a comparatively late date; and enjoyed by no means an equal status with music and gymnastics. Music receives Aristotle's chief attention, as the typically liberal study, pursued for its own sake rather than for an external end. Gymnastics are illiberal in so far as they are introduced for the sake of military efficiency. The Greeks recognized a liberal element in mathematics; and gradually expanded the school curriculum until it became standardized as the seven liberal arts—grammar, rhetoric, dialectic, arithmetic, music, geometry, and astronomy. Thus, the Greeks reduced utilitarian studies to the indispensable minimum.

Nor was this in any respect accidental. Being in no sense goods or ends in themselves, industry and commerce were considered to be unworthy of attention in the schools. The means of reaching the highest good was knowledge. The only right path for the man of leisure and capacity was that of reason. The best life was the life of mental development or culture. The most that industry could do was to change the appearance of things; it could not change reality or truth. The universe, indeed, was regarded by the Greek philosophers as a finished object of contemplation, rather than as a complex of processes which might in a measure be affected by the efforts of man. Industry, therefore, could make no real difference; and the highest use to which the mind of man could apply itself was the contemplation of time and of existence. This end could not be reached through a sordid or utilitarian education. Consequently the Greeks made a deliberate attempt to exclude utilitarian subjects from the curriculum.

The rational life, then, was regarded as distinct from the economic. It was even suggested that as soon as a man had gained by industry enough to live upon, he should retire from his business, and devote himself to the life of reason. It was considered impossible to serve the two masters, virtue and industry. While modern schools incite pupils to work, Greek schools incited them only to virtue. If the Greeks were not exceptionally virtuous, the defect lay rather in the inefficiency of the social and religious sanctions to good living than in any lack of purity and loftiness in their academic ideals. Philosophers never wearied of describing the dangers of excessive wealth. In the words of Plato: 'When riches and virtue are placed together in the scales of the balance, the one rises as the other falls.' Again, to quote Aristotle: 'Property is necessary for States, but property is no part of the State, though many parts of it have life; but a city is a community of equals, for the purpose of enjoying the best life possible.' Wealth, even including slaves, has no part in the best life; with which it is at most an inferior competitor.

Although this way of thinking dominated Greek philosophy and expressed itself in the character of the schools, it was somewhat paradoxical. Property might be an unworthy object of solicitude, yet only those who had it were able to disregard it. The theory was idealistic and doctrinaire. Practical men, in spite of the warnings, condemnations, and exhortations of philosophers, practised business and pursued wealth as much as they do now. Trade must have been held in some esteem in the time of Nicias, who gained much profit thereby. In fact, the Greeks were a great commercial people; and as there were wealthy merchants in Athens, there must have been wealthy artisans. The Rhodians waged several wars in the interests of trade, as did France and England in the eighteenth century. Social and political distinction were closely involved with occupation and wealth. Athens, in the flower of her culture, conferred the freedom of the city upon the banker, Pasion, and his son; but such incidents were distinctly exceptional.

These and similar facts should not be allowed to obscure the main argument, that wealth was placed lower in the scale of goods than at present. As in England during the eighteenth century, no occupation except that of a landowner was regarded as noble. All paid occupations, including that of the teacher, were stigmatized as illiberal, in that they were not followed for their own sake. Greek thought profoundly disliked the obtrusion of necessity into culture.

The objection of the Greeks to utilitarian education is profoundly important, in that it became traditional and influenced the whole course of subsequent thought to the present day. Let us, therefore, briefly review the causes of the Greek attitude towards industry.

For present purposes a somewhat bald enumeration may suffice. Firstly, an aristocratic attitude was natural to the well-born Greek, especially if he were a landowner. Secondly, the influence of the Homeric poems tended to encourage such an attitude. These were court poems, in which no commoner receives mention by name, and which contain no meed of praise for the deeds of the masses. Thirdly, the Greek citizen was essentially a soldier, and, as Herodotus indicated, wherever the military art flourishes the trades are despised. The practice of war, and especially the taste for pillage, unsettled the workers, causing them to be dissatisfied with the meagre wages of peace. Fourthly, the Greeks were not conspicuous for economic virtue, their commercial life being somewhat treacherous and dishonest. Their virtue, as we have seen, was sought in a different direction. Fifthly, their economic genius, if not inconsiderable, by no means equalled their intellectual and artistic genius. Sixthly, their industrial arts were closely connected with the institution of slavery, and could not wholly escape the servile stigma. The Spartans were actually forbidden to exercise a mechanic trade. Similarly Pericles was criticized by Plato on the ground that he catered for the lower and more material desires of the people, the satisfaction of which is the proper care of slaves and artisans.

From these causes, the economic life was held in comparatively low esteem, and utilitarian education was correspondingly restricted. This effect, however, might have been merely temporary, but that it received philosophical justification from the pens of Plato and Aristotle. Their argument rested upon the assumption that the human mind contains two principles of quite a different nature, namely, the reason and the appetites or desires. The reason is satisfied in the life of culture; the appetites in the processes and results of industry. As the reason is higher than the appetite, so is culture higher than industry.

The appetites exist as a mere means to the life of reason, having no value in themselves; but the development of reason is an end in itself. The appetites are to be considered only so far as is necessary, but reason leads to true knowledge and virtue. The necessary is not the good. The good lies in ideas; and the highest life consists in the contemplation of perfection, which is not to be found in reality, but in concepts. From this point of view the life of culture is worth while for its own sake, while the pursuit of trade is in itself of no value, and should be abandoned as soon as possible by all who are intent upon virtue and whose disposition is not slavish.

Until the sixteenth century, at least, the theory of Plato was not seriously challenged. Its influence upon Roman thought is evident in the treatise of Cicero, *De officiis*. Its domination of the medieval curriculum is apparent in text-books like that of Capella upon the Seven Liberal Arts. Medieval and even modern grammar-schools, gymnasia, and public schools of old foundation have clung steadfastly to the separation of culture from usefulness. It was almost in vain that Locke suggested that a gentleman's son might learn a trade, such as gardening or joinery. Even the sciences, because of their economic utility, have been strenuously resisted, and relegated to a more or less secondary place in England's oldest schools. Newman's *Idea of a University* makes little or no advance upon the position of Plato in its exclusion of knowledge not pursued entirely for its own sake. Yet the Greek philosophical theory was unsound. The desires on the whole stimulate rather than hamper the reason; and the industrial arts have placed culture under an obligation which is still but imperfectly acknowledged. Industry has liberated vast numbers of people for a life of study or of cultured leisure. Industry has established great educational endowments and foundations. Industry has afforded a thousand new causes of rational investigation. Success in industry is directly, rather than inversely, proportional to the philosophic conquest of truth.

V

LITERARY STUDIES IN THE GREEK SCHOOLS

FROM their inception the Greek schools were fortunate in possessing a magnificent text-book, the collected poems of Homer. According to Plutarch, the Spartan law-giver Lycurgus interested himself in the Homeric epics, and brought a copy of Homer with him to Sparta (perhaps about 776 B.C.). Peisistratus, who ruled in Athens from 560 to 527 B.C., is credited with having collected the scattered fragments of Homer. Homer, in fact, became the *primum mobile* of Greek literature, and almost of Greek life. Even Hesiod, writing perhaps about 720 B.C., had referred to and imitated Homer; while the age of Pindar was saturated with his influence. The great Athenian dramatists were indebted to Homer for many of their plots. Plato called him 'the educator of Hellas'. In the schools, not only was Homer the standard of literature, but the authority upon religion, morals, philosophy, mythology, history, and geography. In short, the Greeks were the people of a book, almost as were the Hebrews; but the Greek book was Homer.

The first element in the literary education of the Greek was therefore epic poetry. To the *Iliad* and *Odyssey* were added the works of Hesiod. The epic appears to be the most natural form of literary expression in what has been called the heroic age. As in Anglo-Saxon, Germanic, Scandinavian, and Hindu literature, so in Greek literature, the first extant work deals in poetic form with the adventures of heroes. The childhood of the race, like that of the individual, revels in the combination of story with rhythm. Even to-day it is scarcely possible to find reading better adapted to the boyish mind than the Homeric epics.

In general, Homer was praised by philosophers as much as he was loved by schoolboys. He was 'the divine'. All quoted from him, and all regarded him as an authority in every connexion. A few, like Heracleitus and Pythagoras, ventured to be critical; but their strictures merely emphasize the reverence in which his works were held. The criticisms of Plato in the *Republic* are directed against Homer not as a poet, but as the author of a school text-book, a role which the great bard could not have contemplated, as literary schools were non-existent in his day. Nevertheless, all Greek schools taught Homer, and Alcibiades is said to have thrashed a schoolmaster for not having a copy of the Homeric epics in his possession.

The second element in the literary studies of the Greek schoolboy was lyric and elegiac poetry. Literature of this kind is next to the epic in point of antiquity. The principal function of lyric poetry in schools was doubtless to furnish the words of songs. Music was a fundamental element in Greek education, in fact, the term 'music' was used to include both music proper and literature. According to Aristophanes, the schoolboys of the good old age were taught simple, martial lyrics. The Theban Pindar was so widely quoted, and his odes on the Olympic and other games are so obviously suited to the needs of the schoolboy, that one may fairly assume his poems to have been learned in the schools. On similar evidence it is probable that the epigrammatic poems of Theognis formed a part of school reading. Interest in lyric poetry, however, was eclipsed by the fascination of the public drama.

Dramatic poetry furnished the third element of Greek literary education. The Greeks had a habit, which cannot be too much admired, of recording scholastic and other honours upon stone. Among the numerous surviving results of this practice, there is a tablet which shows that at a school in Teos, in the second century B.C., prizes were given to junior boys for 'comedy' and 'tragedy'. Probably a competition in the recitation of selected passages was held, perhaps at some school function or public ceremony. Not only the school, but the State, set great store upon dramatic poetry. In Plutarch's *Life of Nicias*, it is related that some of the Athenian prisoners at Syracuse owed their liberty to the fact that they were able to recite passages from Euripides. Standard copies of the three great tragedians, Aeschylus, Sophocles, and Euripides, are said to have been deposited in the public archives at Athens. Galen relates that these priceless books were borrowed by one of the Ptolemies of Alexandria, on pledge of a large sum of money, fifteen talents, for their return. Ptolemy kept the books for the Alexandrian Library, and forfeited his bond.

No mention has hitherto been made of prose, which comprised the fourth element of school reading. The reason is that prose occupied a comparatively insignificant place in the curriculum of the elementary school. For, although Plato refers to the educational use of strains written in prose, and to composition in prose, without rhythm or harmony, he holds that many such passages are dangerous, while that given in the *Laws* is intended as an example of the most suitable type of discourse for school use. It would appear from a passage in the *Birds* of Aristophanes that the *Fables* of Aesop formed part of the prose read in the schools. The place of prose in elementary education was distinctly subordinate to that of poetry.

With secondary schools it was different. These fell into two main types, the oratorical and the philosophical. The first permanent oratorical school was founded by Isocrates; the first permanent philosophical school, by his contemporary, Plato. Schools of the former type necessarily devoted their attention to forms of prose, and as they received more popular support than the schools of philosophy, prose became an important element in secondary education.

Long before oratory was taken up by the schools it had been a power in Greek life. The pages of Homer glow with the natural rhetoric of Achilles, Nestor, Menelaus, and Odysseus, and there can be no doubt that in every century from Homer to Pericles eloquence had won numerous victories, both in peace and in war. As yet, however, there was no theory of rhetoric. Even Pericles, one of the greatest of orators, appears to have dispensed with formal restrictions, and to have spoken from the fullness of the heart, rather than according to a system of rules. The use of a theory of rhetoric accompanied the rise of democracy in Sicily, beginning in Acragas in 472 B.C., and at Syracuse in 466 B.C. Gorgias introduced rhetorical studies into Athens in 427 B.C. His oratorical style may be compared with the Euphuism which was fashionable in England in the sixteenth century, abounding as it did in antithesis, parallel constructions, and rhyming endings. Isocrates, a pupil of Gorgias and the Sicilian school, aimed at beauty of expression; Protagoras, Prodicus, and Hippias preferred correctness and precision. Plato in the *Gorgias* ridicules the current teaching of rhetoric, but in the *Phaedrus* suggests that it may be founded more firmly upon dialectic and psychology.

In the time of Plato the Athenians were not great readers; their culture arose from what they heard, saw, and participated in rather than from what they read. It was largely due to the excellence of the works of Plato and Aristotle that in later generations books became indispensable to learning. Henceforth, nobody could claim to be a scholar unless he had read the works of the great philosophers. Aristotle himself is said to have collected the first extensive library. His treatise on rhetoric is a most important contribution to the pedagogy of the subject. He complains that the public and deliberative art of speaking is neglected for the judicial or forensic, and that petty devices and unscientific appeals are taking the place of sound reason. Appeals to the feelings are less dangerous in public than in forensic speech; besides, they are justified to a certain extent, since the audience requires this kind of flattery. Rhetoric should be a sort of copy of dialectic, and psychological appeals should not be permitted to obscure the more regular and scientific mode of proof. Aristotle further points out that rhetoric deals with the contingent and probable, rather than with the universal or necessary, and is therefore not an exact science. Nevertheless, like politics, it involves the analysis of human character, notions, and feelings; and on this plea it has won a higher place in education than that to which it is justly entitled. Zeno the Stoic appears to have regarded rhetoric as expanded logic. Logic, he declared, is the closed fist, rhetoric the open hand.

All kinds of prose were influenced by rhetoric. Hence, just as grammar included the criticism of poetry, rhetoric came to include the criticism of prose. The classification of words and their relations was gradually worked out. Plato is the first to classify words, although his distinction is rather between subject and predicate than between noun and verb. Even Aristotle appears to have recognized only three parts of speech—the noun, the verb, and the connecting word. It remained for the Stoics to construct an adequate grammatical terminology. They believed that language is natural, that is to say, that words are the complete expression of things; that the study of language is a path to nature, and a guide to the life of reason. It is chiefly to the Stoics that we owe the analytic study of prose which is now called, in the narrower sense of the word, grammar.

To the Greeks, however, grammar meant literature. The art of the grammarian, or student of literature, is first revealed in the *Cratylus* of Plato and in the *Poetics* of Aristotle. The first to call himself a grammarian was Praxiphanes of Rhodes, *c.* 300 B.C. By the time of Dionysius Thrax (b. *c.* 166 B.C.), whose treatise is extant, grammar had come to be defined as 'in general the practical knowledge of the usage of writers of poetry and prose'. Dionysius divided the subject into six parts, as follows:

(1) Accurate reading.
(2) Explanation of poetic figures of speech.
(3) Exposition of rare words and subject-matter.
(4) Etymology.
(5) Statement of regular grammatical forms.
(6) 'The criticism of poetry, which is the noblest part of all.'

Dionysius of Halicarnassus, however, excludes literary criticism from his analysis.

Enough has been said to indicate the scope of Greek literary education. It included epic, lyric, iambic, and elegiac poetry, the drama, and in later centuries rhetoric and prose. Philology became a competitor of philosophy, and Greece produced a new intellectual type, that of the research student.

VI

THE EDUCATIONAL SYSTEM OF SPARTA

ALTHOUGH much has been written concerning the old Greek education, our information with regard to many of its conditions is meagre. Even when abundant details are furnished, as by Plutarch in his *Life of Lycurgus*, they may be untrustworthy, so that a process of weighing, sifting, and comparing is necessary in order that the truth may be ascertained. Plutarch, writing in the latter half of the first century A.D., ascribed to Lycurgus, an almost legendary law-giver of about the ninth century B.C., the foundation of the Spartan system of education. His knowledge is obviously remote; his material is drawn from sources unknown to us, and probably not always reliable; and some of his illustrations may have been coloured by his own picturesque imagination. On the other hand, it must be remembered that the main principles of Spartan education were widely known; and that Plutarch had access to an ancient literature, the greater part of which has perished. Further, although Plutarch is our most detailed authority on Spartan education, his accounts may be compared with the earlier if less laudatory references of Plato and Aristotle.

The Spartan system of education sought to train all free citizens to be superior to ordinary human weaknesses, not for their individual welfare, but for the good of the State. The most conspicuous features of the system were, (1) the strict limitation of natural wants, desires, and passions, (2) the subordination of the individual to the State, (3) the separation of the free citizens whose only profession was war, from the helots or slaves, to whom the industrial arts were relegated.

1. From their earliest youth the Spartan children were trained in hardihood and obedience. As babes they were made to lie alone in the dark; as boys they were under a threefold discipline, being subject to the captaincy of one of themselves, to the supreme control of a public inspector, and to the commands of a youth called an Iren, about twenty years of age, appointed by the inspector to the charge of a company of boys. In addition, any of the older men might instruct or chastise the lads. Punishments were severe and prompt, and flagellations at the altar appear to have been voluntarily undergone as a part of certain religious ceremonies. In all their undertakings the youth

were taught to prefer death to the dishonour of failure. Plutarch relates that boys above twelve years were clad in a single garment both summer and winter. They slept on beds formed of the tops of reeds gathered by their own hands, without knives, and brought from a distance. They were expected to supplement their scanty meals by the hazardous device of theft, which provided training in several of the practices of warfare. This strict régime continued to manhood, the only relaxation being in time of war. Luxury was curbed by the institution of iron money, which could circulate only in Sparta, and there to a very limited degree. Citizens were not permitted to travel at will, nor strangers to come and go without regulation, lest laxity of discipline and morals, together with new discourse, new opinions, new wants, might creep into the State. Legend relates of Lycurgus that while at the hey-day of his power and influence he deliberately starved himself, thinking that the death as well as the life of a statesman might be a help and inspiration to his country.

The simplicity and alertness of the Spartan discipline was manifested even in speech. Boys were taught to express themselves briefly; but quickness in repartee was highly esteemed. The opinion of Plato and Aristotle, that the intellectual elements of Spartan education were unduly subordinated to the physical, is not confirmed by Plutarch, who depicts ancient Sparta as a city of philosophers. Girls were exercised like boys, whereas in other Greek cities they were secluded after the Oriental fashion.

It will be observed that the Spartans practised asceticism from military and political rather than from religious motives.

2. Spartan education furnishes a unique illustration of the subordination of the individual to the State. Even the question whether an infant should be reared was left not to the parents, as in other Greek cities, but to the ancient men of the State. Marriages were under close State regulation. At the age of seven boys were taken from the control of their parents, and were enrolled in companies, living in State barracks or camps. Thus Sparta, unlike Athens, had a system of public boarding-schools, in certain respects analogous to the great public boarding-schools of England. Among the more obvious similarities are the prefect system, fagging, and emphasis upon manliness and open-air sports. The old men supervised the play and mimic strife of the boys. Military discipline was retained even after a mature age had been reached, so that the city resembled a huge camp—'each man concluding that he was born, not for himself, but

for his country'. The greatest of honours was the right to fight foremost in the ranks of battle.

The life of the Spartan boy, spent in military and other sports, raids, sham fights, &c., though hard, was not uncongenial to the spirit of boyhood. Plutarch describes a lesson given to a company of boys by an Iren, reclining after supper, in the presence of the old men. The Iren would ask such questions as: 'Who is a worthy citizen?' Boys were expected to answer briefly, but to the point. He who answered badly had his thumb bitten by the Iren. Afterwards, if the Iren had been too severe, or not severe enough, he received his own chastisement at the hands of the old men.

Even the men ate at common tables, living the life of soldiers, in barracks. According to Plutarch, they discoursed seldom of money, but generally of ethical and political matters. Boys were permitted to be present at their meals to hear such conversation, and to learn to bear a jest. They might steal from these tables, their own meals being scanty, but only at the risk of dire punishment if caught. They were expected to raid orchards and gardens on the same terms. Thus theft became a branch of moral training, and, clearly, boys trained in this fashion would be the better foragers when sent upon military expeditions. The helots were deliberately goaded into rebellion or flight in order that the bands of young men might practise real warfare against them. There were times, indeed, when great rebellions of the helots threatened the very existence of the Spartan State.

3. The specialization of the military class, which in the case of Sparta consisted of the whole body of free citizens, with its complement, the complete relegation of all industrial functions to the servile class, is characteristic of the philosophical Greek attitude towards industry. War and pillage, the normal conditions of Spartan life, naturally tend to make the soldier despise the producer. A Spartan is reported to have marvelled that an individual brought to court in Athens for idleness should have been admonished 'for keeping up his dignity'. Citizens were forbidden to exercise any mechanic trade, for industrial occupations are allied to the desire for riches and luxury. There was thus no thought of industrial education. According to Aristotle, however, the Spartans brutalized their children, failing to impart that intellectual courage which alone will face a truly noble danger.

VII

ELEMENTARY INSTRUCTION IN ATHENS

ATHENS in her prime possessed three types of schools which may be designated, from a modern point of view, as primary, secondary, and tertiary. Primary and secondary education were not conducted, as in Sparta, by the State; nor were the boys reared in boarding-schools or barracks. They attended private day-schools, which seem to have been controlled in a few respects by State legislation. Only the tertiary or ephebic stage of education was conducted in a State-supported college.

Elementary schools appear to have originated as a means of instructing boys in reading, writing, and counting upon the abacus or bead-frame. By the time that these schools come within our detailed knowledge, however, that is, by the fifth century B.C., they proceeded considerably beyond this minimum of instruction. They took boys from the age of about seven to that of fourteen, teaching them chiefly poetry and music. Thus they received the designation of music-schools. Only half the day was spent by the boys at such schools, the remaining half being occupied at gymnastic schools, which appear to have had little or no connexion with the literary institutions. It is remarkable that there is nothing in Greek literature to show conclusively which half of the day was occupied with music and literature, and which half with gymnastics. Probably, since the work in music was largely individual, some boys came for it in the morning, and some in the afternoon. In that event both the music-school and the palaestra would be open all day. The latter, however, was reserved at certain times for the men, and at other times for boys. Girls did not go to school at all.

Partly owing to the expense and inadequacy of artificial lighting, the ancients kept early hours; and the young pupil appears to have commenced school at or soon after sunrise, returning home for breakfast and other meals. The early Athenian legislator, Solon, is credited with having passed a law against the opening of school before sunrise or after sunset. There were holidays at general and special festivals; but the week-end break to which modern educational establishments are accustomed was wanting.

There is evidence that the masters of music-schools were ill paid, poorly esteemed, and frequently of foreign origin. This does not mean that they were not Greeks, but that they were not usually Athenians. Students from other cities in Greece and on the shores of the Mediterranean would support themselves at Athens by keeping school. The literary master and the music master were usually two different men; and from the fourth century onward their work was supplemented by that of a teacher of drawing and painting. Thus about 300 B.C. the philosopher Teles referred to the gymnastic trainer, the literary master, the music master, and the painter as the four chief burdens of boys.

Representations of school life on early Attic vases show that the master sat upon a high-backed chair, the boys upon stools or benches. Rolls of manuscript constituted the school library, a copy of Homer being considered essential. Among the apparatus of the schoolroom were sometimes included the busts of celebrities, illustrative pictures, and vases. For writing, tablets of wax were used, on which the pupils scratched with the pointed end of a stylus, using the flattened end for smoothing out.

It would appear that every Athenian learned to read; but that some of the poorer section of the community were unwilling to pay the higher fees demanded for musical instruction. Even the sausage-seller depicted in the comedy of Aristophanes, who is selected as the most ignorant type of Athenian citizen, could 'barely read in a kind of way'. The test of education was therefore not literacy, which was taken for granted, but ability to play the lyre. Various devices were employed to make the work of little children easy. Thus the alphabet was presented in a versified form; and songs and even dances were used as aids to spelling. The rediscovery of spelling dances would be a task worthy of the ingenuity of modern teachers. Reading was taught by the method of building up words from simple syllables.

The texts read comprised not only Homer but also all branches of poetry, not excluding comedy. Long passages were committed to memory and recited, sometimes in competition for a prize. Homer was taught not merely for the masterly form of his epics but equally for their intellectual, moral, and religious content. Prose received little attention in elementary schools, but Aesop's fables were not neglected. The boys sometimes received instruction as a group, but said their lessons individually.

The work of the music master consisted essentially of teaching each pupil in turn to play the seven-stringed lyre. It is certain, however, that choruses, mainly of a patriotic character, were sung in unison. Each music pupil also sang, to his own accompaniment, the works of the lyric poets. Early in the fifteenth century B.C., the flute had a short period of vogue in the schools; but was dropped as being more suited to the lover than to the school-boy. There was also an aesthetic objection to the contortion of the face in playing. By the time of Aristotle, the Athenians were beginning to regard the actual performance of music as derogatory to personal dignity; but this feeling does not seem to have immediately prejudiced the teaching of music to boys. On the whole, our modern elementary schools must be regarded as below the standard reached by the Greek in both literature and music, as well as in gymnastics.

In his analysis of the elementary-school curriculum, Aristotle makes no mention of arithmetic. He speaks only of reading and writing, music, gymnastics, and drawing. It would seem, however, that instruction was given in the use of weights and measures, and of the calendar; while counting was done both on the fingers and with the abacus. Plato says that the Egyptians made a game of arithmetic; and number games may have been played in the Greek schools.

Drawing and painting on box-wood were practised, but it is remarkable that drawing is not included by Aristotle among the liberal subjects of the curriculum. Probably it was largely geometrical, and included the making of plans. Support is given to this view by the fact that instruments which seem to be intended for geometrical drawing appear on the walls of schoolrooms as depicted upon Attic vases.

In the palaestra, gymnastic exercises were performed daily by the boys, beginning probably at a later age than that of their first entry to the music-school. Mere infants sometimes attended the latter in order to imbibe its atmosphere, or to be out of the parents' way. Care was taken that exercises for boys should not overtax their strength. The master in charge of gymnastics was called a *paidotribes*, from his duty of rubbing the pupils down. He bore as his rod of office a forked stick, with which to guide the contestants in wrestling and other sports. Among the regular occupations of the palaestra were gesticulation, rope-climbing, leap-frog, wrestling, jumping, running, boxing, discus-throwing, and javelin-casting. All the exercises were performed naked, the place in which they were held being closed to the general public. Teachers like Socrates would sometimes discuss philosophical topics with the older lads while they waited in corridors or ante-rooms.

Athenian gentlemen of the leisured class maintained their devotion to athletics even in mature manhood. They had gymnasia of their own, while in outlying places they seem to have used the palaestra of the boys at stated times. Hunting, swimming, rowing, riding, and dancing were accomplishments upon which they set considerable store; and there were special riding-schools in which feats of horsemanship were practised, such as leaping upon a horse at one bound with arms in the hand. For such pursuits, of course, special opportunities or fees were necessary, so that they cannot be regarded as a part of elementary education. It is important to notice, however, that the well-born Athenian was essentially an athlete, always more or less in training, seldom to be found seated, bronzed of skin, hard of muscle, fond of conversing upon matters of sport, and of witnessing athletic contests.

Throughout the day each Athenian boy, if he came of a well-to-do family, was accompanied by an elderly slave called a pedagogue. The duties of this slave were to see that the boy came to no harm, to be present at his lessons in school, to see that he learned what was expected of him, to accompany him to and from home, and even to chastise him upon occasion. Sometimes the pedagogue helped the boy with his homework, being a kind of tutor who supplemented the lessons heard in school. To judge from contemporary illustrations upon Greek vases, the pedagogue used to sit down cross-legged, a posture not permitted to schoolboys, often holding the boy's dog by a leash while the latter was at his lessons. After the introduction of Christianity the pedagogue's name took on a loftier meaning, being often applied by the earlier fathers to Christ. It thus came to mean not a slave, but a teacher.

The primary cause of the Greek devotion to athletics was the prevalence of war, but the hygienic and aesthetic advantages of bodily exercise were fully appreciated. Frequent protests were made against the tendency towards specialization in some particular performance. Euripides was as hostile to athleticism as Pindar was favourable. The conservative Aristophanes retaliated against Euripides and the intellectuals by satirizing the attention given by the youth of his day to words instead of to deeds.

VIII

SECONDARY EDUCATION IN ANCIENT GREECE

THE permanent schools of Plato and Isocrates mark the beginning of continuous secondary education in Athens. It is clear that the secondary schools developed naturally out of the somewhat casual and periodic lecture-courses of the much-abused Sophists. The golden age of Sophistic education was the Periclean period, when the general thirst for intellectual and aesthetic culture reached the maximum. While it sometimes happened that the masters of elementary schools established a continuation class for advanced pupils, more often pupils left the elementary or music-school at the age of fourteen, and looked to the lectures of wandering sophists for instruction in the more advanced branches of knowledge, such as geometry, astronomy, logic, and rhetoric. The term 'sophist' was generally extended to include even such philosophers as Socrates and Plato, and such well-established teachers as Isocrates.

Of the two main branches of secondary education, namely mathematics and rhetoric, Plato and the philosophical teachers respected only the former. In the fifth century B.C., mathematics included arithmetic, geometry, astronomy, and frequently the theory of music. Rhetoric, on the other hand, was of greater practical value, and not only stood higher in popular esteem, but enabled its professors to command higher fees than the mathematicians and the philosophers. Of the schools of rhetoric, none was as famous as that of Isocrates, a number of whose speeches have come down to the present time. Certain sophists lectured also on Homer and on other literary subjects; and occasionally even on geography, art, prosody, etymology, natural history, politics, ethics, religion, history, mythology, logic, military science, music, and physical culture.

The term 'sophist', at first applied to a poet or one skilled in any craft, came at length to designate the teacher of any advanced subject. The majority of the sophists had no permanent school; but gave their course of lectures, collected their fees, and departed elsewhere. Athens was their Mecca, and success at Athens meant a world-wide reputation. While the accounts of the sophists come exclusively from their enemies, Plato, Isocrates, and Aristophanes, it is clear that their teaching varied greatly in merit and that from it originated most of the intellectual movements of the ancient world. If they lived by fees, they gave many free lectures, and frequently acted as ambassadors on behalf of their native cities. The names of Protagoras, Hippias, Gorgias, Prodicus, and others are perpetuated in the Platonic dialogues, though always mentioned as a foil to Socrates. The descriptions in Plato's dialogue called the *Sophist* cannot apply to such as these, men of undoubted originality and learning, but only to the lesser teachers, some of whom may have been 'hunters after young men of wealth and position, with sham education as their bait and a fee for their object, making money by a scientific use of quibbles in private conversation, while quite aware that what they were teaching was wrong'. Even the best of the secondary teachers, however, were mistrusted by the masses as well for the fact that they tended to promote religious disbelief, as because their pupils were drawn only from the wealthier classes.

The permanent schools of the fourth century B.C. supplanted the lectures of the sophists only in part, and resented both the competition of these teachers on the one hand, and that of written texts on the other. If a certain degree of wealth was necessary in order to study under a sophist, far more was needed to become a member of a permanent school. There were three types of such schools: first, the philosophical type, as represented by the schools of Plato, Aristotle, and others; second, the broad rhetorical type represented by the school of Isocrates; and third, the narrow rhetorical type conducted by the lawyers or *logographoi*.

The lawyers took pupils with no further aim than to make them technically proficient in speaking before the courts. Isocrates, however, aimed at far more; he wished to train cultured gentlemen. He emphasized character as much as eloquence, and to him, as to Plato, were sent the sons of foreign notables, so that Athens became more than ever the centre of instruction for the Greek world. Much care was taken with the matter, as well as with the style, of the pupils' speeches. Each orator had his own style, so that one might distinguish his pupils by their conformity to it. Pupils would write their speeches, mutually criticize and correct them, and commit them to memory before they were actually delivered. The inevitable tendency of the rhetorical schools, however, was to subordinate truth to argument.

It was otherwise in the schools of the philosophers. Plato insisted upon a grounding in mathematics before admitting a pupil, and sought to find the fundamental truths which lie beneath the surface of experience. Music, geometry, and astronomy were regarded as prerequisites to philosophy. Plato charged no fees, but received presents from his pupils, who were, like those of Isocrates, drawn from the leisured and wealthy classes. His deeper tenets were communicated only to an inner circle of friends and old pupils, who were wont to banquet with him, carrying on their discussions sometimes throughout the whole night. His class of boys of about fourteen to eighteen years seems to have been taught chiefly mathematics and logic. Both Isocrates and Plato were jealous of the growing ascendancy of books, to which, by the irony of events, their own writings contributed.

IX

TERTIARY EDUCATION IN ATHENS

DURING the period which we have been considering, the fifth and fourth centuries B.C., higher education at Athens was represented not only by the lectures of sophists and by permanent secondary schools, but also by the Ephebic College, a State institution which prepared the youth for military service. Doubtless, this college should not be regarded, in the first instance, as a continuation of the work done by youths in philosophical and oratorical schools. Its training was primarily, and for a time solely, military and physical in character. Yet many of the pupils of Plato and Isocrates, having studied under their masters from fourteen to eighteen, must have passed into the Ephebic ranks with an increased self-respect and a new consciousness of manhood. The very term Ephebos meant one who had arrived at maturity. Moreover, since the Ephebic College was ultimately to develop into the first ancient institution of university rank, there is a special fitness in describing its activities as a form of tertiary education.

In order to become an Ephebos the youth of eighteen was required to satisfy his deme, and ultimately the Council, as to his age and Athenian parentage. His name was then placed on the roll of his deme, and he took an oath in the temple not to disgrace his weapons nor abandon his comrade, to fight for religion and country, to leave his country better than he found it, to obey the laws, protect the constitution, and honour the religion and temples of his forefathers. There is some evidence, although it may not be conclusive, that candidates may have been required to show knowledge of the laws of the city before being permitted to take the oath.

The discipline of the Ephebi was entrusted to officers known as Sophronistai, elected from each tribe. These superintendents were probably under the supreme control of the higher magistrates or Strategoi. At a later period we hear of a Rector or Kosmetes, whose duty it was to control the students, to accompany them to lectures, to allot them to their respective duties, and to supervise their physical development. Many subordinate masters were employed, instructors in the use of arms, physical exercises, javelin-throwing, archery, the use of the catapult, riding, and other branches of the curriculum.

The Ephebi had an important place in political and religious processions, in escort- and guard-duty, and possibly in maintaining order within the city. At the end of the first year a great review was held, at which each Ephebos was presented by the State with a shield and spear. The second year was spent mainly in field manœuvres, frontier patrols, and garrison-duty. On leaving college at the age of twenty the Ephebi were accustomed to present one hundred books to the library, which was kept in the gymnasium called the Ptolemaion. Of the tests and examinations by which the course was concluded we have, unfortunately, no particulars.

While in Aristotle's lifetime the Ephebic course appears to have been still intact, it is evident that the third and subsequent centuries B.C. witnessed a series of important changes. Bereft of her military power, Athens declined to take military training seriously. The course was reduced to one year and ceased to be compulsory. The number of Ephebi dwindled from perhaps a thousand to twenty or thirty, and the college was only saved from extinction by the admission of foreigners. Books and philosophical lectures took the place of arms; and, although perfunctory visits were still made to the frontiers, the military elements were subordinated and almost disappeared. Many foreign students attended lecture-courses without joining the Ephebic ranks, and the final result was that recognized sophists or advanced teachers attracted to their lectures bands of student supporters, loosely controlled and organized by the civic authorities, constituting in all essentials a university, and sometimes subsidized by the State, but never incorporated in the manner of modern universities, so as to own property as a body, or to sue or be sued at law.

X

SOCRATES AND PLATO

THE greatest minds of all ages have been attracted to education, as the process which furnishes the most practicable means of social betterment. Thus Socrates was even more a teacher than a philosopher, while his pupil Plato, and the latter's pupil, Aristotle, both regarded education as an inseparable part of the art of politics. Socrates would gather a knot of friends about him in the market-place, the porch of the gymnasium, or other public spot, and by skilful questioning lead them to see their own ignorance of fundamental truths. However commonplace the original question, he knew how to invest it with metaphysical dignity, and was ever able to place in the hands of his pupils a clue to a more consistent view of life. One by one he removed many cherished beliefs and customs from the strong room of Athenian tradition, and laid them upon the table of controversy, to be reconsidered and recast in the pitiless light of rational dialectic. For so doing he was condemned as a corrupter of youth, whom indeed he seems to have lured from the arena of sport to the subtler contest of philosophy. Socrates was, as it were, the gadfly of the Athenian people, who stung them out of their self-sufficient ignorance, and did more than any other to bring about the greatest intellectual renaissance which the world has seen.

Socrates wrote nothing; but the golden words of Plato amply justified his memory, and persuaded the Greek public that the alleged corrupter of youth was in fact the model wise man. In Plato's dialogues Socrates appears as the leader of the discussion, to whom the other speakers are but foils. From the standpoint of education, and perhaps from every other, the masterpiece of Plato was the *Republic*, ostensibly a quest for the meaning of justice, but in reality a treatise upon how the just man and just State may be produced by the right process of teaching and training. It is argued that the nature of justice may be perceived better in a State, where it appears upon a large scale, than in an individual. Accordingly an ideal State is constructed upon the basis of division of labour. In such a State each group will perform its own work, without interference with the work of others. Should the people lead a simple life, they will not outgrow their means of support or covet the territory of their neighbours; neither will their neighbours desire to go to war with a community which affords no temptation to rapacity. If, however, the State is to be luxurious, many more citizens will be necessary to cater for its appetites; it will require more territory, and its normal condition will be one of war.

Thus a class of soldiers or guardians becomes necessary, and, since war is an art, the principle of specialization applies to this class as to other forms of labour. Let us, therefore, consider the education of these men. On the physical side they must be swift and strong; and on the mental side they must be fierce towards enemies, but gentle towards their fellow-citizens. Can men be educated to be at once fierce and gentle, courageous yet docile? Yes, for we have just such a combination in a well-bred dog. Moreover, the dog makes knowledge the criterion of his conduct, since he is meek towards those whom he knows, savage towards those with whom he is unacquainted. By this example we apprehend that the guardians must be versed in philosophy, that they may distinguish the friends of the State from its enemies.

At the outset, no better form of education presents itself than the traditional one, music and literature for the mind, gymnastics for the body. Plato generally includes literature under the term music. In this sense musical education should precede the exercises of the palaestra. We begin with fiction, not truth; since the earliest teaching consists of stories from Homer and the other poets. These stories, notwithstanding the wonderful genius of Homer, give wrong impressions of the behaviour of gods and heroes; and for the purposes of an ideal system of education they should be profoundly modified. The gods must not be depicted as authors of evil, unjust, cruel, treacherous, false, immoderate in their desires and in their laughter, greater than men in their frailties. Neither must the heroes fear death, weep and lament like women, resist lawful authority and reproach even the gods themselves. In short, only the good must be told.

From this principle may be deduced the manner of narration. Since only the good is to be told, and only good men are permitted to be poets, the authors will have no temptation to evade responsibility by placing their words in the mouth of another, as in tragedy, comedy, and many parts of epic poetry, e.g. when Homer relinquishes his narrative to the priest Chryses. The method will be that of direct narration, since a good man loves to tell good things in his own person.

Music may be divided into three parts, the words, the harmony and the rhythm. The character of the words has been already determined; they must be simple, moderate, good, expressive only of courage and discipline. The harmonies and rhythms are to be such as befit the words. Hence the Lydian and Ionian melodies must be excluded, expressive as they are of passion and lamentation. Only the Doric and Phrygian remain, the former martial, the latter temperate. Without analysing the various kinds of metre, it is clear that those only which are apt for such moods should be retained.

Ultimately, indeed, words, harmony, and rhythm all depend upon good nature. Neither should the other influences which surround the young be neglected: our architects, sculptors, and painters must be subject to the same censorship as our poets. Thus shall our youth dwell in a land of health; and beauty, the effluence of good works, shall pour upon the eye and ear from every quarter, insensibly moulding the mind to the likeness of the true beauty of reason.

XI

EDUCATION IN AN IDEAL STATE

WHILE Plato's ideal republic provides an elaborate system of education for the military class, it is assumed that the industrial population shall be educated only by the method of imitation, and by the system of apprenticeship. Addressing his aristocratic pupils, Socrates projects a system adapted to their intelligence and stimulating to their moral outlook. The workers are not, indeed, unconsidered; to them, if to any, wealth shall be permitted, nor are they to be denied promotion on account of mean birth, poverty, or any other reason, save the lack of spirit and wisdom. Yet the workers are to have no voice in the government; it is their lot simply to obey. On no account should they attempt to usurp the functions of ruling, though their children, if deemed worthy, may be selected and trained to be the rulers of the succeeding generations.

The education of the soldiers or guardians of the ideal State has already been described; it remains to indicate what will be their proper mode of life. Holding the military power, they must above all things avoid wielding it in their own interests, as individuals or as a class. To this end their life shall be that of the camp; they shall hold all things in common, possess no particle of gold or silver, and be allowed no surplus or profits on their year's expenses. They shall value only that spiritual gold and silver which is within them, having no use for the earthly ore. Under such circumstances they will probably be happy; but in any case, it is not the happiness of a class but that of the whole State which is to be sought.

The function of the guardians, being to preserve the State, does not cease with military service. Dangers of peace, as well as of war, must be countered, and especially wealth, poverty, and educational innovation. The poor man's work suffers for the want of tools, the wealthy man's for the lack of economic stimulus. Moreover, a new kind of music or literature may shake the very foundation of citizenship; therefore, granted a perfect State, the system of education which has made it perfect must, at all costs, be maintained. No stranger, however versatile and brilliant, shall be permitted to subvert it, or to introduce novel ideas and practices.

Obviously, in a perfect State the rulers shall be those most fitted to rule; their peculiar quality being wisdom. The best means of determining who are the wisest is a system by which boys shall be closely and continuously watched and systematically tested in order to discover whether they are capable of resisting the temptations of pleasure, as well as all forms of physical and moral intimidation. This is the first suggestion in literature of mental tests to be devised in a scientific manner for purposes of education. Just as the soldiers have been selected from the whole of the youth for their courage, so the rulers shall be chosen from among the soldiers for their wisdom. They will share the military training of their comrades until its completion at the age of about twenty, but shall continue their studies in a mathematical direction until thirty, whereupon five years should be devoted to philosophy. Then, at thirty-five, the rulers are allotted to the various magisterial positions, holding office for fifteen years, after which, being of a philosophical inclination, they should be permitted to devote the remainder of their lives to the most congenial of all occupations, that of leisured contemplation of all that is true and good.

It now appears that justice depends upon right education. In the individual, justice is the harmony of the lower desires with the higher qualities of spirit and reason; and in the State, it lies in the harmonious discharge of their functions by the rulers, soldiers, and workers. Nor should the rulers rest content with their own possession of truths unknown to the masses. Rather should they retrace the paths that have led them into enlightenment in order to release their fellow-citizens from the atmosphere of cavernous darkness in which their souls lie captive.

The *Republic* has exercised an extraordinary influence upon educational thought. So subtle is its irony that nothing in it, perhaps, is to be taken as a specific practical recommendation. It is a masterly attempt to envisage education as a whole, and in its co-ordinate parts; and the great age of its intellectual wine has but mellowed the flavour of a healthful stimulus.

XII

EDUCATION IN THE POLITICS OF ARISTOTLE

THE educational theories of Plato were reconsidered, and with some amendments approved, by his disciple, Aristotle (384–322 B.C.). This famous teacher, described by Dante as 'The master of those that know', reorganized the whole field of science; and during the Middle Ages was accepted as an ultimate authority upon secular subjects. Our only reliable account of his life is from Apollodorus, a writer of the second century B.C. It would seem that from eighteen to thirty-seven years of age Aristotle studied under Plato; and that for three or more years he attended at the Macedonian court, where he served as tutor to the youthful Alexander, whose subsequent exploits were to be the means of extending panhellenism throughout the Near East. At a later date Aristotle returned to Athens, where he maintained a school, the Lyceum, until 323 B.C., the year prior to his death.

A later account of the fate of the library and manuscripts of Aristotle furnishes an interesting illustration of how easily the books of antiquity, even the works of the most eminent authors, could be corrupted, mutilated, or even lost. Aristotle bequeathed his library, the first extensive collection of books of which there is record, to his pupil, Theophrastus, who carried on his school. Thirty-five years later the books were bequeathed to Neleus, who took them to his home at Scepsis, in Asia Minor. In order that the books might not be 'commandeered' by the King of Pergamus, the heirs of Neleus buried the important documents, which lay hidden for a hundred and eighty-seven years. About the year 100 B.C. they were sold to Apellicon, a collector of books, who took them to Athens. Here they were seized when Sulla occupied the city (86 B.C.), and were removed to Rome. At Rome they found an editor at last in Andronicus of Rhodes 50 B.C.). It is not wonderful that so many of the books of the ancients, and particularly of Aristotle, are fragmentary and impaired by doubtful readings, especially when it is remembered that copying was a manual process, and that the copyists, most of whom were slaves, were rarely competent philosophers or grammarians.

The question of education is considered by Aristotle in the unfinished book with which his *Politics* concludes. The principal topics of this book are: (*a*) the control and organization of education; (*b*) music; and (*c*) gymnastics.

(*a*) Aristotle argues that education should be one and the same for all, since the State has one aim, not many. Hence education should be public, not private. It is the business of the State; indeed, its chief business. The need of education remains to be determined. Is it utility, virtue, or the higher knowledge? Since the end is indeterminate, the means cannot be otherwise; but, on the whole, a liberal education is best, that is to say, an education sought for its own sake, not for the sake of something else. Utilitarian instruction should be imparted only in so far as it does not vulgarize a boy. The received subjects of the elementary curriculum are partly liberal, or worthy of study for their own sake; and partly illiberal, or pursued in order to attain external ends. They are, briefly stated: (1) reading and writing; (2) gymnastic exercises; (3) music, and sometimes (4) drawing. Frequently the term music must be taken as inclusive of literature.

(*b*) Music is generally learned for pleasure; but the original reason for its inclusion in the curriculum is the correct one, namely the best use of leisure, which is the first principle of all action (cf. *N. Eth.* x. 6). Leisure is better than business. It gives true enjoyment, although this varies in quality, for 'the pleasure of the best man is the best, and springs from the noblest sources'. . . . 'There is a sort of education in which parents should train their sons, not as being useful or necessary, but because it is liberal and noble.' . . . 'To be always seeking after the useful does not become free and exalted souls.'

Should music be studied (*a*) for amusement and relaxation, or (*b*) as conducive to virtue, or (*c*) for the enjoyment of leisure and culture? The second is rather the Platonic, the third Aristotle's own solution. In any case, there is the further question, should boys practise music or merely learn to appreciate the performances of others? It cannot be argued that to appreciate music they must perform it. 'If they must learn music (themselves), on the same principle they should learn cookery, which is absurd.' Probably boys should learn music while young; but abandon its performance on reaching manhood. Actual performance does not degrade, except in the case of certain rhythms and melodies. Music is appropriate at social gatherings, if only for amusement. No doubt, also, music has a special moral effect. In hearing musical sounds, our souls undergo a change. No other sense, except sight, has any kinship with moral qualities. Simple music and simple instruments are best. The flute is unsuitable to educational uses, its true function being the relief of the passions. Music has several aims, not one only. Its values are three at least, namely (*a*) education; (*b*) purification; and (*c*) intellectual enjoyment. The melodies should correspond to the minds of the hearers; but from the educational standpoint, ethical strains like the Dorian are best. Others, however, should not be totally excluded. The Dorian mood has the advantage of being a mean between the Phrygian and the Lydian; and education should be based upon the three principles of (*a*) the mean; (*b*) the possible; (*c*) the becoming.

(*c*) Gymnastic education is regarded as productive of courage; not as an end in itself. In education, habit precedes reason, and the body the mind; therefore gymnastic training is appropriate in early boyhood. (Plato had postponed gymnastics to music.) In gymnastics the Lacedaemonians have the greatest reputation; but their exercises brutalize the children, failing to impart that intellectual courage which alone will face a truly noble danger. Gymnastic exercises for children should be light. Excess in athletics is injurious, as is proved by the fact that not more than two or three Olympic victors have won prizes both as boys and as men. After boyhood, three years should be given to other studies. Youths may then go into severe training, but excessive work of mind and body should not be attempted simultaneously.

XIII

ALEXANDRIAN CULTURE

THE period of Aristotle is also the period of Alexander the Great. The independence of the Greek cities had become a glory of the past, which even the frenzied eloquence of Demosthenes had been powerless to restore. Hence education at Athens and elsewhere lost its old social and patriotic character, and was sought for purposes of individual advancement or for abstract knowledge. Greek learning became general rather than political; cosmopolitan rather than local. It is true, of course, that many of the earlier sophists, whose custom it was to tour the Greek states and to deliver courses of literature in various cities, had taught subjects of an abstract character, which were equally acceptable under any government, although at times they must have found it necessary to adjust their instruction to the temper and traditions of the people whose interest they sought to attract. Aristotle himself planned a system of education, not for an Empire, but for a small city-state; but in the meantime Alexander was extending Greek dominion widely throughout Asia and Africa, and many of his conquests became permanent outposts of Greek culture. This was particularly true of the city of Alexandria, which he founded in 322 B.C. The wars of Alexander, like the Crusades, and the victories of Charlemagne, are of no mean importance in the history of civilization.

Their result was, no doubt, to extend rather than to intensify culture. They did not directly produce great philosophers, poets, or scientists; but they did provide a wider reading public, just at the time when the best knowledge of the great creative epoch had been crystallized by the genius of Plato and Aristotle. In the time of Pericles the educated Greek read but little; but after Aristotle nobody could be esteemed a scholar who was not familiar with books. Aristotle is said to have been the first to collect an important library. He surveyed the whole field of knowledge, and produced a timely series of rational and systematic text-books upon the various sciences.

The use of books by no means superseded the sophistic system of higher education, with its brilliant lectures and keen discussions, which remained intact for centuries after the Christian era. Nevertheless, the works of Plato and Aristotle, and subsequently other scientific writings, gained great authority, with the result that education became standardized, every scholar having read the recognized masters. Thus a higher degree of uniformity was introduced into learning than could be attained when almost all instruction depended upon oral speech. Possibly the weight of authority was unduly oppressive, and discouraged originality; but the development of diverse schools, such as the Stoic, Epicurean, and Cynic, although each respected the traditions of Aristotelianism according to its own interpretation, shows that critical and constructive thought was by no means extinguished. Moreover, at Alexandria, as well as in the older Greek cities, considerable progress was effected in science, although the laborious inductive methods of Aristotle were rarely imitated. State support of education and public interest in the lectures of great sophists seem to have increased rather than diminished. The time came when several chairs at Athens were endowed by Roman Emperors, and when the peace of the city was disturbed by serious conflicts between the adherents of rival teachers.

The death of Alexander was followed by a period of turbulence, out of which emerged several independent kingdoms. One of these, Egypt, fell to Ptolemy Soter, who set himself to the task of making Alexandria a centre of Greek culture. Obtaining the support of the greatest Athenian scholar of the age, Demetrius Phalereus, he founded a museum or university, the professors of which were paid by the State; and a library, which developed under his successors into the greatest of the ancient world. Under the second Ptolemy, the poet Callimachus flourished, and much attention was paid to the writings not only of Aristotle but even of Jewish and Egyptian authors. A translation of the Law of Moses into Greek, the Septuagint version, was begun; and Alexandria began to be intellectually, as she already was geographically, a focus of the civilization of Europe, Africa, and Asia. The collection of books became an article of faith with the Ptolemies. No visitor bringing a book to Alexandria was permitted to depart without leaving a copy behind him; and at one period, in order to curb the activity of Pergamus in its endeavour to establish a rival library, the export of papyrus was forbidden. The third Ptolemy is related to have borrowed works of great value from Athens, the standard editions of Aeschylus, Sophocles, and Euripides, depositing a great sum of gold as a pledge of their return. He forfeited the money and retained the books.

It must be recollected that the Ptolemies, and the scholars whose labours they encouraged, were Greeks, living in the midst of a subject race of Egyptians. The system of State support facilitated their researches; but great creative efforts were not to be expected from circles to which no wave of public feeling, no stimulus of national self-consciousness could penetrate. The poems of Alexandria, with the exception of the Idylls of Theocritus, are pedantic and obscure. Progress was made in the more formal sciences, grammar, prosody, mythology, lexicography, archaeology, mathematics. It was at Alexandria that Eratosthenes wrote upon physical and mathematical geography, Euclid upon Geometry, Hipparchus upon astronomy, and Apollonius of Perga upon conic sections.

The death of Cleopatra symbolized the end of Egypt as an independent kingdom, and from 30 B.C. the country became a Roman province. Under the Romans its schools were not eclipsed; but came to be famous for their philosophy rather than for their literature and science. The writings of Philo Judaeus (20 B.C. to A.D. 40) may be regarded as the foundation of Neo-Platonism, which reached its zenith with Plotinus (A.D. 204 to 270). As an educational discipline, Neo-Platonism resembled other mystic forms of philosophical religion. It emphasized the unreality of matter, and the need of developing spiritual life by contemplating the blind intuition of the divine nature which is innate in every soul. 'Everything is good,' writes Plotinus, 'it is not matter, a transitory thing, that rules; it must pass in order that things may be as they are, or else it would have been the cause of reason itself. It is reason that is the principle, reason is everything, it has ordained everything from its origin and birth.' Neo-Platonism became fashionable among the thinkers of the later Roman Empire; and though it would limit philosophical education to the few, its optimism, approval of effort, insistence upon contemplation of the good, wealth of allegory and metaphor, indifference to economic conditions, and emphasis upon the contrast between mind and matter, made it for a time a serious rival to Christian doctrine. It degenerated, however, into the superstitious assumption of a hierarchy of demons, and injured the cause of science by its studied contempt of physical fact.

XIV

THE LATER GREEK SOPHISTS

THE Macedonian conquests closed the classical period of Greek culture. Henceforth Athens in particular was regarded with a reverence which, in modern times, is without a parallel. The Macedonians and their successors in power were Phil-Hellenes; hellenism was represented as an ideal which all should endeavour to attain. When Alexander, having crossed the Hydaspes River, exclaimed: 'O, ye Athenians, will ye believe what dangers I undergo to merit your praise?' he voiced an honour and an aspiration which became dear to the heart of many succeeding centuries. The crowning glory of Athens was her philosophical schools. Four of these at least achieved permanence: the Academic, which Plato had established; the Peripatetic, founded near the Lyceum by Aristotle's pupil Theophrastus; the Stoic, which although not incorporated succeeded in maintaining the continuity of its teaching; and the Epicurean, originally endowed with the house and garden of Epicurus, as the Academy had been endowed with the property of Plato. Notwithstanding the endowments, which all except the Stoics possessed, the teachers of these schools in the generation after Plato adopted the practice of taking fees from their pupils. These philosophical schools, then, rivalled the schools of rhetoric. Many students attended both types of institution concurrently. Schools of grammar or literature were pre-requisite to both. In this field the *grammatistes* taught the elements, while the *kritikos* or *grammatikos* entered upon serious literary criticism, emphasizing the exposition of poetry.

The Greeks admired literature; but they loved the spoken word. The sophists, in truth, were well-skilled platform artists, their voices, carefully attuned to their subjects, conveying such aesthetic pleasure that, when a sophist of reputation had spoken, snatches of his orations were hummed appreciatively in the streets. They were fastidious about their personal appearance. Their distinctive dress, their long hair and onyx rings, their perfect grace of bearing, movement, and gesture, their studied ease and ingenuity in producing oratorical effect, their skill in the dramatic representation of every type of character and situation, and not least their encyclic ability in discussing any theme that might be propounded, filled their pupils with zest for learning, and inspired them with a loyal sentiment that was not incompatible with wide and generous culture.

Until the sack of Athens by Sulla and his Roman army in 86 B.C., though Greece had suffered materially from wars of succession and other troubles, Athens on the whole escaped serious interference with her intellectual pursuits, with the one exception that in 200 B.C. the gymnasia and monuments outside her walls were destroyed by a Macedonian army. Sulla cut down the beautiful groves of the Lyceum and the Academy, wherein for centuries philosophers had delighted to walk, in order to provide materials for his engines of war; and soon afterwards the streets of Athens ran with the blood of her citizens. Yet the city and her schools recovered. Romans as well as others pursued their studies at Athens and at Rhodes, and no Greek could have expressed more reverence for the Academy than did Cicero, who delighted to study philosophy within its precincts. Apart from Cicero and his brother Quintus, Athens attracted such Romans as Quintus Metellus Numidicus, Brutus, and Horace; while Rhodes drew to her halls Marcus Antonius, Julius Caesar, Brutus, Cassius, and Cicero.

It must be added that, although in pre-Christian times education in Athens was private or endowed, there were examples of State education elsewhere. An inscription from Teos in Asia Minor, which may date from the third century B.C., indicates that a citizen had presented an endowment to his fellow-citizens for the education of all free-born children of both sexes in letters, and of all free-born male children in music and in certain military exercises. Instruction was graded, and teachers were to be appointed and paid through the State. Similarly Delphi and Rhodes, apparently during the second century B.C., received large endowments for public education. The Greek historian Polybius, generally an admirer of Roman institutions, criticized the Romans for their lack of a legally established system, a sure indication that the Greek cities had already made large advances in this direction.

As has been related, Athens developed a system of university instruction. When the Ephebic college was thrown open to all, its ancient reputation attracted foreign students in great numbers. With the loss of civic independence, the art of oratory retreated from public life into the schools, but emerged after the Christian era into great popularity. The sophist now ceased to be a master of all knowledge, and became a master primarily of the art of rhetoric. Sophistic addresses dealt with every variety of theme, being divided into two principal types: the speeches for display, and the speeches of a deliberative character. Patronized by the emperors, who endowed a number of chairs at Athens, the sophists gained an extraordinary reputation. At Rome the Emperor Hadrian established the Athenaeum, where both Greek and Roman sophists were wont to give public displays. The same emperor extended his patronage to the museum at Alexandria. Antoninus Pius established many chairs in various cities, probably assisting the municipal authorities as occasion might demand to find the salaries which he had determined. Marcus Aurelius added to the number of endowed Athenian Chairs. Philostratus gives many details of the lives of the sophists of the second and third centuries A.D., and Lucian writes entertainingly of their foibles; both were themselves members of the profession.

During the third century of the Christian era, higher education suffered from the insecurity of many parts of the Empire, and from the weakness, indifference, and even hostility of some of the Roman Emperors. In this period philosophy declined, but rhetoric retained most of its former importance. The period of Constantine witnessed a revival, illustrated by the renewed privileges which were showered upon learning. Subsequently the antagonism between Christian thought and Pagan sophistry became acute. The sophist Libanius discloses the Pagan point of view; he and his followers hailed the apostate Emperor Julian as the restorer not only of the holy rites which had been thrust into the background by the Christian empire, but also of letters. Meanwhile, Christian students like Basil the Great and Gregory Nazianzen could study side by side with pagan students in the university of Athens; so that the conflict, bitter as it sometimes became, was not deemed irreconcilable. Only in A.D. 529 were the pagan schools of Athens closed by an edict of the Emperor Justinian. The endowment of the philosophical schools was confiscated; and the spirit of Hellenism departed.

The golden age of sophistry was the period of the earlier Empire. Its eclipse under certain emperors was but transient. The great sophists of the fourth century A.D., a few of them Christians, rivalled those of the first and second. The sophist was frequently the most important and revered member of a Greek city. He became its ambassador, on important occasions, to other cities; and was made immune from taxation, and from public offices except such as he chose to undertake. His profession far exceeded that of a philosopher in public estimation. The treasury of the city or that of the Empire—probably in some instances both—contributed his salary, the right of appointment being vested, in all probability, in the source from which the emoluments were derived. As time went on the emperors became jealous of the manner in which municipal authorities tended to expend local funds upon salaries, and required ultimately that salaries should not be donated without imperial consent. Sophists lacking an official appointment subsisted upon fees.

Although the ancient universities were not incorporated, parts of them, such as the philosophical schools of Athens, sometimes were. In other cases the appointment and payment of the leading sophists by municipalities constituted them officers of the civic corporation. As need demanded, they employed assistant sophists, attaching these teachers to their schools. In the absence, probably, of degrees or diplomas, the student body was held faithful to its school mainly by the qualities and reputations of the teachers, although in smaller towns, if a youth aspired to enter the public service or a learned profession, there might be no alternative.

In universities the main subjects were rhetoric and philosophy; but teachers of philosophy, astronomy, geography, political science, literature, geometry, law, and medicine were not wanting. There is little doubt that the general tendency was to subordinate such studies to the art of public speaking. Yet never in higher education has impression gone hand in hand so closely with expression, and never has there been greater thoroughness in the treatment of literary niceties.

How did the sophists teach? In their rhetoric each form of discourse was analysed in turn. If an illustration be taken from the treatment of myths or fables, the procedure, although it concerns but one literary form, may be found enlightening. The myth had its own style. It is a primitive story, but anonymous, universal, eternal; and from it had emerged the ancient Greek religion. Clearness, directness, simplicity, naturalness, avoidance of artificiality were the appropriate characteristics of style which the students were enjoined to respect in their disquisitions. Types of the myth were memorized. The method of narration was at one time direct, at another time the story was put into the mouth of another; or, for greater naturalness, direct and indirect narration might be alternated in the one fable. The myth itself mastered, suitable occasions for its employment in oratory had to be discovered. As the camel, wishing for horns, lost even his ears; so did Croesus, in seeking a larger kingdom, forfeit his own. The converse procedure by which the student ransacked his literary resources in order to find a fable appropriate to a given historical fact was unlikely to be neglected. He was expected also to draw morals from fables and to elaborate or condense them. The work was criticized according to definite standards; was it relevant, consistent, co-ordinated, plausible, clear, dignified? Other types of rhetorical composition included the appreciation of solemn crises, application of rigid reasoning, appeals to the gamut of the sentiments, use of easy pleasantry, employment of afflicting diatribe, and even inculcation of ecstatic adoration or production of a romantic vertigo.

Eunapius has left a detailed account of how the sophist Proaeresius, the favourite pupil of his famous predecessor Julian, was driven, after the death of the latter, by the followers of his opponents into exile; but returned and succeeded in obtaining the coveted Headship of the School of Athens. The Roman Pro-consul, having arrived, called the sophists to a conference. They came reluctantly, and made speeches upon set themes. Organized applause followed each oration. They departed; but again were summoned by the Pro-consul, who called in Proaeresius, and stated that all, including Proaeresius, were to speak upon a single theme. All but Proaeresius demurred. He, when called upon, seeing two of his chief enemies in the room, requested that they should propound the theme, that the short-hand writers should be brought in, and that no one should applaud. Speaking and acting as one inspired, Proaeresius made it impossible that the last command should be respected. On completion of his speech, he repeated it without a slip, as the short-hand writers could testify. The Pro-consul, though a Roman, embraced the god-like genius; and after this none dared oppose Proaeresius openly, though his enemies continued to conspire in secret against him.

Such were the sophists of ancient Greece, men who had their country's heritage on the tip of the tongue, as we in modern times store it in the press or in books. They kept schools, more advanced than those of literature, of broad learning, of general culture, of moral judgement, of fluent expression. To an intelligent mind they added a healthful disposition and a peculiar grace of speech. If their profession lent itself to abuses, even to ridicule, as was not unobserved by their contemporaries and by themselves, they never failed to teach their pupils to think, or to couple action with words. As in the Middle Ages, expression was coupled to impression. Where, among the Greeks, the expression was rhetorical, and in the Middle Ages dialectical, in modern times it is literary. Our liberal education finds its expression in essays. The essay fails, for the want of speech, for the want of action, to be as concrete, as replete with satisfaction to the student, as closely in touch with the demands of a professional career, as the misunderstood, the too frequently despised, sophistic culture.

A SELECT BIBLIOGRAPHY

A

Aristotle: *Politics*, trans. Jowett.
—— *Ethics*, trans. Peters.
Becker: *Charicles.*
Bosanquet: *Education of the Young in Plato's Republic.*
Burnet: *Aristotle on Education.*
Butcher: *Some Aspects of Greek Genius.*
Capes, B.: *University Life in Ancient Athens.*
Davidson: *Aristotle and Ancient Educational Ideals.*
—— *Education of the Greek People.*
Drever: *Greek Education.*
Dumont: *Éphèbe Attique.*
Freeman: *Schools of Hellas.*
Grote: *History of Greece* (Chaps. LXVII–LXVIII).
Hobhouse: *Ancient Education.*
Laurie, S.: *Pre-Christian Education.*
Mahaffy: *Old Greek Education.*
Nettleship: 'Theory of Greek Education in Plato's Republic' (in *Hellenica*).
Plato: *Protagoras*, *Laws*, trans. Jowett.
Plato's *Republic*, trans. Jowett.
Plato's *Republic* trans. A. D. Lindsay.
Plato's *Republic*, trans. Vaughan and Davies (Golden Treasury Series).
Sandys: *History of Classical Scholarship.*
Walden: *Universities of Ancient Greece.*
Wilkins: *National Education in Greece in the Fourth Century.*
Xenophon's *Cyropaedia*, trans. F. Watson.

B

Adam: *The Religious Teachers of Greece.*
Anderson: 'Some Facts Regarding Vocational Education among Greeks and Romans' (in *School Review*, vol. xx).
Aristophanes: Comedies.
Bevan: *University Life in Ancient Times.*
Blumner: *Home Life of the Ancient Greeks.*
Botsford and Sihler: *Hellenic Civilisation.*
Burns: *Greek Ideals.*
Cole, P.: *Social Foundations of Greek Education.*
Dickinson: *Greek View of Life.*

Felton: *Ancient and Modern Greece.*
Girard: *L'éducation athénienne au Ve et IVe siècle.*
Gulick: *Life of Ancient Greeks.*
Hatch: *Influence of Greek Ideas and Usages upon the Christian Church.*
Kingsley: *Alexandria and Her Schools.*
Lane: *Elementary Greek Education.*
Livingstone (edited): *The Legacy of Greece.*
Mahaffy *Greek Life and Thought.*
—— *Social Life in Greece.*
Moore: *Religious Thought of the Greeks.*
Nettleship: *Lectures on the Republic of Plato.*
Newman: *University Sketches* (Ed. Sampson—Chaps. IV, VII).
Painter: *Great Pedagogical Essays* (Chaps. I, II, III—Plato, Aristotle, Xenophon).
Plutarch: *Lives*, trans. J. and W. Langhorne.
Ritter et Preller: *Historia Philosophiae Graecae.*
Rusk: *Doctrines of Great Educators* (Chap. on Plato).
St. John: *Manners and Customs of Ancient Greece.*
Tucker, T.: *Life in Ancient Athens.*
Westaway: *Educational Theory of Plutarch.*
Westerman: *Vocational Education Among Greeks and Romans.*
Wright: *Greek Social Life.*
Xenophon's *Cyropaedia*—Selection in Painter's 'Xenophon' in *Great Pedagogical Essays.*
Zimmern, A.: *Home Life of the Ancient Greeks.*

BOOK II

ROMAN EDUCATIONAL THOUGHT

I

EARLY ROMAN EDUCATION

FROM the legendary foundation of the city to the middle of the second century B.C. Rome was content, upon the whole, with her own culture, rudimentary though it was by comparison with that of Greece. The early Romans were less a commercial, more an agricultural people than their neighbours. Neverthelesss, the propinquity of the Greek colonies in Sicily and southern Italy implied an intercourse which must have leavened Roman ideas from the earliest times. The third and second centuries B.C. were a period of transition from indigenous to Græco-Roman culture. The important fact to remember is that Rome, as a small city-state, had a limited and provincial outlook; as an empire, she could not close her eyes to the intellectual superiority of Hellas. Let us briefly review the social standards of the original Roman civilization, and the character of the education which the youthful Roman received prior to the second century B.C., in order that he might realize those standards in his adult life.

Ethically, the early Romans were conspicuous for the virtues of military courage, dignity, industry, piety, and obedience. They were intensely patriotic, being surrounded by a ring of warlike cities, amongst which national self-preservation could only be maintained by a system of almost continual warfare. Like the Spartans, they were trained to subordinate themselves to, and even to sacrifice themselves for, the State. Almost their only industry was agriculture, together with the spinning and weaving of simple clothing, and the construction of serviceable buildings and household utensils. In the finer branches of art and industry they were surpassed by the Etruscans. They had no art or literature worthy of comparison with those of the Greeks, though their priesthood possessed traditions of secret knowledge, the value of which cannot be measured except by mere speculation. Their rude poems and dramas were gross, ill-constructed, unimaginative, and crude in expression. The patricians dwelt in the city, in some luxury, at the expense of the plebeians, and arrogated to their own families the guidance of the state; but were sometimes successfully confronted by the spirit of free republicanism. Their religion exercised little of the aesthetic influence so conspicuous in that of the Greeks, and the rites which they duly performed had generally a concrete and utilitarian end, such as the fruition of the crops, or the preservation of the household, or of the city.

In the rural districts the need of schools was little felt, nor were schools common until the influence of Greece became dominant. The country boy learnt the art of husbandry from his parent. Among the small farmers there was little use for slaves, since their labour was unprofitable, the work of one man being barely sufficient to support himself. The *patria potestas* placed all children under the unlimited control of the head of the family, who might legally put them to death, or sell them into slavery. Not that such things were common; but the legal position must have reinforced those habits of obedience and reverence for which the Roman youth were justly celebrated. Girls learned from their mothers the household arts, and were not segregated after the Greek fashion. When elementary schools became available, the girls seem to have attended along with the boys. Boys and girls were sometimes taught to read and write at their mother's knee, but were unfamiliar with music or any other form of art or literature.

In Rome itself, schools seem to have been conducted in the porches of the forum from a very early period of the Republic. At such a school Virginia is depicted in early Roman legend as a pupil, although writers like Livy were prone to attribute institutions of their own time to a period of whose conditions little was accurately known. Here reading and writing were taught; while simple practical arithmetic, with the use of the abacus, played a larger part, at least in proportion, than in the Greek schools. There was no suitable literary text-book prior to the Latin translation of the *Odyssey*, made by Livius Andronicus, about the middle of the third century B.C. On the other hand, pupils seem to have been taught the simple code of the Twelve Tables, which they doubtless committed to memory, in addition to the rather complicated Roman calendar. School discipline was severe, to the point of brutality; and school life far less congenial and attractive than among the Greeks.

Cicero, seeking in the native culture of Rome something worthy of a comparison with the priceless philosophy of Hellas, was moved to declare that the little book of the Twelve Tables surpasses the libraries of all the philosophers in weight of authority and wealth of utility. However exaggerated the claim may be, it is clear that the Romans possessed an elementary code of civic, moral, and religious law, which came to be regarded with some of the reverence which the Hebrews attached to the Decalogue. The severest penalties were enjoined against crimes. For example, 'The incendiary of a house or of a haystack near a house, if acting intentionally and of sound mind, shall be bound, scourged, and put to death by fire. If by negligence, he shall repair the damage; or, if too poor, shall be chastised moderately.' Sumptuary laws and restrictions upon conduct were included. 'The wood of the funeral pyre shall not be smoothed.' . . . 'Women shall not be allowed to tear their hair nor make immoderate wailings.'

The early Romans did not exercise, like the Greeks, in a gymnasium, nor were they addicted to sumptuous and luxurious baths. These were the innovations of the Imperial period. Yet training in the use of arms seems to have been at all times obligatory upon the Roman youth, and from the city the young men flocked to the Campus Martius for field-sports and military exercises. Grace of action and beauty of form were esteemed little beside the utilitarian ends of strength and martial prowess.

II

ROMAN EDUCATION UNDER GREEK INFLUENCE

THE Latin translation of the *Odyssey*, effected by Livius Andronicus about the middle of the third century B.C., at once became acclimatized in the Roman schools. Livius appears to have been an emancipated Greek slave, who, like so many other Greek slaves and freedmen, was employed by his Roman patrons in educational activities. Harsh as his measures sounded to the cultivated ear of the Augustan period, they made literary education possible in the Latin tongue. Livius was the father of Roman literature. According to Plutarch, about 230 B.C. a Roman named Spurius Carvilius was conducting a regular school with prescribed fees, said to have been the first of its kind, though the statement appears to require some reservation. The first really great grammarian to lecture upon literature in Rome was, on the authority of Suetonius, Crates of Mallos, a distinguished Greek scholar who had been sent upon an embassy from the King of Pergamus, and who was detained in the city by a regrettable accident. Crates fell into an open sewer and broke his leg, a misfortune not without its advantages to Roman culture, as he gave frequent and well-prepared lectures during his enforced sojourn, which were speedily imitated by other scholars.

A Roman schoolmaster with a smattering of learning was called a *literator*. The term *literatus* implied greater skill in reading and writing than belonged to the average teacher, while a *grammaticus* was a recognized master of the criticism of poetry. Seneca, himself a Roman philosopher, and as such a thorough student of 'grammar' or literature, distinguishes between the respective spheres of the *philosophus*, the *philologus*, and the *grammaticus*, in that the first deals with fundamental meanings, the second with historical and archaic aspects of speech, and the third with literature. The art of the *grammaticus*, according to a Greek definition, included accurate reading, explanation of poetic figures of speech, exposition of rare words and subject-matter, etymology, statement of regular grammatical forms, and, above all, criticism of poetry; and it was in this sense that the Romans also understood it. The rhetor was a teacher of oratory, but like the grammarian found it necessary to pay some attention to the attainments of his pupils in logic, mathematics, and even the theory of music.

It was natural that the conservatism of the old Roman habit of mind should react with some vigour against the inevitable encroachments of Hellenic culture and Hellenic institutions. About the middle of the second century B.C., two Epicurean philosophers were banished from Rome, and in 161 B.C. provision was made for the expulsion and exclusion of philosophers and rhetoricians. In 92 B.C. the censors expressed their disapprobation of the new kind of training, which caused young men to waste days at the classes of Latin rhetoricians, when they might have been better employed according to the customs of their ancestors. Yet rhetoric grew in public favour, while grammar was still more firmly entrenched. Augustus, when he expelled other foreigners from Rome, exempted the teachers of the liberal arts, which gradually came to be limited to the number of seven—grammar, rhetoric, dialectic, arithmetic, music, geometry, and astronomy.

Under the Empire a Roman boy destined for the law, for public office, or for the teaching of literature or rhetoric would be taught the rudiments of knowledge by a tutor if his family were wealthy, or otherwise at the local school, which would probably confine its attention to reading, writing, a little Latin literature, practical arithmetic with the aid of the abacus, together with prompt mental calculations, the laws of the Twelve Tables, which, however, gradually became obsolete, but which must have been replaced by some other form of civic and religious instruction, the calendar, and perhaps the elements of military drill. From such a school the boy might be taken, as Horace was taken by his father, to Rome or another centre where he might sit at the feet of a grammaticus of repute. Here he would study chiefly poetry, but also the elements of mathematics, the theory of music, logic, and rhetoric; above all, he would learn Greek. Some of the literary teachers appear to have begun with Greek, taking it for granted that Latin grammar could be learned incidentally. Thus, unlike the Greek secondary schools, those of Rome taught a foreign language; and those students who wished to excel in literature or in oratory sought an opportunity after leaving school of continuing their studies at Athens or some other centre of Greek culture, after the fashion of Cicero and Horace. In many cases, of course, students were not so fortunate as to travel and study in the East; but without leaving Rome or other great western cities they could proceed from the school of the grammaticus to that of the rhetor. The age at which the transition should be made was a matter of some dispute, the grammarian insisting upon a sound basis of literary knowledge, the orator upon the need of an early beginning with the practice of rhetoric. 'As if', remarks Quintilian, greatest of the teachers of oratory, 'one should not learn declamation until he already knows how to declaim!'

The Emperor Vespasian inaugurated a practice whereby the salaries of some of the more eminent rhetoricians were paid by the State. A number of chairs at Athens profited by a similar endowment. According to Pliny, about five thousand children received free education and a dole of corn from the munificence of Trajan. It is clear also that municipalities shared in the control and endowment of higher education, at least under the later Empire. Various honours and immunities began to be conferred upon *grammatici* and *rhetores* from the time of Constantine. The apostate Emperor Julian forbade Christians to teach the classics, on the ground that they could not do justice to themes with which they had no sympathy. The Romans, in fact, were as eager to assimilate Greek culture as the Greeks themselves to propagate it.

The philosophical schools which had arisen after the death of Aristotle, especially the Stoic and Epicurean, and later the Neo-Platonic, flourished at Rome scarcely less than at Athens or Alexandria. The philosopher kept his school less formally than the grammaticus or the rhetor; and his pupils were frequently grown men. Philosophy, in fact, took the place of religion in the lives of the better educated, and offered a considerable resistance to the growth of Christian theology. Neo-Platonism in particular earned the vigorous denunciation of the early Fathers, not merely for the superstitions which became associated with it, but also because the very merit of many of its principles was an abiding danger to faith.

III

QUINTILIAN

MARCUS FABIUS QUINTILIANUS, a native of Calagurris, in Spain, was born about A.D. 35. Quintilian, after practising as a barrister, finally opened a public school at Rome, making a large fortune as a teacher, and receiving a salary from the Emperor Vespasian. According to Juvenal, such success in a pedagogue was as rare as a white crow. Under Domitian he became consul. The *Institutes of Oratory*, his great educational work, became the recognized text-book of the Roman rhetorical schools.

Neglecting the elaborate technical discussion of the art of rhetoric, let us briefly analyse Quintilian's treatment of the following topics:

1. The aim of education.
2. The contents of the curriculum of the oratical schools.
3. The institutional agencies concerned with the purpose of educating an orator.
4. Methods of teaching, and the adaptation of instruction to the age and capacity of the child.

1. The aim is to produce a good man skilled in speaking (Book XII, Chapter I). 'No man, unless he be good, can ever be an orator'; he may speak with great force, but will not reach perfection of eloquence. The aim is indeed to produce a *Roman wise man*, one who mingles in political action, as well as in the discussions of the schools. The orator need not belong to any single philosophical sect; but should learn what is good from all. He is not to be a mere philosopher, since he must needs be acquainted with natural philosophy, ethics, and dialectics, including logic. Logic, however, is often overrated as part of the education of an orator; whereas moral philosophy is above all things to be studied. Right conduct takes precedence of right reasoning.

2. A child should never hear ungrammatical language, even from his nurse. The studies of a schoolboy ought to begin with Greek rather than with Latin, because the latter will be acquired, even though one tried to prevent it (I. i. 12). He must learn reading and writing; and will commit chosen passages to memory, chiefly from the poets (I. i. 36). Next in order follow grammatical studies, including the art of speaking correctly, and that of illustrating the

poets (I. iv. 1, 2). Music, astronomy, philosophy, and eloquence are required to make an efficient *grammaticus*. The range of reading should be widely extended, commencing with Homer and Virgil, and including tragedy and selected portions of lyric poetry, although some lyric and elegiac poetry, being likely to corrupt the morals, should be omitted. When his morals are out of danger, the pupil should study comedy also, especially the Greek of Menander. The circle of instruction preliminary to rhetoric may be completed by geometry, music, and astronomy. Rhetoric itself is apt to be begun rather late; as if a youth should not be taught declamation until he already knows how to declaim!

3. Quintilian neglects nothing that may serve as an institutional means for the education of an orator. (*a*) The nurse is to be chosen with care, first from the moral standpoint, and secondly as a model of speech (I. i. 4, 5). (*b*) Parents themselves, whether learned or unlearned, should be solicitous in all that relates to the education of their children. (*c*) *Paedagogi* should be, if possible, men of learning; if not, conscious of their want of it, lest, by their own misdirected efforts, they hinder the skilled teacher—their conduct should be blameless. (*d*) Up to seven years the child may receive at home some tuition adapted to his infant years, then he should proceed to school. (*e*) Public schools are to be preferred to private, and to domestic tutelage (I. ii.). In public schools emulation is stimulated, friendships are formed, and advantages are gained by the observation of the errors of others. (*f*) Corporal punishment is by no means to be approved, for excellent reasons given (I. iii. 14–17). (*g*) The school of the *grammaticus* is the foundation of all educational superstructures. (*h*) The school of the *rhetor* should follow, not at too late an age. Grammar and rhetoric should not be too completely severed. (*i*) The teacher must be moral, authoritative, neither too austere nor too affable, equable yet uncompromising, attentive to detail, capable of feeding the mind by the living voice (II. ii).

4. Imitation is the first, and always an important method of learning (I. i. 5). Children may be led to commit poems to memory, even in their play; in fact, instruction should be made an amusement to young children (I. i. 20). Rewards and prizes are desirable, and emulation is to be stimulated throughout the whole course. The forms of letters should be learned together with their names and order, not subsequently, as is often the case (I. i. 24–6). Ivory figures of letters may be given to children to play with. The pupil may learn

to write by tracing letters cut in grooves on a board (I. i. 27). In learning syllables, and in reading, progress should be thorough rather than hurried (I. i. 31). Headlines to be copied may include obscure words or moral maxims, that there may be no waste of effort (I. i. 34–6). Exercises in the pronunciation of difficult lines and words are advantageous (I. i. 37). The *paedagogus* ought to see to the boy's homework. The period of infancy should not be enervated by luxuries; too often, indeed, children behold vices in the home before they know that they are vices (I. ii. 6–8). The plan of taking places according to merit is commended (I. ii. 23–5). 'To let himself down to the capacity of the learner' is the master's problem (I. ii. 27). Class teaching is commended as a stimulant to pupils and masters alike.

An acquisitive and retentive memory, and a faculty of imitation, are symptoms of ability in children. Precocious talent is undesirable. Children are to be treated according to their natural dispositions, but all will be found to need play and recreation. 'Nothing too eagerly, nothing dishonestly, nothing without self-control.' Habit is of the greatest consequence.

The only principle in reading is this: Let the pupil understand what he reads (I. viii. 2). There is no great danger of asking the pupil to study too many subjects, for the human mind is so constituted as to be interested in very many things at once (I. xii. 2). Boys can endure a great amount of study, and, indeed, they will never have more time at their disposal. Individual tastes are to be consulted in arranging a course of study; it is ill to fight against nature (II. viii). Able intellects must undertake all the excellences of an orator; feebler minds may study those branches in which they are most likely to succeed. In moderate minds nature contributes more than art; in the most talented art is most often the secret of success.

IV

ROMAN CULTURE AND ROMAN CURRICULUM

IF Rome inherited the civilization of Greece, it was not because the Roman mind was constituted like the Hellenic, but rather from the force of those circumstances which established her power throughout the Mediterranean coasts. For among the Romans there was little evidence of a natural versatility of interest, little power to elevate facts into ideals, or to construct new worlds of imagination, little disposition even to wander into untrodden paths of thought. They looked often to the practical side of life and seldom to the theoretical; their prose was the expression of legal formulae or the practical eloquence of the forum; their very poetry, until the period of so many translations from the Greek, no more than a form of worship.

In the field of drama, the Romans had a native form of comedy, but were indebted to the Greeks for the beginnings of tragedy. The original types of Roman comedy included the Fescenninae practised at rustic festivals and harvesting, the Saturae performed by rural clowns, with music, dancing, or gesticulation, and the Mimi or mountebank representations, scurrilous yet sententious, which held a subordinate place in literature from the period of the fall of the Republic to the final stage of imperial culture. Types of comic characters were developed in the Atellanae, plays of a burlesque sort, often performed as afterpieces. There was no material for the education of the young in the indigenous Roman comedy, which was not only licentious in the extreme, but written always in an undignified plebeian strain.

Roman comedy of the more pretentious kind was an imitation of Greek originals and applied itself to Greek subjects. From Livius Andronicus to Terence, it appears to have gained in refinement of expression rather than in originality of idea. The plays of Terence were favoured by literary students of the empire, and in general the *palliata* or comedies from the Greek were studied in academic circles to the exclusion of the coarser but more national *togata* which dealt with Roman situations and characters of a more realistic, but a baser type.

Tragedy was not indigenous to Rome, but an exotic flower of Greece. At best the tragic poets were few and their genius of a secondary character. Seneca, for example, was read rather than acted; but tragedies furnished a part of the subject-matter of literary studies under the later empire.

Epic poetry began to be used in the Roman schools under the Republic, with the Latinized version of the *Odyssey* by Andronicus. Naevius followed with a poem on the Punic war, and Ennius with an epic version of the Roman Annals. Even Cicero and Octavianus attempted the epic, while the imperial period produced Lucan's *Pharsalia*, together with a host of courtly and antiquarian epics which tended to express ingenuity and scholarship rather than patriotism or feeling. Epics of the heroic rather than the historical type were usually written on Greek subjects which necessitated pedantry, imitativeness, and a laboured recourse to foreign mythology. These limitations were surmounted with great success by Virgil, whose *Aeneid* became the standard text of grammarians, its sonorous lines being recited everywhere in the school. In the meantime numerous Christian epics were written; but, naturally enough, they found no place in the schools as centres of pagan learning.

Certain poems, however, of a purely didactic though seldom of a religious character, were written expressly for the use of students. Some of the poems of Ausonius, such as those on the calendar, belong evidently to this class, while there were also treatises in verse upon letters, prosody, rhetoric, and other subjects which might be schematized and committed to memory. Such verses were written by the grammarians of the later Empire exactly in the spirit and mode which was afterwards to become common among the more enterprising medieval schoolmasters. The so-called *Disticha Catonis*, probably written prior to the period of the official adoption of the Christian religion, comprised a collection of moral sayings arranged in couplets for the use of schools, which actually retained their vogue to the end of the Middle Ages. But it is probable that greater attention was bestowed upon the form of poetry than upon its content. Scholars were practised in the use of various metres, and in the composition of imaginary epistles both in verse and prose. Towards the close of the Empire considerable attention began to be paid to fables, riddles, acrostics, and similar trifles; and hexameters began to be embellished with rhyme.

While *lyric poetry* was less congenial to the Roman disposition than narrative, it is clear that epigrams became extremely fashionable, while elegies were written and studied in schools as exercises in style. The mastery over poetic form appears to have increased as inspiration and power diminished.

Prose occupied a subordinate place in the curriculum of Roman education, as it had in Greek. It had a rhetorical character, owing partly to the practical use that was attached to the command of prose, and partly, perhaps, to the influence of Cicero, who first made it worthy of study in the schools. Prose was employed in history, but so long as this study flourished more in the interests of rhetoric than fact, history meant little for education, although the annalists preserved many facts and traditions that were more often embodied or summarized from their several predecessors than dictated by their own experience or observation.

Antiquarian learning was not without its devotees, and Ausonius depicts for us the type of research student who knew more about recondite studies than about the history and literature of Latium. The most learned of the Romans was M. Varro, the greater part of whose work has perished. From the period of Varro, which was also that of Cicero, an academic and erudite class was rapidly developed which took possession of the schools at the same time that it sacrificed the ancient connexion of theory with the practical affairs of life. Learning became the monopoly of the *grammatici*, who gave themselves largely to etymology, grammar, and the making of dictionaries. The textbooks of Latin grammar written by Donatus in the fourth century, and by Priscian early in the sixth, retained their celebrity throughout the Middle Ages. The *grammatici* were critics as well as grammarians, so that (as Suetonius says) their business was the emendation of texts, the discrimination of meanings, and the compilation of critical notes. They did little, however, beyond the imitation of the Greeks. Each new work on grammar embodied copious extracts from its predecessors, usually without acknowledgement, until there finally arose an incredible confusion of authorities. Meanwhile the *grammatici* taught not only etymology and grammar but also mythology in their schools. The mythology was borrowed from Greece, but the etymology might have either a Greek or a Latin basis according to the grammatical school to which the teacher happened to adhere.

Oratory, more than any other study, occupied the attention of the talented Roman youth. In politics, jurisprudence or war, oratorical skill was equally indispensable. A manual of oratory is ascribed to the elder Cato. In the words of Livy, some were carried forward to the highest offices by jurisprudence, others by eloquence, others by military glory.[1] Oratory then was recognized in the Republic and earlier Empire as a high road to advancement and fame. Cicero

[1] Livy, xxxix, 40.

regretted that whereas for the Greeks it had been an end in itself, for the Romans it was but a means to success at the Bar.[1] The youth trained in oratorical schools would begin to speak in the forum at eighteen or nineteen years of age, at times making his début in a funeral oration. From the time of the elder Cato it became customary for speakers to write down and publish their orations, which had previously been delivered without notes. The speeches of Cicero, Quintilian, and others were taken down by clerks, probably in shorthand, and published with or without the consent of the author, sometimes in garbled versions. Under these conditions the study of rhetoric in Rome was anything but the perfunctory occupation that it seems to be at the present time. It was a practical and profitable thing, frowned upon by the old-fashioned Censors (who decreed the expulsion of the rhetors from Rome in 92 B.C.), but welcomed by the ambitious youth. One reads that only four years after the decree above cited a freedman of Pompey, one Vultacilius Plotus, skilled in Latin rhetoric, had opened a school in the city. There were also numerous teachers of Greek and Asiatic oratory in Rome during and after the age of Cicero.

Under the Empire oratory became less genuine and more servile. Forced to renounce serious topics, the schools became the centre of a host of fictions. The ancients had been orators, the moderns were but rhetoricians; at least such was the judgement of Tacitus. The Empire was never so sure of maintaining a check upon freedom of speech as after it had begun to pay the salaries of eminent professors of rhetoric, the first to benefit being Quintilian in the reign of Vespasian. Gaul and Africa in the third century became important centres of rhetorical study: Gaul being signalized by the skill of her professors in the manipulation of form and style; Africa by the energy of her rhetors, including Tertullian, Arnobius, Cyprian, and Augustine, in the defence of Christianity.

When a pupil had completed his task under the *grammaticus* he would proceed normally to the school of the rhetor, where his work began with demonstrations, and proceeded to declamations, deliberations, and controversies. Controversies included case-law, the subdivision of the subject, and the appeal to mitigating circumstances. But the cases cited in the schools were strangely unreal. Pliny, Petronius, Tacitus, and others ridicule the questions that were accustomed to be raised and disputed, dealing with tyrants, or

[1] Cicero, *de Oratore*, II, 55.

pirates, or the sacrifice of maidens. Contemporary politics were practically taboo. It was the opinion of Petronius that such instruction made youths into fools. Little realism was attached even to historical debates about Sulla and Hannibal; none at all to declamations on subjects taken from Virgil, Ovid, or Homer. But the same stereotyped, empty fictions continued to be treated in the time of Ausonius, the same in the days of Augustine, the same even as late as the sixth century. The subjects appointed for prose composition were no more vital than the topics of debate. In particular, among the favourite exercises of the schools was the composition of fictitious letters; for example, an advanced pupil would be called upon to write a letter from Cicero to Caesar, or from Seneca to the Apostle Paul.

Fairy-tales, romances, and love-stories were licentious and unsuitable for declamation in the schools, but as they had been suggested even in Homer, and by the time of Ovid had come to furnish a part of the staple material of literature, they were actually employed in education to an extent difficult to determine, but certainly appreciable. The romances were at first of the nature of Greek translations, and were generally called 'Milesia'. The metamorphoses of Apuleius were to become the prototype of a certain kind of medieval romance. It was alleged that the schools of the later empire were addicted more to fiction of this kind than to the books of Plato. At least it appears to have been the policy of the emperors to encourage the study of trifles in order to divert attention and criticism from the field of politics.

While the bent of the Roman mind was distinctly more practical than theoretical, and accordingly not so much addicted to *philosophy* as to law, it could not escape from the influence of Greek speculation upon the constitution of the universe and the nature and destiny of man. It was unfortunate that the contact of Rome with Greece was altogether subsequent to the fiery creative epoch of Greek thought. It was but an afterglow of Greek philosophy that warmed the stubborn intellects of the Romans to attempt ambitious flights. Epicureanism, Stoicism, the Peripatetic philosophy, the New Academy, Neo-Platonism, and a degenerate form of the Pythagorean philosophy became domiciled in Rome, but were looked upon with suspicion and regarded as exercises rather than as paths to objective truth. The bare shoulder and cloak of the professional philosopher were often the marks of a mere charlatan. Philosophers were actually banished from Rome by Vespasian and Domitian, but at other times they conducted their informal schools without molestation, and even with honour, so that one philosopher, Marcus Aurelius, came to occupy the throne. In the earlier imperial period Epicureanism, in the later Stoicism, was the most popular form of philosophical creed. The study of philosophy revived in the fourth, fifth, and sixth centuries because of the fact that the pagans were driven to its tenets in order to maintain themselves against the Christian propaganda. A last desperate attempt to preserve the ancient philosophy was made, not without success, in the sixth century by Boethius. His partial translation of Aristotle into Latin and his book on the *Consolations of Philosophy* were studied in the early medieval schools. The opinion of Gellius as to professional philosophical teachers was that they would run and sit at the gates of wealthy youths and persuade them to waste the whole night in drinking wine, ostensibly as a vehicle, no doubt, for discussions and dialectic. The average Roman considered philosophy to be irreligious, a waste of time, and a veil for mercenary motives.

Totally different was the Roman estimation of Law. From the earliest times the Romans had a natural genius for law and order, a shrewd practical intelligence, and a disposition to dispute any conceivable infringement of their individual or collective rights. It is declared among the Roman traditions that there were schools for reading and writing in the forum from the earliest days of the Republic; and whether this be an exaggeration or not, the origin of the custom of teaching the laws of the Twelve Tables to the children is lost in the same obscurity as the origin of these elementary schools. Collections of the sources of law were made as early as 204 B.C., and by degrees the habit of collecting decisions in typical cases developed a new field for study alongside the examination of the laws themselves. For law the Romans were by no means primarily indebted to Greece, and it has been remarked that the more national a Roman poet may be, the more prominent the position the law holds in his writings.[1] The schools of oratory were obliged to devote considerable attention to the study of jurisprudence, but the relative emphasis on good oratory or good law appears to have varied according to the legal knowledge or conscientiousness of the teacher. A consulting lawyer learned his business by accompanying a distinguished juriconsult and listening to his opinions. Cicero's opinion of the jurisprudence of his day is sometimes respectful, but here and there contemptuous. It was not under the Republic, however, but under the later Empire

[1] *History of Roman Literature,* Teuffel and Schwabe, i, p. 78.

that Roman law attained its majority and became the chosen field of the ablest and most honourable minds. Gaius became the first professor of civil law, and began to write his *Institutions* by way of an introduction to the subject. His most notable successor was Ulpian. The codification of the laws ensured their place once for all as a subject of study in the universities of the later Imperial period. Masters of law and students of law are mentioned in inscriptions, the latter with frequency.

For the purposes of this survey, other subjects of study in the Roman schools require no more than a cursory reference. Arithmetic was taught in the schools, as is indicated by Horace, but we know little of what was done in the subject in his day, beyond an emphasis upon mental work with units of money. No advance was made upon the knowledge formerly possessed by the Greeks in arithmetic and geometry, which suffered in the estimation of scholars by their supposed alliance with astrology. The Romans were by no means the equals of the Alexandrian Greeks in mathematical attainments. Neither did they study natural history at first hand, but only from Greek texts, which were gradually corrupted and confused by the introduction of superstitious auguries and credulous allegories and fables.

The study of agriculture flourished among the Romans, but in a private and individual way, and by means of books rather than schools. Medicine was a purely Greek art, although under the later Empire the Arabic physicians had already begun to dispute the palm with the Greeks; this art also depended upon books and individual instruction but not schools. The same general status is characteristic of architecture and military science. Geography, music, and astronomy were actually taught in school, but only in the first of these subjects did the Romans show any originality or tendency to add to the sum of human knowledge. The measurement of land, however, was so important from a legal and military point of view that special schools of surveying were established under the Empire, the first impulse having been given by Caesar, who summoned Greek teachers in this field from Alexandria to Rome.[1]

[1] For a convenient summary of the principal references in extant Roman literature to these studies consult Teuffel, *History of Roman Literature,* ed. London, i, pp. 1–97.

V

AUSONIUS

I

WE should know nothing of the life of Ausonius were it not for his own poems, but these are in fact so studiously autobiographical that each of them celebrates, or introduces in an apparently casual manner, some event of his life; it may be his studies, his professorship, his tutorship of the youthful Caesar, his colleagues in the Gallic universities, or his consulate. We learn that his father, Julius Ausonius, was an eminent physician of Bordeaux, one who had little or no political ambition, no greed of wealth, attending the poor gratuitously, and pleased to guide his life by the example of the seven Sages of Greece. Julius Ausonius was probably a pagan, and even the Christianity of the son was only skin-deep, never colouring his thought or diminishing his allusions to the pagan mythology, but only affording a pretext for a few perfunctory verses upon Easter.

D. Magnus Ausonius was born at Bordeaux about the year 309, and was educated in the city of his birth, and afterwards at Toulouse, under the auspices of his uncle, the rhetorician Arborius. His studies were principally, after the manner of the time, in Latin and Greek grammar, rhetoric, and law. After essaying the practice of law Ausonius turned to the art of teaching, and accepted a chair of grammar at Bordeaux, in which he was eminently successful, finally becoming a rhetorician, and the most conspicuous teacher in Gaul. His fame reached the ears of Valentinian, who called him to the Imperial court, entrusted him with the education of his young son, Gratian, then a lad of eight years, and thus permitted him to compare himself with other tutors of princes, including the great Seneca, Fronto, and Lactantius. It was perhaps at this time that Ausonius first professed himself a Christian, and the shallowness of his profession accorded perfectly with that of the Emperor himself. The good fortune of Ausonius gave a new impulse to his muse, and won him the friendship, besides, of such notables as Symmachus and Probus.

Gratian had barely emerged from the age of tutelage, when he succeeded in 375 to the government of the Empire and soon bestirred himself to reward his teacher. Ausonius became prefect of Africa and Italy, and afterwards of Gaul; and the sum of his honours was completed by the gift of the consulship for the year 379. But the downfall of his protector was near, and with the fall of Gratian Ausonius retired from the court to the nest of his old age in Aquitaine, notwithstanding that, apparently, the favour of Theodosius also would have been extended towards him. Here he superintended the education of his grandson, wrote elegies to his parents and to the professors of Bordeaux, and poems inspired by well-worn remnants of the ancient mythology; and here he may have died about the year 394. He lived in an age when true poetry was impossible; but his verses have delicacy and ingenuity, and traces of an original grace and love of natural beauty; and incidentally, they will be found to reflect a little light on the methods and character of contemporary Roman education.

2

In the first place, this tutor of royalty, this university professor of the fourth century, has bequeathed to posterity the following exhortation to his grandson on the studies of childhood (Idyll IV):

'Even the Muses have their periods of leisure. The imperious voice of the stern master does not always drive his pupils; but fixed hours preserve the alternations of recreation and study. It is enough for the boy with memory to have read with a will, then let him rest. The school is called by a Greek name,[1] to indicate that due leisure should be accorded to the laborious Muses. Since you are sure that play will come in its turn, learn gladly; for we give intervals to wipe out protracted fatigue. The zeal of a boy is wearied unless joyous holidays relieve his days of severe work. Learn gladly, my grandson, and do not curse the rein of a severe master. The aspect of a master is never terrible. Let him be gloomy and old, harsh of voice and always threatening with his furrowed brow, yet he will never be formidable to the pupil who has once become accustomed to his appearance. A child will love the wrinkles of his nurse and avoid his mother. Grandsons prefer grandsires and trembling grandmothers, to whom the late born are a new care, to their fathers. Chiron of Thessaly, who was half horse, did not terrify Achilles, son of Peleus; nor did the son of Amphitryon dread pine-bearing Atlas; but both these preceptors by gentleness and kindly speech conciliated the affections of their young pupils.

'Thyself then do not tremble, though the school resound with many a blow, and thine old master wear a truculent countenance. Fear is a mark of degenerate spirits; but do thou stand firm and fearless; let not the cries, the sounding blows, and the fear of punishment, agitate thee from the morning hour, because he brandishes the ferrule his sceptre, because he is well furnished

[1] The original meaning being 'leisure'.

with a leather thong, and the benches hum with trembling groans. Forget the reputation of the place, and the scene of idle fears.

'Already, following these counsels, your father and mother have assured the calm and happiness of my old age. You also, the first of my grandsons to bear in your childhood the name of your grandsire, to gladden the few days that fate still accords to me in my declining years, give me either deeds or at least hopes. Now I behold you as a boy, soon a youth; and then as a man, if fate has so ordained; but if fate is envious, at the least I hope, and my prayers will not be in vain, that you will not forget your father's example and my own, that you will seek the arduous rewards of the Muses, being eloquent and one day entering on the path in which we have preceded you, and in which are now walking your father the pro-consul, and the prefect your uncle.

'Study all that is worth remembering. I shall recommend each author. You are to read thoroughly the composer of the Iliad, and the works of dear Menander. With inflexions and intonations of the voice put rhythm into the measures, and use correct accentuation. Mark the moods as you read; discrimination adds to the impression, and pauses give vigour to weak passages. When will these gifts gladden my old age? When will you renew for me so many forgotten poems, and histories linked from age to age, and the socks and robes of kings,[1] and melic and lyric measures? When will you make young again the enervated senses of an old man? While you go before me, my grandson, I can learn a second time the modulated poems of Flaccus, and lofty-sounding Virgil. You also, O Terence, who adorn with chosen speech, the Latin tongue, and tread the stage with tightly drawn sock,[2] conduct my worn out memory to dialogues almost new to it. And now I read your crime, O Catiline, and the insurrection of Lepidus, and anon leaving Lepidus and Catulus I now read the story of affairs and life at Rome during twelve years; I read the war half-foreign, half-civil, which the exiled Sertorius waged in company with his Iberian allies.

'And this advice I do not give as an ignorant grandsire, but as one experienced in teaching a thousand minds. I myself have nourished many in their suckling years, cherishing them in my bosom, and teaching them to speak; I have plucked their tender years from their fond nurses. Then I have attracted them as boys by gentle admonition and a moderate fear to seek pleasure through difficulty, and to pluck the sweet fruits of a bitter root. And as they become men under the impulse of the age of puberty, I have guided them towards morality, the fine arts, and the force of eloquence, although they declined to give obedience to the yoke, or to offer their mouth for the insertion of the bit. A difficult moderation, a hard experience, a rare success to be expected only after long trial, a gentle censure to rule intractable youth—I had much to bear until my sorrow became a pleasure, and my labour was softened by habit and use; and then I was called to the pious task

[1] i.e. tragedy and comedy.

[2] i.e. finished comedy.

of educating a prince,[1] and was invested with various honours, and had the right to command in golden palaces. May Nemesis pardon me, and Fortune tolerate my jests! I presided over the empire, when Augustus was still a boy, and though he had the purple, the sceptre, and the throne, submitted to the commands of his teacher, thinking my honours greater than his own. Reaching maturity he increased these honours by a sublime addition, when I was created quaestor by the two Emperors, father and son, and was endowed with a double prefecture, a curule chair, a robe of state,[2] and a painted toga as the reward of my labours, and finally became consul, and my name was placed first on the calendar in my year.[3] Thus I have tried to win as great an honour as possible for my grandson, and my life will be the torch to lighten yours. Although you are already distinguished by your father's name, which may well be an honour and responsibility to you, yet a marked honour comes from me also; but let it not be a burden to your own efforts, and if you become consul, owe the fasces to yourself.'

3

Gaul was the home of Ausonius, and in his day the home of learning. In his own words, Gaul had his love, Rome his worship. Among the poet's works there is a series of commemorations of the professors of Bordeaux, his birth-place, of which the first, perhaps, will serve as a sufficiently good example, as it is not least characteristic of the academic standards and interests of the day. This, then, is an elegy addressed to *Tiberius Victor Minervius, orator.*

'My first speech is of you, Minervius, O pride of Bordeaux, second Quintilian of the rhetorical toga. Your teaching formerly shed lustre on Constantinople and Rome, and latterly on your native land. Let Calagurris[4] boast its native Fabius; yet the chair of Bordeaux is not inferior. It has given to the forum a thousand youths; it has added two thousand to the numbers of the senate, to the numbers of the purple toga, myself included; but I shall not speak of the numerous wearers of the purple toga, but will sing of you for your own sake, not for the honour that I owe to you. If you are compared with the panegyrists, you should be numbered among the panathenaics; if you care to develop the fictitious controversies of the schools, Quintilian has but a disputed palm. You have a flow of words like a torrent, yet one which rolls down gold and not a flood of mire; and the talent which Demosthenes thrice called the first thing in an orator[5] is so potent in you that he himself is surpassed by you. Shall I refer also to that divine gift of nature, your memory? You would hold fast in your mind anything you had once heard or read, so that people

[2] Gratian. [2] *trabeam*

[3] i.e. the name Ausonius was written before that of his colleague in indicating the year.

[4] Calahorra, the birthplace of Quintilian.

[5] i.e. action. Cf. Quintilian, Book XI, ch. 3; Cicero, *de Oratore,* Book III, section 56.

could rely upon your ear as upon a book. Once I saw you enumerate all the throws of the game[1] after a long contest, all the dice that were poured forth in rapid rotation by the steps cut out in the hollow boxtree, narrating with exactness all the points played or recalled in that prolonged period. No malice ever darkened your soul, your tongue was witty and spicy,[2] but gentle and without bitterness. Your table was distinguished in a way not culpable according to the censorial regulations, such as Frugi Piso would not have disowned as his. Sometimes on your birthday or on festive occasions it displayed abundance, but never such as to impair your moderate fortune. Though dying heirless at sixty years, you are mourned by us as a father and a friend. And now, if there is aught of us left after our last fate, you still live mindful of the life which has perished; but if nothing is left, if the long rest of death have no sensations, you have lived unto yourself, and our consolation is your fame.'

In the estimation of Ausonius, and of men of culture in his day, the title of *Grammaticus* was extremely honourable. Under these circumstances it was not unnatural that the attempts of pseudo-grammarians to claim the name were regarded with jealous disfavour. Ausonius looked upon such impostors in the same way as a modern university graduate regards the man who has purchased his degree, not earned it. It must have been in this spirit that the epigram to Philomusus the grammarian was written: 'Because your library is stuffed with books that you have bought, do you think yourself a savant and a grammarian, O Philomusus? According to this reasoning you have only to provide cords, bows, and instruments, and to-morrow will see you a musician.'[3] It was not that the grammarian was a lucky fellow, that men should imitate him so. 'The fortunate man is not a grammarian, he never was so, and no grammarian was ever described as fortunate. But if in spite of fate, there was ever a fortunate grammarian, he must have passed beyond the canons of grammar.'[4] The grammarian, of course, taught Virgil's epic, high among his courses of lectures; and this is the cry of the unhappy husband, grammarian though he be: 'Though I teach *arms and the man*, and know *arms and the man* well, I have married *arms* rather than a wife.'[5]

From a social point of view, upon the whole, to be a *grammaticus* was no slight distinction; it was to be a university professor of recognized academic status; and many a candidate for such a position must have lived and died a sub-doctor or assistant professor, a mere

[1] *Omnes bolos.* [2] *sale multo.* [3] Epigram 44.
[4] Epigram 136. [5] Epigram 137.

proscholus. Accordingly Ausonius writes of such an assistant professor, Victorius, a man apparently addicted to antiquarian researches, in the not uninteresting words which follow. (We know little or nothing of the Castor or Rhodope of the text, whose books, though apparently still in existence at the time, were already rare.)

'Studious Victorius, gifted with memory and facility, an assiduous reader of unknown books, perusing only what is recondite, you care more for studying papers eaten by bookworms and mice than for those that are more familiar. The pontifical law, the treaties and origin, before the time of Numa, of Cures the city of sacrifices; what Castor says of all the little known kings; what Rhodope published of her husband's writings; our pontifical law; the decrees of the ancient Quirites; those of the senate; the laws of Draco and Solon; those which Zaleucus gave to the Locrians; those of Minos under Jupiter; those of Themis before Jupiter; are better known to you than the books of our Cicero and Virgil, and the facts of the history of Latium. Perhaps further reading would have given you these also, if Lachesis had not accelerated your last journey. You had but the bare libation of the name of *grammaticus*, the mere varnish of the honour of our chair. You died finally on the distant coasts of Rome, whither you had crossed from the Sicilian shore. But now rejoice, if this pious tribute reaches your Manes, for you are remembered in the company of celebrated masters.'

The labours of an educated Roman included a good deal more, in one respect at least, than the work of a modern scholar. He was at his wits' end to get copies of books; and again, his friends would request copies of such as he had, and would expect to have them, not infrequently, within an unreasonably short period of time. Ausonius, poor man, had to write to the pretorian prefect Probus: 'O most worthy Probus, the copyists have caused me delay, and I know that I have kept you waiting so long that you will not thank me for the fulfilment of my promise. Fortunately, however, I have not failed you. I have sent your nobility the *Apologues* of Titian and *Chronicles* of Nepos, which are a sort of apologues, too, since they are very like fables, and I am glad, nay proud, that my efforts to serve you will contribute something to the education of your children.' The slaves who were unfortunate enough to be employed as copyists were probably driven early and late, so that, sometimes, they would run away, although the work of a clerk must have been preferable in many ways to that of a labourer in the field. Ausonius has some epigrams on one of these fellows, named Pergamus. 'As lazy a writer as you are a slow runner, Pergamus, you have fled only to be taken in the first couple of hundred yards. So, Pergamus, you bear the marks of writing on your face, and your forehead carries the letters neglected by your hand.' This was indeed a cruel jest, for the wretched copyist had evidently been branded with a hot iron. But the epigrammatic Ausonius goes on to remark that an injustice had been perpetrated, the innocent forehead suffering for the hands, guilty of idleness, and the feet, of running away.

Far more pleasant is it to turn to some verses of appreciation written to a really excellent clerk, who was evidently a stenographer, as indeed it appears from many references that shorthand-writing was practised by the Roman scribes, long before the time of Ausonius.[1]

'Slave, skilful minister of swift notes, come hither. Open the double page of your tablets, where a great number of words, each expressed by different points, is written like a single word. I go through great volumes; and like dense hail the words are hurled from my noisy lips, but your ears are not troubled, nor is your page filled. Your hand, scarcely moving, flies over the surface of the wax, but if my speech runs into a long circumlocution, you put the ideas on the tablets as if I had already spoken them. I wish my mind had as swift a flight as your right hand when you anticipate my words. Who, pray, has betrayed me? Who has told you what I was just meditating about saying? How does your winged right hand steal the secrets of my inmost thoughts? What is this order of things so new that what the tongue has not yet uttered has come to your ears? Schooling has not taught you this; no other hand is so skilled at swift abbreviation. Nature and God have bestowed this gift upon you, to know beforehand what I am going to say and to anticipate my desires.'[2]

[1] See especially Manilius, *Astronom.*, Bk. IV, v. 197.
[2] Epigram CXLVI.

VI

MARTIANUS CAPELLA

THERE are some men of whom we should care to know little, if the intrinsic merit of their work were the only thing concerned, but of whom we cannot know enough, because of the influence they have exerted upon the subsequent course of human affairs. Such a one is Martianus Minneius Felix Capella, the author, it is said, of the most successful text-book ever written, of whom if we conclude that he was an advocate, resided at Carthage, and wrote between A.D. 410 and 429, we have determined not less but rather more than is known by positive evidence. As to when he wrote, there is indeed the greatest diversity of opinion, but it appears to have been while Carthage flourished and had proconsuls, and if so, before 429, when Genseric landed in Africa and led his host of Vandals to the capture of the city (439). Capella appears, on the other hand, to have alluded to the capture of Rome by Alaric in 410, but the interpretation of this passage is at least doubtful. One can only conclude with certainty that since he used the works of Aquila Romanus and Aristides Quintilianus, Martianus must have written after the fourth century, and probably later than Augustine's book on the liberal arts, published in 387.

In the pages of any other author, writing at the beginning of the fifth century, it would have been strange to find no mention of Christianity, but it is not strange in Martianus. Prolix and self-satisfied, he seems to have cared less for the historical events that were going on about him than even the Christian writers of those times; and indeed, although the Roman Empire, as we have been accustomed to consider it, was toppling to ruins all about him, it is a fact that neither he nor other writers of the time appear to have grasped or appreciated the mighty phenomenon. His only care is to amuse himself and his readers with neo-Platonic mythology and allegory, and facts and events have little interest for him except as symbols. The empirical details which he was compelled to include in his work upon the seven liberal arts were too tiresome to occupy much of his personal attention, and it was fortunate, perhaps, for succeeding generations, that Capella preferred to cull them directly from Varro on grammar, dialectic, geometry, and astronomy, from Aquila Romanus upon rhetoric, from Solinus and Pliny on geometry and geography, and from Aristides Quintilianus on music.

The *Marriage of Philology and Mercury* is the title of the extant work of Martianus, but the true occasion of this strange ceremony, one reluctantly admits, is no more than the compilation of a text-book. The author appears to have drawn his personal satisfaction from the compilation of the allegorical setting of the books on the arts, wherein he is pedantically allegorical and obscurely humorous; while the actual subject-matter, as has been suggested, was compiled from older Latin sources. But most of the writers of the fourth century dearly loved to mingle sterile facts with fantastic allegories; therefore if Martianus amused himself in this way, it was but natural. And, consequently, why not take his facts from the nearest older text-book? For in those days of dogmatic temper, and a scarcity of books, it was barely possible to question the veracity of the written word. Seldom indeed did the verdict of experience presume to compete with the sanctity of a written authority. This attitude of the later Romans has been attributed to the influence of the Christian doctrine; on the contrary, however, it was characteristically both Greek and Roman, from the time when Theophrastus succeeded Aristotle in the government of the Lyceum, and inherited his master's books. Martianus, then, troubled no more to investigate his facts than frequently does the writer of a modern text-book for schools. Moreover, he made many mistakes, which may have been due to either haste or ignorance. But, when all is said, he could not go far astray with the formalism of grammar, dialectic, and rhetoric, so long as he copied the words of his originals carefully.

There is something ungrateful about discussing an author whom you cannot praise, something paradoxical about translating him at all, if there be no good in him. For why not be patient until some one arises to treat his work appreciatively? On the other hand, in the case of Martianus these arguments are not conclusive, for what is intrinsically trivial becomes historically of the greatest importance, and the *Marriage of Philology and Mercury* continued to be the principal fountain of the learning of the schools of western Europe during several centuries. And again, if one should wait for another to appreciate Martianus, before translating him, it is very probable that his work may never come into English at all. He is not wholly uninteresting, even to the modern reader, for his allegory is strange enough to attract attention, and in his accounts of the liberal arts one is brought face to face with an odd mixture of the curious and the familiar.

To expect originality of Martianus is as unfair as it is futile. There was no originality either in himself or his times. The fact is, perhaps, that apart from science, which was foreign to the spirit of the day, there was nothing new for the unfortunate Romans of the decadence to think about, except theological dogma. For, with that exception, the earlier Greek philosophers had exhausted all the speculative questions of the natural and supernatural worlds. Indeed, as I imagine, one of the reasons, though doubtless a minor one, that the scholars of the Middle Ages gave over philosophy for theology, was that theology represented a wood less denuded of its attractive foliage. Thus, had Martianus been a theologian, he might easily have diversified his argument by a more powerful motive than allegory. For example, he might have exercised his imagination, like Augustine, by speculations on the probable scheme of eternal punishment or the nature of the happiness of the blessed; or again he might have proceeded with a series of easy refutations of heresies, or the elaboration of a diversity of picturesque phrases of invective. This would have been in the spirit of the contemporary Christian literature, which had in its favour emotion if not reason, strength if not mercy. Far as the precepts of the later Latin fathers were removed from those of the original gospels, they infused into the Christian literature a simplicity, naturalness, and vigour that the work of a pagan writer of the fifth century, such as Martianus Capella, could not possibly have reproduced. Martianus had only his allegory to sustain the interest of his readers, and his own; and even in the allegory he merely succeeded in ringing the changes on the ideals of the mythology of earlier and greater masters. Thus, on the whole, Martianus achieved the obscurity of symbolism without its beauty; and just as the form of his occasional verse is more or less vitiated by errors, so the allegorical movement of the whole work is impaired by numerous lapses into the crudest improprieties of literary expression.

In reading the book of Martianus an almost absolute distinction ought to be drawn between the character of the setting, which was mainly his own, and that of the material for study, which was incorporated, not without error, from other sources. As the first two books are given to the setting alone, and are entirely allegorical, these are more original than the others, but in so far as one may speak of their originality at all, it consists only in giving new forms and combinations to other people's facts and ideas. Apparently Martianus had at first intended to limit his allegory to the first two books, as in the verse at the end of the second book he affirms the termination of the myth; but immediately the child of his imagination claims his sympathy once more, and regulates the tone and form of the work until the very end, where music, as is proper, conducts the bride to the nuptial couch. Meantime, apart from the setting, the seven later books have been sufficiently well described as 'strictly instructive, and sapless as the rods of medieval schoolmasters', for by their side the scholasticism of the later Middle Ages, much abused as it has been, would appear to a reader to be fresh, humane, and beautiful.

2. *An Extract from Book IV, on Dialectic* [1]

Binding her propositions in intricate knots, she without whom there is neither sequence nor opposition in argumentation, coming into the assembly of the Gods, brings forward the fundamental principles of speech and lays the foundation of the propositions of the schools, calling to mind that an expression consists of ambiguous words, and that nothing is normal, unless it is associated. But although pale Aristotle speaking in ten categories impetuously change his moods, although the Stoic sophisms circumvent and mock the senses, although they bear the never-lost horns on the forehead,[2] although Chrysippus accumulate and consume his own sorites, and although Carneades wield equal power with the aid of hellebore,[3] yet no such dignity has ever fallen to the children of men, nor has such a happy lot befallen thee, for now, Dialectica, thou mayest speak in the temples of the gods, and practise the laws of teaching in the sight of Jove.[4]

Thereupon entered at the call of Apollo a woman rather pale, but very keen of sight and with vibrant eyes continually in motion. Her locks were curly, with becoming waves, and had the appearance of being crimped and bound, yet they were let down in certain regular steps and encircled the whole form of the head so that they seemed to be neither too scant nor too abundant. She wore indeed the cloak and garment of Athens, but she carried something in her hands that was strange and quite untried in any gymnasium. For in her left hand a serpent was coiled in monstrous folds; inside her right certain formulae skilfully devised on flowering tablets, charmingly variegated, were

[1] Ed. Kopp, Frankfort-on-Main, 1836, pp. 325–41. Cf. Teubner text.

[2] Referring to the ancient sophism: 'What you have not lost you have; you have not lost horns, therefore you have horns.'

[3] Carneades the academician, when about to write a polemic against the books of the Stoic Zeno, is said to have used hellebore as a purgative, so that no crass humours in the stomach might distract his mind or diminish its powers.

[4] Thus far the metrical invocation. A prose description follows.

held beneath by the curve of a hidden hook. But while she hid the insidious reptile under her cloak in her left hand, she offered her right to everybody. Thus if any one took any of these formulae, he was soon seized by the hook and drawn to the venomous folds of the hidden snake, which quickly emerging first wounded him with eager bites by the venomed point of his piercing tooth, and then surrounded him with a number of folds and constrained him to the conditions offered him; but if any one did not wish to accept any of the formulae, she either caught them with certain contrary questions or quietly stimulated the snake to creep against them, until the binding folds strangled their captives according to the will of the questioner. But the woman herself was slight of figure, and dusky in her dress,[1] but her hair was like brier-thorns and she spoke somewhat that is unintelligible to the vulgar. For she asserted that the universal is dedicative to the particular, but in transverse opposition to the abdicative, and that both can be converted, by connecting equivocals with univocals,[2] and she declared that she alone could discern the true and the false as though by a kind of gift of divination. She said that she had been educated on the rock of Egypt, and then had descended to the school of Parmenides and Greece, and by proposing herself to speak on either side of a question had arrogated to herself the greatness of a Socrates and a Plato. 'Why, then', said Bacchus, the most jocular of the gods, and one who did not know Dialectica very well, since the twin snake of Mercury rising on his staff attempted to lick her, versed as she was in argumentation, and boasting of her victories over many, with frequent and rapid flashes of his tongue, and then also the Tritonian Gorgon hissed with the joy of recognition, 'doubtless she has either been brought here from the sands of gasping Lybia, as her twisted hair and friendship for snakes testify, or else we must credit her with being a poisonmonger of the Marsic nation. For in viprous caressing recognition she is loved with the adulation of snakes, or, if not, she is caught by the trick of the hook yonder, because that most seductive circlet is also an inhabitant of the Marsic territories.' When most of the gods had laughed at this as much as was proper,[3] Pallas, a little annoyed, forbade the ridicule of the newcomer, suggesting that this sober personage (a thing that could not be said of some of the gods[4]) could be

[1] Probably signifying the obscurity of the art.

[2] This sample of technical logical jargon is evidently chosen with the deliberate intent to create a formidable impression.

[3] Compare Plato, *Republic*, III; *Laws*, V; and Aristotle, *Nichomachean Ethics* IV, 8, 10, for the classical view of the indecency of immoderate laughter.

[4] Alluding to Bacchus

derided by none when once she had brought forward her propositions, even among kinsfolk that may be expected to be critical. And then Pallas ordered Dialectica to tell them what she had related in the trial of venomed assertion and bitterness, and to put herself in readiness to instil her wisdom. Then when Grammar, who having got through her discussion was standing near, feared to take the circled coils and gaping mouths of the slippery snake, they were entrusted to the goddess herself, who had tamed even the Medusa's hair, with their seductive figures and hooked formulae. Then by the dressing of her hair she was proven to be genuinely Athenian and Attic, especially as the wearers of the pallium and the choice of the Athenian youth follow her, wondering at the wisdom and mental power she displays. But Jupiter, who thought that the superficiality of the Greeks was inferior to the Roman strength not only when it came to practice but even in the judgement of virtues, commanded her to express her knowledge in the Latin tongue. Then Dialectica, although she thought that she could not do herself justice in Latin, with ready confidence, her aspect rendered formidable even before she spoke by the vibrant tension of her eye, thus began:

Were I not assisted by the learning and industry of Varro, a man famous among the glories of Rome, as a woman of the Greek nation I might be found very unskilled or barbarous upon an examination of my way of speaking Latin. For after the golden stream of Plato and the genius of Aristotle the work of Marcus Terentius (Varro) was the first to entice me into speaking Latin, and to make it possible to speak in the Ausonian[1] schools. Striving therefore to be consistent with these precedents, I shall not refuse to speak in Latin. And first I wish it understood that the Romans, wearers of the toga, could not have yet prepared a new vocabulary for my purposes, and therefore it is quite justifiable if I use the terminology for the science of dialectic that I am accustomed to in Athens, however the other arts express themselves. For, as nobody doubts, neither Grammar, whom your ears have heard, nor she who is renowned for the gift of the fertile mouth,[2] nor she who outlines the diversity of forms with a stick in the dust,[3] could be explained without my ratiocinations. For within my power and sway are six principles that are fundamental to the other arts. The first is speech,[4] the second interpretation,[5] the third propositions,[6] the

[1] i.e. Latin. [2] Rhetoric.
[3] Geometry. (Compare the occupation of Archimedes in Livy XXV, 31.)
[4] *de loquendo.* [5] *de eloquendo* (*de interpretatione*). [6] *de proloquendo.*

fourth the sum of propositions,[1] the fifth judgement, concerned with the criticism of the poets and their songs, the sixth as to what it is suitable for rhetoricians to say. Now in the first part the questions must be asked, what is genus, what form, difference, accident, property, definition, the whole, the part, the mode of division, the mode of partition, the equivocal, the univocal, and so to speak the plurivocal. Indeed, you ought to bear with these unusual terms, since you have compelled a Greek to speak Latin. Thus the first part of our division will consider what words are literal, what metaphorical, what are substance, quality, relativity, place, time, situation, character,[2] doing, suffering, opposites, and how many kinds of opposition there may be. But in the second, concerning interpretation, we shall ask what is a noun, a verb, the two in conjunction, which of them is the substantive and which the predicative part of the sentence, how far the noun is accepted, how far the verb, how far the sentence is perfect, so as to be a proposition. The third part, on propositions, follows this. In it the investigation is made, as far as time allows, as to how propositions differ in quantity and quality, what is a universal, a particular, an indefinite proposition, what are affirmative and negative propositions, what force have particulars, and how do they affect each other. Then follows the fourth part, which, as we have said, deals with the sum of propositions. In it the questions are asked, what is an assumption, an inference, a syllogism, a conclusion; what is a predicative syllogism, what a conditional, and what is the difference between them; how many forms are of the predicative kind, and what are they; do they follow a certain order, and if so, what is its nature; how many moods has each, and have these moods a certain sequence, and if so, what is its nature; finally, what are the primary and necessary moods of the conditional syllogism, what is their order, and how do they differ from each other. I think that this is enough for our present theme and thesis. I shall first indicate what genus is, going back to the beginning in order to run over the whole field.

Genus is the comprehension of many forms under a single name, as animal, whose forms are man or horse or the like. But sometimes certain forms comprehended under a genus are such that they themselves may be in the relation of genus to other forms, as the genus man, which is a form to *animal*, but a genus to *barbarians* and *Romans*. And one may go on dividing the forms of a genus in this way until one comes to an individual thing. For if you divide *man* into male and

[1] i.e. the syllogism.
[2] *Habitus*, any state of acquired perfection.

female, *male* into young and old, *young* into those who can and those who cannot speak, and if then you divide the young into Ganymede or any other youth of a known character, then he is not a genus, because we have now come to an individual. But we ought to use whatever genus is nearest to the business in hand, so that if the question is about *man*, we ought to assume his genus to be *animal*, because that is the most relevant.

By *forms* we mean the same as what we call species. Forms therefore are such that when substituted for the genus they retain its essence and name, as man, horse, lion; for since these are forms of animal, both man, horse, and lion can be called animal, and their name and substance participate in the essence that is ascribed by definition to the genus.

Difference is a discrimination adequate for the purpose in hand, as if it be asked what is the difference between *man* and *horse*, it is sufficient to say that man is a biped and horse a quadruped. But we ought to notice that since there are many differences in individual things, anything may be differentiated in as many different ways as we can find differences. For if we wished to divide *animal*, we can do so as to sexes, since some are male and others female; as to age because some are infantile, others old; as to size because some are small, others large, others middling; as to modes of locomotion because some walk, others creep, swim, or fly; as to diversity of habitation because some are aquatic while others are dwellers on the earth or in the air, and some say even in the fire; or we can divide them by their utterance, since some talk, others groan, bark, or yell. Yet we should see that each division is perfect and that everything is included in the particulars. For male animals may be new-born, small, walking, terrestrial, bipeds, and talkers at once. Therefore you may use what differentiation you please, but it ought to be suited to the purpose in hand. Thus if you are to speak in praise of mankind, it is advisable to divide animals into rational and irrational, so that it may be readily seen how high among the animals has nature set men, to whom alone she has granted powers of reasoning adapted to self-knowledge.

Accident is what does not occur except in a certain species, yet does not always occur even in that species, as rhetoric only belongs to man, but need not belong to him, since any one may be a man without being an orator.

Property is what occurs, and occurs invariably in the same species, so as to distinguish anything from what is common to all things, as laughter in man. For neither can any one but a man laugh, nor can a man avoid laughing according to his nature even if he should so wish. *Difference* is distinguished from property in that difference distinguishes anything only from the subject under discussion, whereas property distinguishes it from everything else. For if we wished to discriminate *man* from *lion* as to violence, by the fact that a lion is ferocious and a man gentle, we only discriminate as to what concerns the business in hand. For in calling the lion fierce and man mild we do not separate man from other gentle animals, nor the lion from other beasts, but when we have called man a laughing animal we have discriminated him thereby from the generality of other living creatures.

Definition is the clear and brief explication of the inner meaning of anything. In defining, three things are to be avoided, the false, the greater and the less. The false is in this wise; man is an immortal or an irrational animal. For though it be true that man is an animal, it is false that he is immortal or irrational. The greater is this wise: man is a mortal animal. For although this is concise, it is too extensive, because it applies to all animals. The less is indicated in this form: man is a grammatical animal. For though no animal except man is grammatical, yet not every man is a grammarian. The perfect definition is this: man is a rational and mortal animal. For by adding *mortal* we have separated him from the gods, and by adding *rational*, from the beasts.

VII

IMPERIAL EDICTS: WITH REGARD TO PROFESSORS, GRAMMARIANS, DOCTORS, AND STUDENTS[1]

1. *The Emperor Constantine Augustus to Volusianus*

WE ordain that doctors, grammarians, and other professors of letters, and the goods which they possess in their cities, shall be exempt from taxation and shall have the honours due to their functions. We forbid their citation to court, or the infliction of any injury upon them. If any one harasses them, he shall pay one hundred thousand *nummi* to the treasury, exacted by the magistrates or the quinquennials, or else they themselves shall be subject to this penalty. If a slave has done them injury, he shall be beaten with rods by his master in the presence of the injured party; but if the master shall have consented to the injury, he shall pay twenty thousand pieces to the treasury, and the slave shall be retained as a pledge until this sum is paid. We order that their goods and salaries shall be duly paid. And since like parents, masters, and tutors they ought not to be loaded with onerous offices, we permit them to discharge public offices if they are willing; but we do not compel them to do so contrary to their inclination. Given on the Kalends of August, at Sirmium, in the consulate of Crispus and Constantinus, Caesars (1st August, A.D. 321).

2. *The Emperor Constantine Augustus to the People*

In confirmation of the benefits of our divine predecessors, we ordain that doctors and professors of letters, with their wives and children, shall be exempt from every public function and from all public charges. They shall not be forced into military duty, they shall not have people billeted upon them, nor discharge any function of a public character; in order that they may the more readily instruct many students in liberal studies and in the arts to which we have referred. Given the fifth day of the Kalends of October, at Constantinople, in the Consulate of Dalmatius and of Zenophilus (27th September, A.D. 333).

[1] Translated from *Cod. Theodos,* Book XIII, tit. 3, ll. 1, 3, and 10: Book XIV, tit. 9, l. 1. Cf. Appendix, *Œuvres Complètes d'Ausone,* tome ii, seconde série de la bibliothèque latine-française, v. 5.

3. *The Emperors Valentine, Valens, and Gratian, Augusti, to Principius, Praefect of the City*

Let all men know that immunity is granted to the doctors and the professors of the city of Rome, so that even their wives may rest exempt from all disquietude; they shall be free from all public charges, they shall not be forced into military service, and soldiers shall not be billeted upon them. Given the third day of the Kalends of May, in the third consulate of Valentinian and Valens, Augusti (29th April, A.D. 370).

4. *The Emperors Valentinian, Valens, and Gratian, Augusti, to Olybrius, Praefect of the City*

(NOTE: *Sunt etiam Musis sua ludicra*—even the Muses have their relaxations—says Ausonius, Idyll 4. The discipline of the schools was severe, yet students were frequently given to diversions such as are restricted by the law which follows (*Cod. Theod.* Book XIV, t. 9, l. 1), which was passed while Ausonius himself was at court, so that it is not impossible that the hand of the famous professor may itself be traced in its provisions. This law indicates some interesting manners.)

All those who come to the city in the pursuit of learning should present to the master of the Census in the first place a letter from the provincial judges whose function it is to give them permission to come. The letter will mention the towns, the birth, and the merits of the individuals concerned. Thereupon, on their first entrance, they shall declare to what studies in particular they propose to devote their attention. In the third place, the office of the Censuales shall carefully take note of their residences, to ensure that they direct their endeavours towards the end which they have claimed to pursue. The Censuales shall also see that each of them behaves in conferences as men who should avoid a shameful and dishonourable reputation, and associations which we regard as bordering upon crime; and that they should not go too often to the spectacles, nor frequent untimely banquets. Nay, rather, if any one has not conducted himself in the city in such a way as the dignity of liberal studies demands, we give power that he be publicly beaten with rods, expelled from the city, and at once placed on shipboard and returned to his home. But to those who carefully devote their attention to their studies, permission is given to remain at Rome until the twentieth year of their age; but, after this time, he who shall have neglected to withdraw voluntarily shall be sent back to his country by the care of the prefect even though his education be unfinished.[1] But for fear that these measures should be taken in a perfunctory way, your high Sincerity is to instruct the Office of Censuales to take note every month of the names of the students, whence they come, and which ones ought to be sent back to Africa or to other provinces because of the time of their sojourn, those only being exempted who are attached to the offices of corporations. Similar notes will be addressed every year to the archives of our Mansuetudo, in order that we may be able to know the merits and aptitudes of each, and judge how and when they will be serviceable to us. Given the fourth of the Ides of March, at Treves, in the third consulate of Valentinian and Valens, Augusti (12th March, A.D. 370).

[1] Conjecturing *imperitus* for *impurius*.

VIII

EARLY CHRISTIAN SCHOOLS

1. *Catechumenal Schools*

CHRISTIANITY, bringing into the world of antiquity the concept of one great human family, in which the wife is elevated to a spiritual equality with the husband, the slave to the spiritual footing of the master, and the child to the spiritual value of the adult, produced a new system of schools and a new curriculum of instruction. Influenced as the Christian schools were by the methods and learning of Greece, they yet had a positive character of their own which was derived from their essential nature and purpose. Catechumenal schools existed possibly in apostolic times, certainly in the period immediately following, for the purpose of instructing candidates, chiefly adults, in the Christian faith prior to baptism. For some time nothing further was attempted, for the Christian expectation of an early return of Christ tended to prevent the development of settled institutions.

The substance of instruction in catechumenal schools consisted of the Lord's Prayer, together with the exposition of the Old and New Testaments, and of the doctrines of the Trinity, Grace, the Eucharist, Eternal Life, Eternal Punishment, &c., some knowledge of which, in those days of unsettled dogma, seemed desirable before baptism. Instruction was given either by the bishop or presbyter himself, or, should the number of disciples be too great, by a priest, deacon, or even a lay teacher designated by him. While the method was essentially that of exposition followed by catechism, it was varied by narrative and exhortation. Catechumenal instruction was offered only for a limited period; thus for a time it occupied the forty days of the Lenten fast. The tendency was for the duration of the catechumenal school to be extended, even to two or three years, although in the fifth century the customary period was reduced to eight months. Finally, infant baptism having become general before the end of the fifth century, the catechumenal schools were allowed to lapse.

At all times their limitations had been such as to render it necessary for Christians desiring a secular education to attend the heathen schools. Being purely religious in their curricula, and essentially catechetical in method, the catechumenal schools failed to teach even reading and writing. Secular subjects were taught in a few cases by

Christian teachers in the ordinary schools; but generally only by pagan masters, most of the content studied being drawn from the ancient mythology as embodied in classical poetry and prose.

2. *Catechetical Schools*

Schools of a higher type than the catechumenal, schools which even welcomed Jews and heathen in order that they might be instructed in the Christian theology, answering their doubts and objections and winning them to the Christian faith, were first established in the eastern parts of the Roman Empire. These catechetical schools were in many respects similar to the existing Hellenic schools for advanced instruction in literature and philosophy.

At Alexandria, about the year 181 or 182, there arose the first and most famous of such schools, conveniently situated at the very centre of Judaic and Hellenic learning. Among the teachers of this school were the founder, Pantaenus (died 202), Clement of Alexandria (born at Athens, died about 220), Origen (185–254), at a later period Heracles, and finally the wonderful Didymus the Blind (310–95), who, though afflicted with blindness from birth, had learned reading and mathematics by means of symbols shaped in metal, and became famous for his proficiency in all the liberal arts. This catechetical school, if indeed it may be regarded as continuous rather than as a succession of independent schools, seems to have flourished until the end of the third century, only to be rent asunder by polemics in the ensuing age. Other catechetical schools are known to have existed at Antioch, Edessa, Caesarea, Jerusalem, Rome, Carthage, and Constantinople.

The earliest set of instructions from a Latin pen for the teaching of the young in a Christian school is contained in the *De Catechizandis Rudibus* of St. Augustine, a treatise written at the request of Deogratia, a deacon who conducted a catechetical school at Carthage.

'In education,' says St. Augustine, 'love and fear, fear and love must ever be coupled together. Bad company, evil examples, are the worst enemies of good training. Children must be taught humility; and girls especially must be brought up in the fear of God. Severe words will be necessary. "A hard word is like the knife of a surgeon, that cuts away the ulcer at one stroke." None the less the instruction should be made agreeable, lest it be beyond the pupil's power of assimilation; moreover, it should be understood as well as learned. Although force and fear cannot be dispensed with, a better stimulus to the understanding than either is to be found in interest and self-denial. Teaching should take the form of a narrative, supplemented by questions, exposition, and exhortation. There should be no gaps in the instruction. The principal points should be brought into relief and emphasized, the facts thoroughly grounded and the matter selected in accordance with the individuality of the learner. The great aim is to convince the pupil that there is no rest for the heart but in God.'

Such is the view taken by St. Augustine of the scope, method, and significance of the catechetical school.

In general, the early Christians either attended pagan schools for their secular education, or went without it. Gregory of Nazianzus and Basil attended the lectures of pagan teachers at Athens; Jerome studied under Victorinus prior to the latter's conversion. A few Christians, indeed, such as Origen, had from the beginning retained their philosopher's cloak and continued to teach the secular subjects. Many, like Cyprian, abandoned the teaching of rhetoric upon their conversion. By the middle of the fourth century, Christianity having become widespread, many Christians had begun to engage in secular teaching, their activities in this direction being only temporarily checked by the famous edict of Julian in 362, which forbade Christians from teaching the classics on the ground that their belief prevented them from doing justice to the work. This edict was repealed in 364.

Augustine, and especially Jerome, whose influence upon ecclesiastical thought can scarcely be overrated, emphasized the dangerous fascination of secular learning without altogether denying its necessity. Jerome himself taught the works of Virgil in his monastery at Bethlehem. The catechetical school might have solved the difficulty, but unfortunately it never became a universalized institution.

IX

CHRISTIAN, STOIC, AND NEO-PLATONIC EDUCATION

1. *The Christian Attitude*

IT should not be supposed that when the Emperor Constantine embraced Christianity, and enjoined the observance of the Christian religion upon all his subjects, this was the end of Greek and Roman paganism. Many philosophers and teachers knew little or nothing of the new official faith, many accepted it only in name, and many refused to have anything to do with it. One emperor, Julian, actually reverted to paganism and attempted to exclude Christian teachers from the schools altogether. Pagan poetry, rhetoric, and mythology were still taught in the grammar-schools, to be superseded gradually and partially by Christian adaptations and imitations. Philosophers still gathered youths about them, to whom they taught their systems, the most important of which were the Stoic and Neo-Platonic. It was necessary and inevitable that even Christian scholars and teachers should make themselves acquainted with Stoic and Neo-Platonic thought, both to incorporate with their own doctrines what was not out of harmony with the Christian faith and to be able to answer objections to their own views, or to reveal flaws in the teachings of their pagan rivals.

A knowledge of Greek logic and philosophy is discernible in the Gospel of St. John and in the Epistles of St. Paul, but the first definite alliance between Greek culture and Christian propaganda was effected in the catechetical schools of Alexandria. Naturally many devout Christians dreaded the lewdness and idolatry which defiled the pagan classics. Yet a knowledge of Virgil and of Tacitus was obviously indispensable to the grammarian and to the rhetorician, and indeed to all who could claim to be educated, whether Christian or not. A Christian apologist like St. Augustine, however he might decry Neo-Platonism, was the better and the stronger for his own studies in the classical literature and philosophy. The great theologian, St. Jerome, though he seems to have entertained a doubt as to the compatibility of Christianity with classical culture, was a profound scholar for his time, unequalled in learning among the Latin fathers. Even the earlier thunders of Tertullian against everything pagan were made possible by the forensic eloquence of the rhetorical schools.

It is not from the Latin fathers, however, that the sanest exposition of the relation of Christianity to classical education is to be drawn. The Greek fathers of the Church, possessing as their racial inheritance a more profound instinct for knowledge, wisdom, and beauty, discussed the question with greater moderation and dignity. Passages from the writings of Clement of Alexandria (*c.* 160–220 A.D.) may serve to show his opinion, first that philosophy is necessary, secondly, that it proceeds from God, and thirdly that it is pursued by good men (*Ante-Nicene Fathers*, vol. ii, Misc. B. VII, ii; B. VI, xviii; B. VI, xvii.):

1. 'By giving to the Jews commandments and to the Greeks philosophy, he confined unbelief (Rom. xi. 32) to the period of His own presence on earth, in which everyone who believed not is without excuse' (Rom. i. 20).

2. 'For truly it appears to me to be a proper point for discussion, whether we ought to philosophize; for its terms are consistent. But if we are not to philosophize, what then? (For no one can condemn a thing without first knowing it.) The consequence, even in that case, is that we must philosophize.'

3. 'Logical discussion, then, of intellectual subjects, with selection and assent, is called Dialectics; which establishes, by demonstration, allegations respecting truth, and demolishes the doubts brought forward.'

'Those, then, who assert that philosophy did not come hither from God, all but say that God does not know each particular thing, and that He is not the cause of all good things; if, indeed, each of these belongs to the class of individual things. But nothing that exists could have subsisted at all, had God not willed. And if He willed, then philosophy is from God, He having willed it to be such as it is, for the sake of those who not otherwise but by its means would abstain from what is evil. . . . Now, then, many things in life take their rise in some exercise of human reason, having received the kindling spark from God. For instance, health by medicine, and soundness of body through gymnastics, and wealth by trade, have their origin and existence in consequence, too, of human co-operation. Understanding also is from God.'

'Philosophy is not, then, the product of vice, since it makes men virtuous; it follows, then, that it is the work of God, whose work it is solely to do good. And all things given by God are given and received well.'

'Further, if the practice of philosophy does not belong to the wicked, but was accorded to the best of the Greeks, it is clear also from what source it was bestowed—manifestly from Providence, which assigns to each what is befitting in accordance with his deserts.'

'Rightly, then, to the Jews belonged the Law, and to the Greeks Philosophy, until the Advent; and after that came the universal calling to be a people of righteousness, through the teaching which flows from faith, brought together by one Lord, the only God of both Greeks and barbarians, or rather of the whole race of men. We have often called by the name philosophy that portion of truth attained through philosophy, although but partial.'

Such was the view of Clement, whose catechetical school at Alexandria was an introduction not only to the Christian faith; but also to Christian philosophy. A more detailed exegesis has reached us from the pen of St. Basil, in his Homily to the young on the value of reading secular books. The substance of his view is that faith is the one thing necessary to the soul; yet secular education may by no means be neglected.

St. Basil the Great was born at Cesarea in Cappadocia in A.D. 329 He came of Christian parentage, but was sent to Athens to study philosophy and rhetoric. Returning, he became a pleader in the courts of his native town; but soon went abroad to Egypt and then retired from the world to meditate in solitude on the Christian faith. He entered the priesthood, and for twenty years occupied the bishopric of Cesarea. He died in 379, honoured and mourned by all. It is related of St. Basil that in a year of famine, he gave all his goods to the poor, desiring that even Jews and pagans should be allowed to share in his bounty. The date and place of the homily on reading secular books are unknown; but the advice is evidently intended for a number of Christian scholars who studied under him, probably with a view to entering the ranks of the priesthood.

The following is a brief digest of Basil's *Homily*:

1. Secular books are a useful preparation for understanding the sacred writings.

2. Secular learning is not a necessity, but only an ornament to the soul; yet the examples of Moses and Daniel indicate that this is no reason why it should be despised.

3. Secular books must be studied with discrimination; and as the bee sucks not from every flower, so the Christian scholar must study only those portions of the secular writings which are not prejudicial to purity and virtue. Passages from Hesiod, Homer, Theognis, and Prodicus are to be commended.

4. The virtuous precepts of these writers are not only to be studied, but to be put into practice, since there is no worse vice than hypocrisy.

5. The lessons of secular writers in many places coincide with the precepts of the Gospel.

6. We must train like athletes if we are to wear a crown like athletes, renouncing ease and exercising unceasingly. (The ancient thinkers are unanimous in approving the cultivation of the soul and the curbing of the appetites.)

7. Let us not neglect any factor that may aid us in our march towards eternal life; let us, therefore, study and practise the wisdom of the ancients.

On the whole the Homily represents the attitude of the Greek Fathers towards pagan literature That of the Latin Fathers was more grudging; yet they did not entirely condemn the pagan learning.

2. *The Stoic Attitude*

Like Christianity, Stoicism was an educational discipline. Though Greek and pre-Christian in its origin, the Stoic theory of life flourished in the hardy soil of the Roman temperament. Under the Empire, its doctrine of self-sufficiency was a congenial refuge to noble minds which revolted inwardly against their slavish environment. Epictetus, born in Phrygia about A.D. 45, was responsible for the most perfect Stoic discourses which have survived. This philosopher is believed to have been a slave under Nero; but was afterwards one of the recognized teachers of philosophy in Rome until compelled to leave the city by the edict of Domitian. His teaching was at the same time practical and in the highest degree ideal. It has profoundly influenced many of the finest characters of all subsequent epochs. The Discourses of Epictetus were put into literary form by one of his disciples, Arrian, who seems to have performed the task both faithfully and well. The unsystematic form in which they are cast is doubtless a reflex of the conversational method of the best philosophical teaching of the period.

'Follow Nature' was the educational axiom of the Stoics. It was a similar doctrine which in the eighteenth century inspired Rousseau and his naturalistic school of followers in their attempt to revolutionize the processes of teaching and learning. Nature, according to Epictetus, is the criterion of right and wrong. But what is Nature? As used by the Stoics, the term is practically interchangeable with Reason, and sometimes with Deity. From the Stoic standpoint, it is not every affection or desire that can be called natural, but only such as coincide with reason. When the affections and reason are leagued together, we have what is natural and therefore what is right. Luxury, insincerity, vanity, flattery, falsehood, these are not from the Stoic point of view natural, but are the target of philosophic scorn. The philosopher who boasts of the size of his classes, weighs the sonorous quality of the applause at the end of his speeches, praises his own eloquence, or solicits friends to join his audience, is severely satirized. Epictetus praises the method of Socrates, remarking: 'Who ever heard Socrates say, "I know, or teach, anything?" ' Thus in theory at least the Stoic was as free of affectation, and as austere in his mode of life, as the Christian. He did not, however, teach that vanity and indulgence are sinful; but merely that they are inconsistent with the character of a wise man.

The attitude of the Stoics towards theoretical knowledge was well defined. It was but a means to an end. The only end or ultimate good in life is virtue, or conformity with Nature. The ideal of knowledge for its own sake was deliberately discarded, but not more so than by the early Christian Fathers. To one of the liberal arts, however, the Stoics paid close attention. They devoted themselves assiduously to grammar. In the *Cratylus*, Plato had discussed the question whether words originate by mutual agreement or whether they arise out of some natural resemblance to the things which they represent. The Stoics held that language had originated not by convention but by nature. Hence the analytical study of language might well be the path to Nature and the clue to Reason. Logic, as the art which deals directly with rational processes, also received a share of attention in the schools of the Stoic philosophers. To a modern reader the *Discourses* of Epictetus appear at their worst in the passages devoted to the formal minutiae of dialectic. Yet Epictetus himself clearly teaches that there is no need of study on its own account; but only for the sake of the one great and admirable thing, which is to understand the will of Nature. This must take precedence even of the works of Chrysippus, the great protagonist of Stoicism. For although to most minds the guidance of Chrysippus may be indispensable, he is but an interpreter. Nature reveals to man his own will as a thing utterly independent of all external influence. None can compel him to assert a falsehood, or to deny a truth. Things which are independent of his will are matters of indifference, even though they may involve pleasure or pain. Such things have nothing to do with morality. Virtue is the only good, and man is self-sufficient to attain it. Herein the spiritual pride of the Stoics is in contrast with the Christian doctrine of humility and dependence upon the will of God.

The Stoic teaching contained so much that is noble, so much that is vital, as to make it in the fourth century of the Empire a formidable competitor with the Christian theology. It was no mere diversion for the learned, but a system of education, of life, of religion. The Stoics held that a philosopher is tested not in the discussion of virtue but in the practice of it; not in the peaceful atmosphere of the schools but in the perilous chances of shipwreck and danger. In reality the Stoics appear to have over-estimated the independence of the will. According to their theory a well-disciplined mind may be happy though the body is suffering torture, while the death of a father or a son, a husband, or a wife, should be a matter of indifference, because not dependent upon the will. They followed Nature to the point of the unnatural.

Moral philosophy, according to Epictetus, is capable of being classified under three heads:

(*a*) The desires and aversions, which are to be so regulated that the former should never be disappointed, nor the latter incurred. This can be done only by the strict limitation of the desires to matters dependent upon the will. Externals, things independent of the will, are purely indifferent.

(*b*) The pursuits and avoidances, the activities founded upon desires and aversions.

(*c*) The assents, which in the case of the wise man will be so regulated as to produce an infallible judgement.

Independence, self-help, self-reliance, self-control, with an abundance of that intellectual and spiritual pride which distinguishes the Stoic from the Christian teaching, these were the most prominent features of Stoic education. In things dependent on the will, man is responsible; and being of a rational and divine nature, is self-sufficient unto virtue. To things independent of the will, the wise man preserves an attitude of indifference.

3. *The Neo-Platonic Attitude*

Plotinus, born in Egypt in A.D. 205, dying in Italy in 270, is regarded as the true founder and the finest exponent in ancient times of the Neo-Platonic system of philosophy. It is true that Plotinus himself was indebted to such predecessors as Ammonius Saccas and even to Philo Judaeus, a contemporary of Christ. In the hands of later Neo-Platonists like Iamblichus (d. 330) the system degenerated into a circle of myths, magic, polytheism, and superstition; the rallying-point of the adversaries of Christianity. Like Stoicism and Epicureanism, however, it must be regarded in part as an educational system, since there is no doubt that it became the intellectual and religious refuge of many of the finest minds of the later Roman period.

Neo-Platonism as an educational discipline was similar to other forms of mysticism. The immense distance of man from God is emphasized, but at the same time a blind intuition of the divine is held to exist in the soul, so that if it be contemplated the whole nature of man may at last be reduced to this divine element. The mystic seeks to fan the inward flame of his soul until all its grosser elements shall be consumed. The result is an ecstatic trance during which the soul becomes at one with the divine nature. For this purpose effort is needed. 'We must be like God; we become like God by virtue; God is the soul of the world' (Plotinus, *Enneades* I. Bk. II. Ch. i.). 'Let every one become divine, become beautiful, if he wishes to contemplate God and the beautiful' (I, Bk. VI). 'It is not by prayers that one obtains the fruits of the earth, it is by cultivating it' (III. II. viii). The Neo-Platonist was an optimist, since material changes seemed unreal to him. 'Everything is good; it is not matter, a transitory thing, that rules; it must pass in order that things may be as they are, or else it would have been the cause of reason itself. It is reason that is the principle, reason is everything from its origin and birth.' Effort, optimism, contemplation of the good, limitation of philosophical education to the few, free use of allegory and metaphor, disregard of all material things and concrete facts, indifference to wealth, poverty, and other economic conditions, emphasis upon the contrast between reason and matter, and the invention of a vast hierarchy of demons to bridge the gap between the human and the divine, these may be regarded as the most prominent features of the Neo-Platonic system. Its weakness lay in the indifference to fact which had so much to do with the decadence of science in the ancient and medieval civilizations of western Europe.

A letter of Longinus to Porphyry illustrates the scholarly attitude of critics under the Roman Empire. These two were both engaged in the study of the great Neo-Platonist, Plotinus. 'Unless by some happy chance, do not expect to find anything new here; you will not even find all the past, of which, as you say, a part has perished. Copyists are so rare here that in all the time that I have entirely occupied myself with the works left by Plotinus I have hardly been able to get them all. I have even had to take my secretary away from his ordinary duties to attend solely to this. Finally, I have included in the collection, I think, all that you have sent me. But still I only half possess them, they are so full of mistakes, in spite of the care of our friend Amelius to remove the errors of copyists.'

Neo-Platonism was a mystic rather than a strictly rational discipline. It had enough in common with Christianity to make it a formidable rival to the Christian faith in the minds of some, and to influence at a later date the Christian mystics of the middle Ages, but its practical influence towards a virtuous life does not appear to have been comparable to either the Christian or the Stoic. Though widespread, Neo-Platonism appealed deeply only to a few; and the Emperor Julian failed utterly in his attempt to make it a State religion.

Stoicism was an education of self-control and of the reason; Neo-Platonism an education of the intuition; but Christianity an education of life as a whole, and especially a training in faith and charity, according to a pattern unexampled in pagan antiquity.

A SELECT BIBLIOGRAPHY

ROMAN EDUCATION

A

Becker: *Gallus*, Sc. III (on Roman Libraries and Books).
Clarke, S.: *Education of Children at Rome.*
Cole, P.: *Later Roman Education.*
Dill: *Roman Society in the Last Century of the Western Empire*, Bk. IV, Chap. V.
Fowler, W.: *Social Life in Rome in Age of Cicero*, Chap. VI.
Haarhoff: *Schools of Gaul.*
Hobhouse: *Ancient Education.*
Laurie, S.: *Pre-Christian Education.*
Quintilian: *Institutes of Oratory* (trans. Watson).
Sandys: *History of Classical Scholarship.*
Wilkins: *Roman Education.*

B

Abbott: *Society and Politics in Ancient Rome.*
Anderson: 'Some Facts Regarding Vocational Education Among Greeks and Romans' (in *School Review*, vol. xx).
Bailey (edited): *The Legacy of Rome.*
Bury, E. G.: *Student's Roman Empire.*
Church, A.: *Roman Life in the Days of Cicero*, Chap. 1.
Davidson: *Aristotle and the Ancient Educational Ideal.*
Gwynn, A: *Roman Education from Cicero to Quintilian.*
Johnston: *Private Life of the Romans*, Chap. IV.

Jullien: *Les Professeurs de Littérature dans l'ancienne Rome et leur Enseignement.*
Mommsen, T. (trans. Dickson): *History of Rome*, vol. i, Bk. I; vol. i, Bk. I, Chaps. 11–24; vol. ii, Bk. 4, Chaps. 12–13, &c.
Newman: *University Sketches* (ed. Sampson), Chap. 8.
Painter: *Great Pedagogical Essays*—Chaps. I–VIII. (Cicero, Seneca, Quintilian, Plutarch, Jerome).
Preston and Dodge: *Private Life of the Romans.*
Sellar: *Roman Poets.*
Teuffel: *Roman Literature.*
Tucker, T.: *Life in the Roman World of Nero and St. Paul*, Chap. 17.
Webster: *History of the Ancient World.*
Westerman: 'Vocational Education in Antiquity' (in *School Review*, vol. xxii).

EARLY CHRISTIAN EDUCATION UNDER THE ROMAN EMPIRE
(Transition Period)

A

Bigg: *The Christian Platonists of Alexandria.*
Hodgson, G.: *Primitive Christian Education.*
St. Augustine: *Confessions.*

B

Clarke: *St. Basil the Great.*
Cubberley, E.: *History of Education*, Chap. IV.
Currey: *Tertullian.*
Cutts: *St. Jerome.*
Davidson, T.: *History of Education*, Bk. II, Chaps. 2–3.
Leblanc: *L'Étude et l'Enseignement des Lettres profanes dans les premiers Siècles de l'Église.*
Roger: *L'Enseignement des Lettres classiques d'Ausone à Alcuin.*
St. Augustine: *Writings.*
St. Basil: *Homily on Reading Profane Authors.*
St. Jerome: (in Painter's *Great Pedagogical Essays*).
Seeley, L.: *History of Education*, Chaps. 13–18.
Spear: *Influence of Plato on St. Basil.*
Whitaker: *The Neo-Platonists.*
Zeller: *The Stoics, Epicureans, and Sceptics.*

See also the 'Library of the Fathers'.
The Fathers for English Readers: Basil, Athanasius, Ambrose.
Also various Histories of the Church, e.g.
Johnson, E.: *Rise of Christendom.*
Spence-Jones: *Early Christians in Rome.*

BOOK III

EDUCATIONAL THOUGHT IN THE MIDDLE AGES

I

THE GREAT TRANSITION

'ORBIS Romanus ruit', wrote Jerome. Strictly speaking, the Roman Empire did not fall, it declined, was overrun, gradually broke in sunder, and melted away. The sack of Rome by Alaric in A.D. 410 was not regarded by contemporaries as the end of ancient times nor as the beginning of a new age. Of the many causes which led to the disruption of the greatest of all ancient empires, the chief was the superiority of hardier and more warlike races over a population which relied upon other arms than its own to protect it. By a process of infiltration Goths and other barbarians who bore no devotion save to their immediate leader had come to constitute an important part of the Roman armies, and their weapons were turned readily against Rome herself. At first the issue lay between leaders rather than between nations, but in time the cohesion of barbarian tribes bordering upon the confines of the Empire, tribes which had learned the art of war from the Romans, led to the mastery of all the Roman provinces and of Italy herself. The barbarians behaved differently in accordance with the varying knowledge which they had of Roman civilization, and with the degree of appreciation which they bore towards Roman institutions. In Germany, Britain, and Africa the invaders left little of the ancient culture; in Italy, Gaul, and Spain they showed a certain respect for Roman institutions, some admiration for Christianity, some toleration of schools, and some understanding of Roman local government and of Roman law. The churches, the monasteries, the schools and other institutions of the Empire endured many acts of violence, contempt, and persecution; but they survived. The great lay schools of law and rhetoric which had been patronized by the Empire and controlled by municipal governments as late as the beginning of the fifth century disappeared or were reduced to insignificant and dwindling proportions; but the schools of the monasteries and those of some cathedrals remained. Moreover, the Eastern or Greek Empire was still intact, while in Rome, Gothic chieftains like Theodoric imagined themselves to be the successors of the divine Caesars. In the East pagan teachers remained side by side with Christian at least until the schools of Athens were closed in 529 by an edict of Justinian, who desired to reorganize and strengthen the schools of Constantinople.

It is with western Europe that the modern student is primarily concerned. Here the problem was whether only Christian teaching as such should be preserved, or whether the elements of the ancient classics and the ideas of the pagan philosophers should be transmitted to an age that was rapidly becoming ignorant of Greek. The continuity of classical scholarship was secured by the efforts of a group of 'great transmitters'. Cassiodorus was born about 470, and about 480 Boethius and Benedict saw the light.

Cassiodorus, the descendant of a distinguished political family at Rome, advanced under the Emperor Theodoric and his successors to the important position of Quaestor and subsequently to that of Consul, supporting as he did the imperial policy of uniting the Goths and the Romans into a homogeneous people. In 540 he retired to the pleasant seclusion of a cloister of his own foundation at Vivarium. His work, *Institutions of Sacred and Secular Learning*, contains in its second part a brief treatment of the seven liberal arts, in which, however, nothing original appears. His ecclesiastical history, founded upon the Christian histories of Socrates, Sozomenus, and Theodoret, was widely studied in the Middle Ages. The most important contribution of Cassiodorus to education, however, was his monastic rule, in which the substitution of literary for manual labour on the part of the monks was permitted and apparently encouraged. Without such provision the reading and copying of books might have practically ceased.

Still more celebrated is the contemporary of Cassiodorus, Boethius, chief of the 'great transmitters'. An eminent counsellor and favourite of Theodoric, he was accused unjustly of conspiring to restore the ancient Roman form of government. The charge led to his imprisonment and to his execution in 525. While in prison Boethius produced the *Consolations of Philosophy*, a work still widely read, and universally studied in the Middle Ages, conveying as it does an excellent summary of Greek moral philosophy. Realizing that Greek scholarship in the West was doomed, Boethius rendered into Latin a large part of the writings of Aristotle, together with a number of valuable commentaries upon Aristotle, Porphyry, and Cicero. Although his writings do not convey as much, Boethius was accepted in the Middle Ages as a Christian and as a martyr. Without the translations of Boethius the Middle Ages would have long remained ignorant of Plato and Aristotle. He wrote also upon the liberal arts, being regarded as an eminent authority on the subjects of music and dialectic. Boethius was, according to Gibbon (c. xxxix), 'the last of the Romans whom Cato or Tully could have acknowledged for their countryman'. The appreciation of his contemporary Cassiodorus epitomizes the influence of his writing: 'Through your translations the music of Pythagoras and the astronomy of Ptolemy are read by the Italians, the arithmetic of Nichomachus and the geometry of Euclid are heard by the Westerners; the theology of Plato and the logic of Aristotle dispute in the tongue of Quintilian; even the mechanical Archimedes you have restored in a Latin garb to the Sicilians, and all the training and the art which fertile Greece has produced by the efforts of individuals, Rome has revived in her own tongue thanks to yourself alone.'

About the same time as Boethius, was born St. Benedict, patriarch of Western monasticism. Fleeing at an early age from the worldliness of Rome, Benedict founded a number of communities consisting of men who were prepared to forsake the world for God. It was well for the development of education that western Europe avoided in large measure the solitary eremitic life which flourished in the East. In 529 Benedict founded the important monastery of Monte Cassino. About 530 appeared his famous *regula* or rule, which gradually became general, reaching England with St. Augustine of Canterbury in 597. Maintaining that 'Idleness is the enemy of the soul', St. Benedict demanded of the monks both 'the labour of their hands' and 'holy reading'. It was upon this foundation that Cassiodorus seems to have built when about 540 he introduced the teaching of both sacred and profane literature at Vivarium. Later we find the Benedictine monks reading and studying, teaching boys who were to become monks and sometimes external pupils also, and, in the case of those who were qualified for the work, copying manuscripts. Profane learning, however, was regarded as a handmaid of religion, not as a worthy end in itself. Hence the monastic schools were content to mark time without advancing. It is to their credit that they built up libraries in which many classical works of the utmost value were saved from extinction. The Venerable Bede and Rhabanus Maurus were products of the Benedictine schools. In other directions too, socially, agriculturally, and artistically, the Benedictines were the teachers of the early Middle Ages.

In that dark period the natural refuge of peace, learning, and piety was the monastery. It is true that the privileges of monastic life were abused by some communities as a cloak to cover sin and worldliness. Such examples, however, were not typical. In general, the monastery was a place for the service of God by a life of asceticism. Now asceticism is literally an exercise in holiness. In the East it was carried to extremes, the material world and the pleasures of the senses being regarded as allies or servants of the devil. No doubt the influence of Egyptian and other pagan practices may be traced in the frightful self-punishments of many of the Eastern hermits. There was a tendency to disparage the married estate and to idealize a life of almost Platonic contemplation, though the Christian *vita contemplativa* was a more emotional condition than the 'theoretic life' of Aristotle. The same features may be distinguished in western monasticism. In the west, however, there were fewer solitaries. The western monastic communities evinced a higher degree of sanity, and a greater capacity for self-government than the eastern. There is no certainty that if they had not chosen to preserve the essentials of classical culture any other institution would have done so in their place.

Gradually the Middle Ages created an atmosphere of their own. All the elements of this atmosphere had been distinguishable during the period of the Roman Empire in competition with classical Greek thought; but in the fifth century this competition was eliminated from western Europe. Henceforth the liberal studies, though they survived, were subservient to theology. A compendium of the liberal arts, such as that of Martianus Capella, was considered sufficient. Even the Roman law was abridged and provincialized. In northern France, for example, it dwindled and became of little more than academic interest. It is true that the old personal law of Rome as applied to the clergy grew and widened in significance under the name of the canon law. Moreover, the barbaric codes, even the ancient Salic law, were affected in various ways by Roman law, which from the time of Constantine included penalties against heresy, restrictions upon divorce, and other innovations of Christian origin. The ethics of Augustine triumphed over the rationalistic theories of paganism. Until the time of Augustine many Christian fathers, even as late as Ambrose, had preserved the doctrines of Cicero. Augustine, however, was content to seek the soul's rest in God. He mistrusted the unaided power of human reason, seeking simplicity and appealing to emotion. It is true that the Neo-Platonism of Synesius and the mystic transcendentalism of Dionysius the Areopagite were never sufficiently intelligible to become universal.

Mysteries now took on a magic character. The appetite for miracles was whetted; and the natural tended to be ignored even by the most intellectual Christian bodies in favour of the supernatural. Statements of fact were interpreted allegorically. Miraculous legends of the saints were more widely appreciated than demonstrable facts. Piety was exalted even above truth.

The Alexandrians had approached the Gospel through philosophy. Now the sources of Greek philosophy were neglected. Until the twelfth century all that was read in the Western schools of Plato and Aristotle consisted of an incomplete Latin version of the *Timaeus* and the more elementary of the translations made by Boethius from Greek to Latin.

Beauty, according to the Christian view, was the expression of the soul, a reflection of the beauty of God. Logically this was a more complete view than that of paganism; but in practice it became narrower, beauty being mistrusted except when, as in the Gothic architecture, it was directly impressed into the divine service. Even the Christian doctrine of love, while more powerful morally than the Platonic conception of justice, was employed rather in the suppression than in the sanctification of the emotions. The realities of life were ignored, and celibacy became an ideal.

Literature tended to be almost exclusively religious. Christian hymns became more emotional and less philosophical than formerly. Classical Latin prose was still attempted by a few, but in general Latin style was christianized. As such it is more direct and more fluid than the classical. The language of theology had to introduce terms unknown in the age of Cicero. The tendency was to discard *oratio obliqua* and other troublesome constructions in favour of a simplicity which could be understood by the average reader.

It has been seen that owing to the labours of a few such as Boethius, Benedict, and Cassiodorus, the learning of the ancients did not disappear from western Europe with the disappearance of the Western Empire. In the course of the sixth century the tendencies of medieval thought are reflected in the writings of Gregory of Tours, Pope Gregory the Great, and Isidore of Seville.

Gregory, Bishop of Tours, born in 538, the author of the *History of the Franks*, preserved in his work a knowledge of Merovingian times which would otherwise have been lost. From the educational standpoint his history is of interest chiefly for its style. Gregory wrote a crude kind of Latin far below the classical standard of literary taste and precision. His mode of expression was already tending towards the Romance language which developed in the end into French. Gregory, however, aware of the faults of his Latin style, used it for the sake of fluency. It should not be inferred that he was ignorant of the Latin classics. Yet it is clear that in his time educated persons no longer wrote classical Latin with any degree of ease, and that the study of the classics as such had become a mere intellectual luxury. Neither Rome under the Empire nor Italy during the fifteenth-century renaissance would have tolerated such laxity of grammar or such degeneracy of construction.

Pope Gregory the Great, the most prominent European figure of the sixth century (b. 540, d. 604), was in some respects almost the maker of medieval opinion. A great administrator, as Pope between 590 and 604 he exerted the beginnings of that mighty influence which so many of his successors were to wield in western politics. Lombardy, France, Germany, Constantinople, and even distant England were under the spell of his influence, although no man and no office in that troublous period could inspire universal obedience.

Well as Gregory merited the epithet Great, it was rather as a stern moralist, an ardent Christian, and a determined organizer and administrator than as an intellectualist. Gregory is reputed to have 'founded a school of singers, endowed it with some estates and built for it two habitations, one under the steps of the Basilica of St. Peter the Apostle, the other under the houses of the Lateran Palace', and to have taught in it himself. The training of singers in school to take part in service at the altar involved the teaching of reading and of elementary Latin. The Gregorian style of music, however, was a later development for which the Pope himself could not have been responsible. Gregory disparaged classical studies. Although he had lived in Constantinople as papal legate for some years, he knew no Greek, nor was he interested in literary excellence. His letter to Desiderius, Bishop of Vienne, had a lasting influence which was contrary to the interests of higher education. He despised correctness of style and was proud of his own contempt for the rules of Latin syntax. After Gregory, because of his great name and authority as an ecclesiastical writer, it became the monastic fashion to deprecate classical culture. It was unworthy, he wrote to the Bishop of Vienne, who devoted too much pains to the teaching of rhetoric and literature, that the praises of Jupiter should be in the same mouth that praises Christ.

Few books had greater influence during the centuries which followed than Gregory's *Cura Pastoralis* (Pastoral Rule). In it were set out the duties of a bishop, and especially the treatment of such moral problems as were likely to arise. Not only in the Latin, but in vernacular forms such as the Anglo-Saxon version of King Alfred, the Pastoral Rule became popular. In the ninth century a copy was presented to bishops as a part of the ceremony of their consecration.

Another writer of the period, a Spanish bishop of the sixth and seventh centuries, was Isidore of Seville. His *Etymologies* or *Origins* was an encyclopaedic treatment in twenty books of the whole range of knowledge as it existed in the Dark Ages. Although uncritical and compiled from inexact and secondary materials, the Etymologies remained through the Middle Ages one of the principal text-books of higher education. The scheme of the work was sufficiently comprehensive. It included books upon (1) Grammar, (2) Rhetoric and Dialectic, (3) Arithmetic, Geometry, Music, and Astronomy, (4) Medicine, (5) Law and Chronology, (6) Ecclesiastical Books and Offices, (7) God, Angels, and the Orders of the Faithful, (8) Church and the Sect, (9) Language, (10) Society and Relationship, (11) Man and Habits, (12) Animals, (13) The World and its Parts, (14) The Earth and its Parts, (15) Buildings, Fields, and Their Measures, (16) Stones and Metals, (17) Agriculture, (18) War and Games, (19) Ships, Building, and Garments, (20) Provisions, Domestic and Rustic Implements.

It will be seen that the new Europe which emerged from the dissolution of the Roman Empire preserved the outlines of the ancient Greek treatment of the seven liberal arts, adding a broad field of Christian and supernatural interest to which the secular studies were made entirely subservient. The character of medieval education in general may be inferred from a study of its development in England.

II

THE IRISH EDUCATIONAL TRADITION

AT a period which cannot be fixed with reliability, Celtic tribes had established themselves throughout Britain. The Gaul became the Gael. In time all sense of historical continuity was lost; the Celtic inhabitants of Ireland and Wales forgot their kinship with the Continent.

Christianized, in large part, by St. Patrick and his companions, in the fifth century, in the sixth the Irish extended Christianity to the Picts, radiating their faith from the monastery founded by St. Columba, at Iona.

The conquest of the Picts by the Irish Gaels was completed in the ninth century. The Scoti were originally Irish, and during the Middle Ages the term Scotus is to be translated Irish rather than Scotch. For several centuries Ireland herself remained the principal home of Celtic missionary effort, and of that branch of the Graeco-Roman civilization which accompanied it.

The Gaels were ardent scholars. The monks of many Irish monasteries excelled the standards of their time in the Graeco-Roman arts. With the current Roman antipathy to the heathen classics they had very little sympathy. The Caledonian Scots, being a branch of the Irish race, maintained similar traditions. Thus, from medieval records, it is frequently impossible to determine whether Scotus, the name applied to so many eminent scholars, denotes birth in Ireland, in Scotland, or even in Wales. The Gaelic heritage in each of these countries was essentially the same. The term Irish, so frequently applied to all the medieval Gaels, must, therefore, be interpreted liberally—it means belonging to the Gaelic race and tradition. Those Western schoolmen of the Middle Ages who knew Greek were, generally speaking, Gaelic, although it may be unwise to infer, with Fitzpatrick and other historians, that the phenomenon of a schoolman knowing Greek is sufficient evidence to connote him an Irishman.

It is hardly possible to avoid a comparison between the Byzantine and the Irish educational traditions. Constantinople and Ireland lay at the extremes of the ancient Roman Empire; they survived the wreck of its mighty centre; their scholarship was uninterrupted if not unimpaired by the heathen storms that beat against their coasts.

Greek became the language of the Eastern Empire; Greek was still read in Ireland. The otiose spirit of the Byzantines, and the slavish adherence of their scholars to the writings of the past, left the field of original thought and of missionary endeavour mainly to the Irish, whose confident and enthusiastic spirit built up many seminaries of learning in connexion with their monasteries. The Irish Church differed in certain respects from the Roman, and Irish divines defended their views before the chair of St. Peter. From Columbanus, in the sixth century, to Duns Scotus, in the thirteenth, Irish scholarship was remarkable for its energy and culture. In the ninth century it culminated in the first of the great schoolmen, John Scotus Erigena. Irish missionaries helped to convert the Anglo-Saxons. They founded Melrose, Lindisfarne, Whitby, Malmesbury, and Glastonbury. St. Columba in Scotland, Burgundy, and Italy; Fursa in Gaul; Aidan, Finan, and Colman in England; these are but a few of the eminent Gaelic apostles who contributed to the rebirth of European civilization. The monastery established by Columbanus, at Luxeuil, in Burgundy, and that founded by his disciple, St. Gall, on the Upper Rhine, became two of the chief nurseries of European learning. Established in the fifth, sixth, and seventh centuries, from thirty to forty important Irish schools, despite the Danes, for centuries continued to pour out a stream of missionaries over Europe, receiving in return a considerable influx of foreign students. On the Continent, some monasteries, such as Péronne, were founded exclusively for the Irish.

The age of Charlemagne saw the restoration of a strong central government to a great part of the old Roman Empire. Nor did the Irish neglect this opportunity. According to Einhard, they became a burden on the country—evidently their numbers and their privileged position aroused local jealousies. The Irishman, Clement, who came to Gaul 'to sell wisdom', after the manner of a Greek sophist, became one of the chief organizers employed by Charles in his intellectual reforms. The presence of Irish scholars implied facilities for the study of Greek. If Alcuin and Rhabanus Maurus belonged to other races, they were sufficiently familiar with the Irish tradition to lend it their co-operation. Courtesies, which Einhard interpreted as an offer of allegiance, were extended from the Irish kings to the Emperor. A number of Irish monasteries on the Continent received signal marks of Charlemagne's esteem, and Clement, apparently in succession to Alcuin, was made Master of the Palace School. Other great Irish scholars associated with Charlemagne were Joseph Scotus, Dungal, and Donatus of Fiesole. The successors of the great Emperor continued his policy of patronizing notable Irish scholars, including the geographer and astronomer, Dicuil, and the great philosopher, John Scotus Erigena, who seems to have been a layman, but who pioneered that process of applying the Aristotelian dialectic to Medieval speculation, which is generally known under the name of scholasticism.

'What is the difference between a Scot and a sot?' asked Charles the Bald, of Erigena, when they were dining. 'The difference of a table,' was the reply. Such were the privileges enjoyed by the subtlest of Gaelic philosophers at the Court of Charlemagne's grandson. Greece was reputed by contemporaries to have been jealous of Irish learning, although how much of this was rhetoric may be only vaguely inferred. Erigena probed the deepest metaphysical and theological questions, and was the translator of the Greek treatises which, appearing in Constantinople in the sixth century, under the name of Dionysius the Areopagite, tended to amalgamate Neo-Platonic with Christian thought. Erigena held that true philosophy is true religion, and conversely, that true religion is true philosophy. He towers on the sky-line of his period like a solitary intellectual giant in an age of pigmies, but there can be little doubt that his learning, like that of his contemporary, Sedulius Scotus, was a product of the Irish schools.

Erigena and Sedulius were closely associated with two notable intellectual centres of the ninth century, Laon and Liége. Another Scot, or Irishman, Martinus 'the Greek', lectured on the Greek philosophy and language, at Laon, and was able to write Greek poetry. Yet apart from the Irish tradition, Hellenism at the time scarcely breathed in western Europe. Laon was in part an Irish centre; it became the home of a limited but real renaissance. In the tenth century the scholarship of the Irish flourished better in Germany than in France. St. Gall became the leading European school for the production of books, seconded ably by another monastery in which Irish activities played a very large part, Fulda. In Italy, Bobbio, which Columbanus had founded, became an important metropolis of Irish learning, and its library long remained the richest in Italy. Among the greatest services rendered by the monasteries which have been mentioned, and by others in which Irish *peregrini* played a leading part, to modern generations, was the presentation of great libraries in which the pagan classics, elsewhere deprecated on all sides, were carefully cherished and preserved alongside the more customary collections of sacred books. Among the schoolmen of later centuries, a number of Gaelic scholars, including Richard of St. Victor, Michael Scotus, Peter Hibernicus, and Duns Scotus were prominent in maintaining the continuity of Irish scholarship, of whom Richard was placed with Bede, by Dante, in the third heaven. In their time, however, learning of the scholastic trend had become more general; it was during the so-called 'dark' ages, from the sixth to the ninth century, that Irish learning fulfilled its most glorious apostolate. It was at once vigorous, fecund, and stable, a notable example of what Christianity and scholarship could attain by persistent and indomitable striving.

III

ANGLO-SAXON EDUCATION

THE conquest of Britain by the Anglo-Saxon tribes led to the annihilation of Roman schools throughout England. Having no respect for any Roman institution, the invaders seem to have exterminated almost all the Britons, except those who found refuge in Wales, Caledonia, or Ireland, where Christian traditions and classical learning were still maintained, chiefly in the seclusion of the Celtic monasteries. Whether the Anglo-Saxon races possessed any system of education prior to their invasion of Britain is unknown. The existence of such an epic as *Beowulf* at the period of the invasion points to a stage of civilization comparable to that of Greece in the Homeric period, when songs and music were appreciated, and were passed from one to another informally and without the mediation of schools. The arts of reading and writing do not appear to have been practised until the influence of the Roman civilization became felt among the early English, although there can be little doubt that at the courts of kings they were introduced before the coming of Augustine and his monks to Kent in 597, while a runic writing was not unknown to the Anglo-Saxon priesthood.

The first school in England of which there is record was established at Canterbury by St. Augustine, who had been sent by Pope Gregory the Great to convert the English to Christianity. In 631, according to Bede, a Grammar-School was established in East Anglia, provided 'with pedagogues and masters after the fashion of the Canterbury men.' At such schools not only Latin but the classical authors, especially the poets, were studied. Canterbury school was probably founded with Canterbury church in 598, while the East Anglian school was almost certainly at Dunwich.

'In England from the first,' writes Leach in his valuable *Educational Charters*, 'education was the creature of religion, the school was an adjunct of the church, and the schoolmaster was an ecclesiastical officer. For close on eleven hundred years, from 598 to 1670, all educational institutions were under exclusively ecclesiastical control. The law of education was a branch of the canon law. The church courts had exclusive jurisdiction over schools and universities and colleges, and until 1540 all schoolmasters and scholars were clerks, or clerics, or clergy, and in orders, though not necessarily holy orders.'

The arrival of Archbishop Theodore and Abbot Hadrian in England in 668 marked an epoch in Anglo-Saxon education. Both were highly skilled in Greek as well as Latin, and in secular as well as in sacred literature. Theodore united the whole English church and brought the celebration of Easter into conformity with Roman practice, although for some time the Christian Britons to the north and west adhered to different customs. Theodore and Hadrian taught to many pupils a knowledge of the art of metre, astronomy, ecclesiastical arithmetic, and church music, and Bede relates that more than sixty years later a sound knowledge of Greek and Latin still remained in England as a result of their efforts. Bede's own profound scholarship was directly or indirectly a product of this school. Nor did the pupils of these learned churchmen neglect to study the Saxon language and literature, which gradually rose to considerable height and dignity.

Writing about 680, Aldhelm, a scion of the royal West Saxon house, describes his studies, which appear to have been founded less upon Roman than upon Irish sources. Aldhelm mentions a catalogue of subjects with which his acquaintance does not appear to have been profound. His difficulty with arithmetic is intelligible when it is remembered that the Arabic notation did not come into general use until the twelfth century.

'For indeed no small time must be spent in the study of reading, especially by one who, inflamed by the desire of knowledge, wishes at the same time to explore Roman law to the marrow, and examine in the most intimate fashion all the mysteries of the Roman lawyers; and what is much more difficult and perplexing, to digest the hundred kinds of metres into prose rules, and illustrate the mixed modulations of song into the straight path of syllables. And in this subject the obscurity is so much the harder for the studious reader to penetrate because of the small number of teachers to be found.

'But the restricted space of a letter does not permit of a long dissertation on this matter; how, for instance, the secret instruments of the art of metre are collected in letters, syllables, feet, poetical figures, verses, accents, and quantities; how the art of prosody too, is divided into a sevenfold division, the headless hexameter, the weak line, and the rest; how the balance of verse is weighed by a certain measure in single lines, or stanzas of 5 to 10 lines; and on what principles the catalectic, brachycatalectic or hypercatalectic verses are recognized by clever proof. All this methinks and other like learning cannot be grasped in a mere interval of time and a momentary application.

'As to the principles of arithmetic what shall be said? When the despair of doing sums oppressed my mind so that all the previous labour spent on learning, whose most secret chamber I thought I already knew, seemed nothing, and to use Jerome's expression, I, who before thought myself a past master began again to be a pupil, until the difficulty solved itself, and at last, by God's grace, I grasped after incessant study the most difficult of all things, what they call fractions. As to the Zodiac and its twelve signs, which circle in the height of heaven, I think it better to say nothing, lest any matter so obscure and deep, which needs a long and reasoned exposition, should be made to seem cheap and worthless by a perfunctory explanation.' [1]

Alcuin, who was sought out by Charlemagne to assist him in promoting learning and religion in his dominions, gives a picture of the cathedral school at York under Albert, who was not one of the regular clergy or monks, but a secular, and Alcuin's own teacher. Brought up at the Minster from his earliest years, Albert became a master, supporting some pupils at the school apparently at his own expense. He travelled abroad seeking new knowledge and new books, and on his return was called to the position of Archbishop of York. He still remained master of the cathedral school, but ultimately bequeathed to his favourite pupil, Alcuin, 'the sphere of wisdom, the master's chair, the books, which the illustrious master had collected from all sides, piling up glorious treasures under one roof'. On the death of Albert, Alcuin succeeded to the school only, not to the archbishopric. In Latin verse Alcuin describes the teaching of Albert, which was sufficiently versatile. There is no indication, however, that the Anglo-Saxons flocked with a Grecian zeal to hear such a notable teacher, or that many went to school at all unless they contemplated a career in clerical orders. To the Anglo-Saxon mind, learning was still an exotic.

'There he moistened thirsty hearts with diverse streams of teaching and the varied dews of learning, giving to these the art of the science of grammar, pouring on those the rivers of rhetoric. Some he polished on the whetstone of law, some he taught to sing together in Aeonian chant, making others play on the flute of Castaly, and run with the feet of lyric poets over the hills of Parnassus. Others the said master made to know the harmony of heaven, the labours of sun and moon, the five belts of the sky, the seven planets, the laws of the fixed stars, their rising and setting, the movements of the air, the quaking of sea and earth, the nature of men, cattle, birds, and beasts, the divers kinds of numbers and various shapes. He gave certainty to the solemnity of Easter's return; above all, opening the mysteries of holy writ and disclosing the abysses of the rude and ancient law. Whatever youths he saw of conspicuous intelligence, those he joined to himself, he taught, he fed, he loved; and so the teacher had many disciples in the sacred volumes, advanced in

[1] Leach's translation.

various arts. Soon he went in triumph abroad, led by the love of wisdom, to see if he could find in other lands anything novel in books or schools, which he could bring home with him. He went also devoutly to the city of Romulus, rich in God's love, wandering far and wide through the holy places. Then returning home he was received everywhere by kings and princes as a prince of doctors, whom great kings tried to keep that he might irrigate their lands with learning. But the master hurrying to his appointed work, returned home to his fatherland, by God's ordinance. For no sooner had he been borne to his own shores, than he was compelled to take on him the pastoral care, and made high priest at the people's demand.'[1]

In 796 Alcuin, though no longer schoolmaster, recommended the Archbishop of York to separate the classes for grammar, singing, and writing, and to have a different master for each. In 797, referring to Hexham School, he wrote: 'It is a great work of charity to feed the poor with food for the body, but a greater to fill the hungry soul with spiritual learning . . . For the increase of the flock is the glory of the shepherd, and the multitude of learned men is the safety of the world.' Sacred studies are always mentioned as prior to profane learning, which suffered all through the Middle Ages by its position of subordination. The subsequent career of Alcuin may be briefly noticed. On his way to Rome to receive the pallium for the Archbishop of York he met Charles the Great at Pavia, and was persuaded, at first temporarily, afterwards permanently, to transfer his services to the Frankish kingdom. After some years spent at Charlemagne's palace Alcuin was allowed to establish a model monastic school at Tours, occasionally visiting the court. He was an able and prolific writer and controversialist. The seven liberal arts, upon most, if not all of which he wrote, he regarded as essential to wisdom. To Charles he was a kind of Minister of Education who infused life and earnestness into many a moribund school and abbey. Alcuin died in 804.

In 826, the provision of masters and teachers of the liberal arts in grammar-schools was enforced by the Council of Pope Eugenius. The duty related not only to England, but to Christendom as a whole, and confirmed what was already a custom in most bishoprics, although complaints of the absence of masters and of endowment for grammar-schools had reached the Holy See.

It is evident that the Danish invasions and conquests were a sore blow to the grammar-schools and to learning in England generally. The heathen Danes ravaged towns and countryside; but were staved

[1] Leach's translation.

off for a time by the genius of Alfred the Great. His preface to the translation of Gregory's *Pastoral Rule* into Anglo-Saxon contrasts the degeneracy of Latin education in his day with the greatness of the period of Alcuin. Alfred acceded to the throne in 871; and the preface may be dated about 893.

'I let it be known to them that it has very often come into my mind, what wise men there formerly were throughout the English nation, both of sacred and secular orders . . . and also the sacred orders how zealous they were both in teaching and learning, and in all the services they owed to God; and how foreigners came to this land in search of wisdom and learning, and how we should now have to get them from abroad if we would have them. So general was its decay among the English people that there were very few on this side of the Humber who could understand their services in English, or translate a letter from Latin into English; and I believe that there were not many beyond the Humber. There were so few of them that I cannot remember a single one south of the Thames when I came to the throne. Thanks be to God Almighty that we have any teachers among us now. . . . When I considered all this I remembered also how I saw, before it had been all ravaged and burnt, how the churches throughout the whole of England stood filled with treasures and books, and there was also a great multitude of God's servants, but they had very little knowledge of the books, for they could not understand anything of them, because they were not written in their own language.

'Therefore I think it is better, if you think so too, that we also should translate some of the books, which are most useful for all men to know, into the language which we can all understand, and should do as we very easily can with God's help if we have peace, that all the youth of our English freemen, who are rich enough to be able to devote themselves to it, should be set to learning, as long as they are not fit for any other occupation, until they are well able to read English writing; and further let those afterwards learn Latin who will continue in learning, and go to a higher rank. When I remembered how the knowledge of Latin had formerly decayed among the English, and yet many could read English writing, I began, among other various and manifold troubles of this kingdom, to translate into English the Herd's Book, sometimes word for word and sometimes meaning for meaning as I had learnt it from Plegmund my archbishop, and Asser my bishop, and Brimbold my mass-priest, and John my mass-priest. And when I had learnt it to the best of my ability, and as I could most clearly interpret it, I translated it into English; and I will send a copy to every bishopric in my kingdom; with a clasp on each worth fifty mancuses. And I forbid in God's name anyone to take the clasp from the book or the book from the Minster.'[1]

[1] Leach's translation.

The life of Alfred, wrongly attributed by subsequent generations to Bishop Asser, describes the great king's early education. It is related that he did not learn to read until about twelve years of age; but as a boy learned many Saxon poems by heart, and anticipated his elder brothers in learning to decipher a book of Saxon poetry, beautifully illuminated, which his mother offered as a prize to whichever of her sons could first read to her. He learned the hours, some psalms and prayers, which he collected and carried about with him in a book, but found no master who could instruct him properly in Latin grammar in the whole of Wessex. Yet his insatiable desire to learn never ceased during his lifetime. It was said that in his thirtieth year he began miraculously to read and construe Latin in one day. Then he began to collect in a little handbook which was always with him the flowers of holy scripture. This account, though inconsistent and irreconcilable with historical facts, illustrates some of the educational customs of the age. The King saw to it, after the manner of Charlemagne, that his sons and near relations should receive a more systematic Latin education than his own, and established a court or palace school. The children of kings and nobles in Anglo-Saxon times seem to have attended Latin grammar-schools along with the sons of ordinary freemen. Moreover it is evident that mothers sometimes taught their children to read Anglo-Saxon poetry.

Anglo-Saxon learning may have reached its zenith in the time of King Edgar. The learning of the Celtic monks as well as the practice of the Roman schools was by this time firmly rooted; the Danish invasions had been stayed, and peace and Christianity reigned in the land. Not only the bishops but the parish priests concerned themselves with education, and the general ignorance of Latin, referred to by Alfred, had disappeared. It would seem that fees were paid to priests by children whose parents could afford it, otherwise the provision requiring a scholar who studied under a priest to obtain the leave of his former master or tutor (if also a priest, as seems to be taken for granted) would be scarcely intelligible. It was always the custom, however, that intelligent sons of the poor should be taught freely, often with a view to entering the priesthood at a later time. The Anglo-Saxons generally showed more love for their native literature than for Latin, except when the latter tongue was necessary to their future career. Passages in Ælfric's *Colloquy* of 1005, which indicate that the sons of ploughmen, shepherds, cow-herds, hunters, fishermen, hawkers, merchants, shoemakers, salters, and bakers all attended

Latin grammar-schools together, should not be taken too literally. The names of occupations are clearly introduced by the grammarian so that their Latin equivalents might be learned. Yet where boys were destined for the priesthood they might come of any class in the community, nor was Anglo-Saxon life as highly feudalized or as clearly marked by class-division as Norman-French. The church was the one medieval career in which humble birth offered little hindrance to advancement.

King Edgar's Canons of about 960 are quoted from Leach, *Educational Charters*:

'10. And we enjoin that no priest receive another's scholar without the leave of him whom he formerly followed.

11. And we enjoin that every priest in addition to lore, do diligently learn a handicraft.

12. And we enjoin that no learned priest put to shame the half-learned, but amend him, if he know better.

17. And that every Christian man zealously accustom his children to Christianity and teach them the Pater Noster and Creed.

22. And we enjoin that every man learn so that he know the Pater Noster and Creed, if he wish to lie in a hallowed grave, or to be worthy of housel; because he is not truly a Christian who will not learn them, nor may he who knows them not receive another man at baptism, nor at the bishop's hand, ere he learn them.

51. And we enjoin that priests diligently teach youth, and educate them in crafts that they may have ecclesiastical support.'

The *Colloquy* of Ælfric, 1005, is an example of a method of teaching Latin which remained popular until the eighteenth century. The Latin is given along with the vernacular rendering. After a study-period, the master would ask the questions, and the pupils give the answers, in Latin without the book. It was still important to speak as well as to read and write Latin. Ælfric, a clerk of Winchester, who became bishop of Evesham, translated many Latin works into Anglo-Saxon, a fact which illustrates the probability that Anglo-Saxon reading was taught in village schools. The Latin original may have descended from the time of the old Roman public schools. Another work of Ælfric, his *Grammar*, is taken in the main from Priscian's *Ars Major*, an elaborate work by a schoolmaster of Constantinople of the early sixth century A.D. Before reading Ælfric's *Grammar* a pupil was expected to study his Donatus. The *Ars Minor* of Donatus, the universal school Latin grammar of the Middle

Ages, was a more elementary work written in the latter half of the fourth century at Rome. The *Grammar* of Ælfric not only shows that considerable classical learning existed among the Anglo-Saxons, but also that girls, at least the high-born and the nuns, were taught Latin, a practice which seems to have declined after the Norman Conquest. An example in the *Grammar* reads: 'The nun is awake teaching little girls. A man is taught by reading and by reading a woman is taught.' In the Middle Ages, as Leach points out, monks were addressed in Latin, but nuns in the vernacular.

The conquest of England by the Danes, when it came, interrupted the march of education less than their fierce incursions had done during and preceding the time of Alfred. This was the result of their speedy acceptance of Christianity. Canute is depicted as the founder of a number of scholarships for the sons not only of freemen, but of freedmen also. 'Canute', reports an eleventh-century chronicler, 'is related to have been so pious, so charitable, so great a lover of religion that he established public schools in the cities and boroughs and appointed masters to them, and sent to them to be taught grammar not only noble boys of good promise, but also the freed sons of slaves, charging the expense on the royal purse.'

It must be recollected that public education was not the business of the regular clergy or monks, but of the secular clergy, including bishops, secular canons, and parish priests. A monk indeed might become an archbishop or even a pope, but in such a case took on the duties of a secular. Hence the public grammar-schools of Anglo-Saxon times are found in connexion with cathedrals or with great collegiate churches, such as the church of the Holy Cross at Waltham. This was enlarged by the last of the English kings, Harold, before his accession to the throne, into a college with a dean and chapter of twelve canons. The canon next in rank to the Dean was the schoolmaster. After Senlac it was the schoolmaster who sought Harold's body and brought it back to Waltham for burial. After the year 1170 Henry II turned out the secular canons on the ground of luxury (marriage), and established regulars in their place. This was a part of his atonement—though at other people's expense—for the murder of Beckett. But the secular clergy had maintained good schools, though research, such as it was, had been left to the monasteries. The intellectual sluggishness of the early English was a figment of the Norman imagination.

IV

INTELLECTUAL DEVELOPMENT OF THE AGE OF CHARLEMAGNE

CHARLEMAGNE ascended the Frankish throne in 768, was crowned Emperor of the Romans by the Pope at Rome in 800, and occupied an unrivalled position in western Europe until his death in 814 A.D. A Frank, not a Roman, he perceived neverthless the advantages of the principles of order embodied in Roman institutions, law, customs, and education. Thinking highly of learning, he enticed Alcuin from England to his court, patronized other notable scholars, established a notable Palace School, stimulated the abbots and bishops of his dominions to improve the existing schools and to add new ones, and even made heroic efforts, probably with but moderate success, to raise the standard of his personal culture. None the less the picture of an adult emperor struggling to learn to read does not convey an impression of general intellectual activity.

The following instructions to Abbot Bangulfus are embodied in the Capitulary of 787:

'During past years we have often received letters from different monasteries, informing us that at their sacred service the brethren offered up prayers on our behalf; and we have observed that the thoughts contained in these letters, though in themselves most just, were expressed in uncouth language, and while pious devotion dictated the sentiments, the unlettered tongue was unable to express them aright. Hence there has arisen in our minds the fear lest, if the skill to write rightly were thus lacking, so too, would the power of rightly comprehending the sacred Scriptures be far less than was fitting; and we all know that though verbal errors be dangerous, errors of the understanding are yet more so. We exhort you, therefore, not only not to neglect the study of letters, but to apply yourselves thereto with perseverance and with that humility which is well pleasing to God; so that you may be able to penetrate with greater ease and certainty the mysteries of the Holy Scriptures. For as these contain images, tropes, and similar figures, it is impossible to doubt that the reader will arrive far more readily at the spiritual sense according as he is the better instructed in learning. Let there, therefore, be chosen for this work men who are both able and willing to learn, and also desirous of instructing others; and let them apply themselves to the work with a zeal equalling the earnestness with which we recommend it to them. It is our wish that you may be what it behoves the soldiers of the Church to be—

religious in heart, learned in discourse, pure in act, eloquent in speech; so that all who approach your house, in order to invoke the Divine Master or to behold the excellence of the religious life, may be edified in beholding you, and instructed in hearing you discourse or chant, and may return home rendering thanks to God most high.

Fail not, as thou regardest our favour, to send a copy of this letter to all thy suffragans and to all the monasteries; and let no monk go beyond his monastery to administer justice, or to enter the assemblies and the voting-places' (Painter, *Great Pedagogical Essays*, pp. 156–7).

One of the most distinguished intellectual products of the Carolingian era was Rhabanus Maurus, born at Mainz about 776 A.D. He studied at the great monastery at Fulda, at length becoming the head of the monastic school. To Fulda came pilgrims in search of learning, not only the seven liberal arts, but even physics, philosophy, and theology. Among the numerous works of Rhabanus were treatises on the Education of the Clergy, The Reckoning of Time, On the Soul, and The Study of Wisdom and the Divine Law. The following passage is from the *Education of the Clergy*:

'Arithmetic is the science of pure extension determinable by number; it is the science of numbers. Writers on secular science assign it, under the head of mathematics, to the first place, because it does not pre-suppose any of the other departments. Music, geometry, and astronomy, on the contrary, need the help of arithmetic; without it they cannot arise or exist. We should know, however, that the learned Hebrew Josephus, in his work *Antiquities*, Chapter VIII of Book I, makes the statement that Abraham brought arithmetic and astronomy to the Egyptians; but that they as a people of penetrating mind, extensively developed from these germs the other sciences. The Holy Fathers were right in advising those eager for knowledge to cultivate arithmetic, because in large measure it turns the mind from fleshly desires and furthermore awakens the wish to comprehend what with God's help we can merely receive with the heart. Therefore, the significance of number is not to be underestimated. Its very great value for an interpretation of many passages of Holy Scripture is manifest to all who exhibit zeal in their investigations. Not without good reason is it said in praise of God, "Thou hast ordained all things by measure, number and weight"' (*Book of Wisdom*, xi. 21).

'But every number, through its peculiar qualities, is so definite that none of the others can be like it. They are unequal and different. The single numbers are different; the single numbers are limited; but all are infinite.

'Those with whom Plato stands in especial honour will not make bold to esteem numbers lightly, as if they were of no consequence for the knowledge of God. He teaches that God made the world out of numbers. And among us the prophet said of God, "He forms the world by number". And in the

Gospel the Saviour says, "The very hairs of your head are all numbered." . . . Ignorance of numbers leaves many things unintelligible that are expressed in the Holy Scripture in a derivative sense or with a mystical meaning. (Painter, *Great Pedagogical Essays*, pp. 164–5).

In the same work appears a discussion of all the seven liberal arts:

Grammar, Rhetoric, Dialectic—The Trivium.

Arithmetic, Geometry, Music, Astronomy—The Quadrivium.

The work of Capella appears to have influenced both the order and treatment of the subjects of the curriculum outlined. Rhabanus attained the dignity of Archbishop of Mainz and the reputation of *preceptor Germaniae.*

Einhard, an intimate and trusted contemporary of Charlemagne, has left an account of the Emperor's life which throws additional light upon educational customs. Charlemagne's children were educated with care. 'As for children he thought they should be so brought up, both sons and daughters, as to be first informed of those liberal studies to which he himself devoted his attention. For his sons, as soon as their age permitted it, he ordered riding in the Frankish style, the practice of arms, and the chase; for his daughters wool-spinning, the use of distaff and spindle; they were to beware of becoming slothful by reason of their leisure, they were to be instructed in every virtuous occupation.'

Such was the intellectual atmosphere of the age of Charles. It was a time of herculean efforts to meet a dire need; but a permanent revival of western culture was impossible until Roman institutions should have become firmly established throughout Christendom. An unbroken succession of eminent teachers from the age of Charles made possible the variety, brilliance, and originality of the twelfth-century renaissance.

V

PETER ABELARD

PETER ABELARD, whose parents occupied a small *château* in Brittany, was born towards the close of the eleventh century. His life presents an example of the scholastic fever which caused many another like himself to leave the favour of Mars and to woo the gentler Minerva. Peter's first master was the rationalist Roscellin, whose heretical views of the nature of the Trinity had been the cause of his banishment from England and from the French kingdom. He went, he says, wherever dialectics flourished; indeed he seems to have been successful in all branches of learning, except mathematics. The curriculum which he pursued in the monastic or episcopal schools, and especially in the schools maintained in large towns, was that of the seven liberal arts. About the opening year of the twelfth century Abelard visited Paris, already the centre to which the students of Europe were beginning to repair in quest of knowledge. At that time the great abbeys of Paris had each a school; one hears even of a school of Jews and a school for women; for the decline of opposition to the Church on the part of heathen and heretics had made the Church for the time being tolerant.

The chief school in Paris was that of William of Champeaux, the greatest dialectician in France, destined to be overshadowed in that age only by his new pupil, Abelard. William's school was none other than that of old Notre Dame. The great question which agitated the scholars of the age was a controversy which arose from a passage in the Latin translation by Boethius of Porphyry's Introduction to Aristotle, as to whether species as well as individuals could be said to have a real existence. The affirmative answer was considered to be orthodox, although Roscellin had declared that universals are mere words. Anselm attacked Roscellin on the theological, William of Champeaux, on the philosophical side. It was in debate upon this question that Abelard was to secure the homage of intellectual Europe, as a result of his discovery that the true theory of genera and species, in relation to individuals, is neither realism nor nominalism, but conceptualism. Universals are not independent entities nor yet mere names, but generalized ideas. Thirty miles away, at Melun, Abelard soon opened a school of his own. Later, he removed near to

Paris; and ultimately displaced William of Champeaux in public estimation as the greatest dialectician of the day.

In the autobiography entitled *The Story of My Calamities*, Abelard narrates that he was almost cut off from France for several years on account of the failure of his own health. Returning to Paris, he found that William had adopted the black cassock of the canon regular and had been instrumental in the foundation of the Abbey of St. Victor, afterwards the principal stronghold of medieval mysticism. William had left a substitute in the school of Notre Dame. The new master, who was perhaps Peter the Eater, so called for his greed of study, decided to exchange the teacher's seat for a place on the hay-strewn floor under Abelard's tuition. The arrangement was not tolerated by William, who drove Abelard again to Melun, only to find that the anger of the scholarly world soon made his own position intolerable. In his turn, William quitted Paris. Abelard, returning to the city, pitched his camp, as he expresses it, on the hill of Ste Geneviève, formerly the seat of a school of Roscellin. Here stood an abbey of secular canons who had little love for the regular orders. A fierce academic war was waged henceforth between Notre Dame and Ste Geneviève. One hears in the *Life of Saint Goswin* written by two monks of the twelfth century, in what manner Abelard was beginning to be regarded by the orthodox school whose strength lay partly in its ignorance.

In the end Abelard completely vanquished and broke up the rival school at Notre Dame. Later he returned to Brittany to visit his mother who was about to take the veil; then retired for a time to study theology, probably with ambitious intent, although the school at Notre Dame, the former object of his ambition, was now his for the taking. He decided, however, to go to Anselm of Laon, recognized as the greatest theological teacher of the time—just as William of Champeaux, and later Abelard himself, had been esteemed the greatest dialectician. Anselm possessed a remarkable memory and an extraordinary knowledge of patristic literature; but showed no spark of originality. Once more the pupil became teacher, this time in theology, beginning his lectures with the book of Ezekiel. The essay was too successful to be permitted to continue. Abelard was summarily suppressed, and returned to Paris.

The heyday of his life had now arrived. He is said to have attracted five thousand students of all nationalities to the city, and there is nothing incredible in the claim. Paris itself was developing with wonderful rapidity at the time so that by the end of the twelfth century the city contained some two hundred thousand people; and part of this growth must be attributed to its fame as a university town. In Abelard's days there was not yet a university, but certainly no single individual did as much as he to bring the university about. Few parts of Europe were as benighted as Brittany; yet one finds a prior writing to Abelard: 'Distant Brittany sent you its animals to be instructed.'

Abelard would lecture for some six hours, beginning almost at sunrise, his scholars sitting tablet on knee, in the hay upon the floor. English, French, Normans, Burgundians, Bretons, Flemings, Germans, and Romans were represented among his pupils, none having a very savoury reputation as a body. Battles between the student-nations were frequent and sanguinary enough, giving the governor and his archers much ado to establish peace. The ability and fame of Abelard may be gathered from the epithets of his contemporary enemies, especially St. Bernard.

Abelard departed from the narrow texts of Boethius, Cassiodorus, and Martianus Capella, being familiar with Lucan, Ovid, Horace, Virgil, and Cicero; and apparently knowing Juvenal, Persius, Statius, Suetonius, Valerius, Quintilian, and Priscian. He knew little Greek and probably less Hebrew; though many Greek works were known to him through Latin translations and by the references of the Fathers.

About 1118 came about Abelard's unhappy passion for Heloise. The story is too well known to be embodied here. Abelard's sin and its punishment were followed by a complete change in his life. Heloise entered a nunnery; Abelard tried to hide his shame in the monastery of St. Denis, at a distance of six miles from Paris.

The life at St. Denis was worldly and disgraceful; and Abelard, now a reformer in spirit, made himself so disagreeable to his fellow Benedictines that he was again detailed to teach. Though a small village was selected as his province, it soon swarmed with three thousand students. Old and new enmities were excited by the master's success; and the charge of heresy soon appeared as a great and terrible cloud over his head. Peter was a rationalist; and in that age no rationalist could survive the indictment. One of his works was a treatise on the Unity and Trinity of God, into which almost inevitably heretical illustrations found their way. Abelard was given a trial at the Council of Soissons. His book was burnt, himself refused a hearing and committed to monastic confinement at St. Medard. The imprisonment did not last long, for there was now a scholarly public which insisted vehemently on Abelard's release.

Having returned to St. Denis, Abelard was unfortunate enough to make his position intolerable by attacking the legend of the martyrdom of Denis the Areopagite at Paris. He was referred to the king's justice; but aided by some of his sympathizers among the brethren escaped to Champagne. He was saved from inevitable recapture and punishment by the death of the abbot, whose successor, the famous Suger, permitted him to lead the life of a hermit. In this he rejoiced until necessity impelled him again to teach. The animosity of St. Bernard was now aroused against him; but a path to safety seemed open when a monastery in Brittany invited the great scholar to become its abbot. Having at length barely escaped with his life from this 'monastery', which consisted practically of a band of robbers, whose hatred the new abbot had earned by unexpected efforts at reform, Abelard returned to Paris, and taught in the vicinity. St. Bernard, who now organized a campaign of orthodoxy against him, was foiled momentarily by Abelard's request for a debate, and again by his appeal to Rome. At Rome, however, Bernard was all powerful, and was given a bull of excommunication against Abelard, the effect of which was diminished by the efforts of the venerable Peter of Clugny. This notable monk induced an apology and partial retractation from the overbold theologian, now an elderly and broken-spirited monk, destined to pass his final days in the quiet routine of Clugny and in the instruction of the monastic brethren. Here, although condemned by the Council of Sens, 1141, Abelard was permitted to live in retirement until his death in 1142.

The career of Abelard illustrates many of the conditions of education in one of its most important periods of transition—the awakening of new theological and philosophical interests, the great congregations of students which were soon to organize themselves as Universities, the conflict between reason and piety, a way out of which was discovered by later schoolmen such as Thomas Aquinas, the rivalry of monks and seculars in the field of education, and in fact the beginnings of the twelfth-century renaissance.

VI

ELEMENTARY AND GRAMMAR SCHOOLS OF THE MIDDLE AGES

A. *Monasticism and Education*

IN the earliest centuries of the Christian era, the recognized test of excellence was essentially morals. From the third to the fifth century it tended to become orthodoxy. From that century to perhaps the thirteenth, though faith and morals were by no means neglected, a new stress came to be laid upon effectiveness in securing power and wealth for the Church, and especially for the monasteries. The pure Hebraic influence of apostolic religion was responsible for the first period, the Hellenic influence and the opposition of pagan philosophies for the second, the disappearance of all serious opposition for the third.

In the third period, the earlier Middle Age, the monasteries contributed little that was new to the world's culture. Their main function was religious, not intellectual, service. They preserved rather than added to literature. They taught the disparagement of secular writings. They tended to exalt piety even above truth. At the same time, they made positive advances in theology, and provided an ideal refuge for the scholar or writer who could find no peace elsewhere; as well as a perfect stimulus to those saintly souls who, like the English Caedmon, could derive inspiration rather from sacred history and legend than from the conditions of the ferocious and semi-barbarous society of men. Moreover, within their inevitable limitations, they promoted learning, though in a conservative spirit.

The Benedictine Schools.—The pupils were, in most monasteries, oblates who were destined to become monks. In some centres, especially in large cities such as Paris, the tendency was for 'externs' also to be welcomed, on payment of fees. In general, the teaching of the laity was regarded as the function, not of monks, but of the secular clergy.

Children were received into the monasteries at a very early age, and at seven years were expected to recite the Latin Psalter. At this stage they entered the monastic school, where the seven liberal arts were taught. Greek was practically unknown, although preserved in a measure by the influence of Irish monks, which extended to some of the great European monasteries, notably St. Gall and Laon. The vernacular received some attention, although never esteemed equal to the eternal and sacred Latin. The names of Bede, Alcuin, and Rhabanus Maurus bear witness to the pre-eminence of the Benedictine educational system during the Dark Ages. If little or no advance was made, the ancient learning was not suffered to perish, though the monks were under no obligation to preserve it, except what was self-imposed. Neither is it to be forgotten that the pioneers and exemplars in such arts as painting, book-making, architecture, and agriculture were to be found in the monasteries.

On the other hand, the scientific spirit as now understood had little or no place. There was little attempt to seek truth as such, other than religious truth. Sacred legends, however distorted or false they might appear under the test of reason, were regarded as better food for the mind than the facts of secular science. The monastic rules demanded sacred, not secular reading, the latter being merely ancillary to the former.

The following is the section of the Benedictine Rule relating to Manual Labour and Reading (Cubberley, *Readings in the History of Education*, pp. 57–9).

'*Concerning the daily manual labour.*—Idleness is the enemy of the soul. And, therefore, at fixed times, the brothers ought to be occupied in manual labour; and, again, at fixed times, in sacred reading. Therefore we believe that, according to this disposition, both seasons ought to be arranged; so that, from Easter until the Calends of October, going out early, from the first until the fourth hour, they shall do what labour shall be necessary. Moreover, from the fourth hour until about the sixth, they shall be free for reading. After the meal of the sixth hour, moreover, rising from table, they shall rest in their beds with all silence; or, perchance, he that wishes to read may so read to himself that he do not disturb another. And the nona (the second meal) shall be gone through with more moderately about the middle of the eighth hour; and again they shall work at what is to be done until Vespers. But, if the exigency or poverty of the place demands that they be occupied by themselves in picking fruits, they shall not be dismayed: for then they are truly monks if they live by the labours of their hands; as did also our fathers and the apostles. Let all things be done with moderation, however, on account of the faint-hearted. From the Calends of October, moreover, until the beginning of Lent, they shall be free for reading until the second full hour. At the second hour the tertia (morning service) shall be held, and all shall labour at the task which is enjoined upon them until the ninth. The first signal, moreover, of the ninth hour having been given, they shall each one leave off his work;

and be ready when the second signal strikes. Moreover, after the refection they shall be free for their readings or for psalms. But in the days of Lent, from dawn until the third full hour, they shall do the labour that is enjoined on them. In which days of Lent they shall all receive separate books from the library; which they shall read entirely through in order. These books are to be given out on the first day of Lent. Above all, there shall certainly be appointed one or two elders, who shall go round the monastery at the hours in which the brothers are engaged in reading, and see to it that no troublesome brother chance to be found who is open to idleness and trifling, and is not intent on his reading; being not only of no use to himself, but also stirring up others. If such a one—may it not happen—be found, he shall be admonished once and a second time. If he do not amend, he shall be subject under the Rule to such punishment that the others may have fear. Nor shall brother join brother at unsuitable hours. Moreover, on Sunday all shall engage in reading; excepting those who are deputed to various duties. But if any one be so negligent and lazy that he will not or can not read, some task shall be imposed upon him that he can do; so that he be not idle. On feeble or delicate brothers such a labour or art is to be imposed, that they shall neither be idle, nor shall they be so oppressed by the violence of labour as to be driven to take flight. Their weakness is to be taken into consideration by the abbot.'

B. *Types of Medieval Schools*

1. *Monastic or Cloistral Schools.*—It cannot be too clearly understood that the monasteries represented a withdrawal from the concerns of the world, and that general education was considered to be no part of their duty. The monastic schools educated those who were to become monks, both in sacred learning and in such preliminary knowledge of the liberal arts as might be deemed necessary. At times 'externs' were somewhat illegally admitted; at times a monk might be permitted to act as tutor to a nobleman's children, though a secular was often employed at large monasteries for the instruction of pages; sometimes a monk might even be delegated to keep a public school, though this was, properly speaking, not a monastic school but a grammar-school conducted under the auspices of the monastery. At the same time the best scholars of the early ages were monks; they undertook researches and wrote books, notwithstanding that owing to the institution of celibacy the tendency was for the learning of any monk, or indeed of any clergyman, to perish with him.

Quite a wrong impression is to be gathered from many standard histories as to the function of monastic schools in imparting general education. Known as Abbey Schools in England, as Cloistral Schools in Germany, they promoted monkish scholarship rather than public instruction; and were careful at all times to deprecate profane learning. Although in the time of Charlemagne an attempt was made under the influence of Alcuin to have schools in monasteries as well as cathedrals in which music, arithmetic, grammar, and writing should be taught, although this was decreed by the Council of Aachen in 789, yet another Council of Aachen in 817, under Lewis the Pious, forbade schools for externs: 'No school shall be kept in a monastery, except for oblates.' When grammar-schools were handed over to monasteries, as not infrequently happened, they were taught by delegated masters who were seculars—'always', writes Mr. Leach (article on Abbey Schools in the *Cyclopedia of Education*), although this is going too far in view of the fact that Abelard when a monk was deputed to keep a public school. Young ladies and small boys were not infrequently taken into Abbeys for women. But nuns knew little Latin, and unlike monks were addressed in the vernacular. Notwithstanding attempts made in the later Middle Ages to enforce an adequate education upon monasteries, by the time of the Reformation their members were notoriously ignorant. In 1335 Benedict XII ordered the Augustinians and Benedictines to provide a grammar master, who might be a secular; and in the same year it was required that five per cent. of English monks should go to Oxford or Cambridge University; but the results of such measures did not fulfil expectations, while the necessity of them is a proof of that intellectual idleness for which they were indicted by Erasmus and many others.

2. *Cathedral Schools.*—Cathedral schools, on the other hand, were provided mainly for those who would enter the ranks of the secular clergy, and carry on the work of the Church in the world, not apart from it. Each bishop saw to it that there was at least one school in his diocese, in connexion with his Cathedral, at which a Latin education could be obtained. Some of the cathedral schools appear to have had a continuous existence from the times of the later Roman Empire. The cathedral school included at least two parts, the grammar and the song schools, which developed into separate institutions under different masters. From about the last quarter of the twelfth century the theological school was discriminated from both. The choristers of the song school might only learn enough Latin to be able to sing Latin hymns and psalms; but the grammar department taught all the liberal arts. In the early Middle Ages the cathedral schools were the highest educational institutions open to members of the public. But few

attended them except with a view to an ecclesiastical career; and many poor boys were supported by foundations or from the munificence of bishops or other patrons, so that they might be educated at the cathedral school and subsequently enter upon the service of the Church.

Originally the cathedral schools were bishops' schools; but by the end of the eleventh century the Bishop was relieved by a Dean, next to whom in the Cathedral Chapter ranked in order the Precentor, the Chancellor, and the Sacrist or Treasurer. Of these, the Precentor controlled the song school and the Chancellor the grammar-school; but the latter type of school was always regarded as the most important of the educational agencies in connexion with a Cathedral Church.

3. *Collegiate Schools.*—The collegiate schools were conducted on the model of cathedral schools, being in the hands of Colleges of Secular Canons, and in some cases being survivals of schools held when the Collegiate Church had itself been a Cathedral. Several of the English collegiate schools antedate the Norman Conquest, e.g. Warwick and Waltham, while others, as at Hastings, were established shortly after this epoch. Some of the colleges, including Waltham Holy Cross, were ousted in favour of monks or 'regulars' as a result of a movement in favour of monachism during the eleventh and twelfth centuries. About 1260 the swing of the pendulum brought the foundation of colleges again into favour; and Mr. Leach estimates that by 1547 England possessed about 200 collegiate schools. All of these would include a Latin grammar-school and a song or choir school; but the foundations of many were not restored subsequent to their confiscation under Henry VIII and Edward VI.

4. *Chantry Schools.*—A Chantry, like many monasteries, was an endowed institution, the essence of which was that one or more priests were to be supported in order to say masses for the dead. Many chantries were established in connexion with cathedrals or other large institutions. Since the saying of masses occupied but a small portion of the day, other duties tended to be laid upon chantry priests, especially that of teaching. The chantry schools which thus arose were generally free of tuition fees, either to children of the poor, or of parishioners. Many chantry foundations provided for both a grammar and a song school—that is to say, for a Latin and an elementary school in some sort of co-ordination. The dissolution of Chantries by the Act of 1547 involved the disappearance of most of the chantry schools, which during the later Middle Ages had been widely diffused, especially throughout England.

5. *Gild and Municipal Schools.*—By the close of the twelfth century the rise of an industrial class in the cities, accompanied by a new sense of citizenship, had led to the development of a third estate, to the comparative independence of the towns, and to the foundation of new schools in the cities. Many were established by the gilds; and on the Continent some were municipal schools, the municipal council being sometimes indistinguishable from a gild.

The city schools were of several types, civic Latin schools, civic vernacular schools, and private schools. Private schools for girls became not uncommon. While the teachers were still under ecclesiastical control and theoretically ranked as clerics, laymen and laywomen gradually became more numerous in the teaching ranks. Village schools were sometimes taught by a delegated master instead of by the priest of the parish himself, who might have to administer to the needs of several villages.

Like the older cathedral and cloistral schools, the city schools were specially endowed. The head of the school known as Rector, Master, or *Ludimagister*, was usually qualified for his position by a course at the university, and received his appointment and salary from the civic authorities. His assistants, entitled *socii* or *locati*, were chosen and paid by him. The Rector, usually the town clerk, sometimes delegated his duties in large measure to a Provisor, frequently the Cantor. To an increasing extent, merchants and others who could afford to do so sent their sons to the town Latin School.

Pupils were divided into classes called *lectiones* or *locationes*, which sometimes had the advantage of separate class-rooms.

The main divisions were three:

(1) Elementary—reading and writing.
(2) Middle—Latin grammar, from Donatus.
(3) Higher—logic, classics.

Latin was the staple subject of the curriculum; all text-books being in Latin. Owing to the universal use of Latin throughout Christendom, learning possessed an international character which has since been partly lost. Other subjects were religion, reading, writing, and counting; and in some schools philosophy, higher arithmetic, music, geography, history, and natural history.

Discipline continued to be severe, as may be gathered from the institution of rod-holidays and the carrying of 'the horse' for talking in the vernacular. On rod-holidays the boys gathered birch twigs for use throughout the year. Wandering scholars, known as Bacchantes and their attendant 'A B C shooters', are described by the Schoolman Thomas Platter (b. at Basle, 1499), who attended seven parish schools in Breslau, but has not left us an account of his text-books. Such scholars lived frequently by licensed begging, supplemented by minor thefts; but some found hospitality at the hands of charitable persons.

6. *Elementary Schools.*—The elementary schools of the Middle Ages are shrouded in mystery. Until recently, historians appear to have been under the impression that during this long period there were few except Latin schools, which, of course, must be regarded as secondary. Certainly throughout the Middle Ages many boys went to a Latin or grammar-school without having studied the mother tongue, just as Quintilian had recommended that the Roman boy of his time should study Greek before Latin. But it is certain that most of Quintilian's pupils had Latin literature before Greek; and probably the average medieval schoolboy could read his own language before he began upon that of the Church and of learning.

Our difficulties in describing the elementary schools of the Middle Ages arise from three causes. The first is that such schools were unendowed and ephemeral, and such as had endowments failed to safeguard them during crises such as that of the Reformation. Thus the elementary schools left few traces upon legal documents. The second difficulty is that the vernacular schools were poorly esteemed—the national languages and dialects lacked the permanence, the standardization, the universality, and the literary pre-eminence of the Latin tongue. Hence they are seldom mentioned either in poetry or in prose literature. The third difficulty is the obvious one, that the Middle Ages covered many centuries, that they showed, contrary to the current belief, an important degree of intellectual progress, both intensive and extensive, and that the conditions which may have been in vogue during one part of the Middle Ages were not necessarily characteristic of another.

These difficulties are not, however, fatal to our inquiry. Some elementary schools, that is to say, schools which did not teach Latin grammar, had endowments; and a considerable number have been traced by Mr. A. F. Leach in his historical study of the schools of England. Most of the endowments appear to have been confiscated along with those of the various institutions under whose auspices the schools were conducted. Neither is there any certainty that endowed elementary schools existed very early in the Middle Ages. As to mention in literature, although the elementary schools of the Middle Ages are not, so far as we have been able to discover, described by medieval writers in detail—indeed, there was only too little to be said about their curriculum and organization—yet there is ample proof that a great body of people in England and elsewhere could read and write the mother tongue, even during the so-called 'Dark Ages', and this fact presupposes elementary schooling. We believe, indeed, that the darkness of those ages exists chiefly in our own want of knowledge about them. Alfred caused several standard works to be translated into Anglo-Saxon as 'the language which we all can understand', the implication being that we can all read it. Ælfric's *Colloquy* was written with an interlinear translation in Old English—evidently the pupils could read the latter, although they were mere beginners in the classics. Anglo-Saxon books were read more widely and more freely than Latin. Indeed, in large cities such as London, ability to read and write English must have been almost as indispensable to the commercial class as it is at the present time; and, in addition, books of Anglo-Saxon poetry certainly had a wide vogue. Elsewhere throughout Christendom, conditions seem to have been parallel. The intellectual sluggishness attributed to the Anglo-Saxons by their Norman conquerors was a myth.

From whom did the Anglo-Saxons learn to read and write? When they first came to Britain, these arts may not have been totally strange to them. Runic inscriptions were at that time, in all probability, a secret of the priestly craft. But the contact of the Germanic peoples with the Roman civilization must have led to reading and writing by means of the Roman alphabet, among a few of the English, long before Augustine and his monks founded a Latin grammar-school at Canterbury. Even from the conquered Britons, and certainly through trade with the Continent, English writing could not fail to have been instituted. It may never be known when the epic poem, *Beowulf*, which the English appear to have brought with them from the Continent, was first committed to paper, but doubtless at some time prior to the introduction of grammar-schools in England.

The agencies by which elementary instruction was given remained, throughout the Middle Ages, varied and often informal. Some children learned to read and write at home. Others went to a master, no doubt often to a priest. The schools which priests were enjoined to keep were probably, in most cases, elementary, though some parish priests, as in the suburbs of London, sought to found grammar-schools. Ordinarily a parish school was conducted by the parish clerk under the priest's supervision. The 'Dame Schools' which abounded at the end of the Middle Ages were kept for small fees in some kitchen or cellar, by old women who could teach to infants the alphabet, the Lord's Prayer and Creed, and the numerals, but little else. No doubt such schools were of ancient lineage—they were too insignificant for the Dame to require a formal ecclesiastical licence. Song schools taught boys to read sufficiently for the purpose of singing from music; but did not attempt Latin grammar, though the Church with which they were affiliated would usually provide a grammar-school as an alternative or complement to the song school. In some grammar-schools there was an elementary department in which the vernacular was read and written by boys, the majority of whom would afterwards proceed to the higher or Latin grades. In the later Middle Ages every township provided ample facilities for both elementary and higher learning. The elementary scholar was nicknamed Abecedarius. Only in rural districts was complete illiteracy prevalent; and in general, there was no obstacle to either vernacular or Latin education other than that of poverty, or, in a limited degree, that of servile status. For the sons of villeins rarely attended school except with a view to the priesthood.

C. *London Schools of the Twelfth Century*

In London the principal medieval schools were attached to churches of ancient foundation. For a long time the grammar-schools of St. Paul's, the Arches, and St. Martin's claimed a monopoly of higher education within the city precincts.

Fitz Stephen, in his *Life of Becket*, describes the London schools as they existed in 1118. His account is thus rendered by Leach (*Educational Charters*, pp. 83, 84):

'The chief suburban wells near London are on the north, of sweet water, health-giving, clear and "with stream hurrying over clear pebbles"; among which Holywell, Clerkenwell, St. Clement's well, are thought the best known, and are more frequented by the more celebrated of the scholars and youth of the town when they walk out in summer time to take the air. A good city indeed when it has a good lord.

'*The Schools.*

'In London the three principal churches have celebrated schools of privilege and ancient dignity. Often, however, through personal favour to some noted philosopher, more schools are allowed there. On feast days the masters celebrate assemblies at the churches, *en fête*. The scholars hold disputations, some declaiming, others by way of question and answer. These roll out enthymemes, those use the better form of perfect syllogisms. Some dispute merely for show, as they do at collections; others for truth, which is the grace of perfection. The sophists, using the Socratic irony, are pronounced happy because of the mass and volume of their words; others play upon words. Those learning rhetoric, with rhetorical speeches, speak to the point with a view to persuasion, being careful to observe the precepts of their art, and to leave out nothing that belongs to it. The boys of the different schools vie with each other in verses; or dispute on the principles of grammar, or the rules of preterites and supines. Others in epigrams, rhymes and verses, use the old freedom of the highway, with Fescennine licence freely scourge their schoolfellows without mentioning names, hurl abuse and fun at each other, with Socratic wit gird at the failings of their schoolfellows, or even of their elders, or bite them more deeply with the tooth of Theon in audacious dithyrambics. The audience, "ready for much laughter, wrinkle their noses as they redouble their shaking guffaws".

'*Games.*

'Every year, on the day which is called the Carnival (Shrove Tuesday), to begin with the boys' games (for we were all boys once), all the boys in each school bring their masters their game-cocks, and the whole morning is devoted to the boys' play, they having a holiday to look on at the cock-fights in their schools. In the afternoon the whole youth of the city goes into the suburban level for a solemn game of ball. Each school has its own ball, and nearly all the holders of civic offices also provide one. The grown-up people, the fathers and rich men of the city, come on horseback to look on at the struggles of the young, and in their ways grow young with the young; and the motion of natural heat seems to be excited in them by looking on at so much motion and by sharing in the delight of the freedom of youth.'

VII

EDUCATIONAL POLICIES IN MEDIEVAL ENGLAND

A. *Attitude of the Church*

MEDIEVAL education was highly standardized. The schools of one western European country resembled those of another, with minor variations only. Hence the student, disposed to make a survey of the relation of education to the Church, the Crown, and the nobility, may confine his attention if he so desires to conditions in England. The problems of other countries were on the whole similar, the educational system of Christendom being a unity; and although many local differences existed, in general it remains true that the history of English paralleled that of Continental education.

For some time after the Norman Conquest the control of the Church over education appears to have been absolute. Both the scholasticus or schoolmaster, and the clerici or scholars, of the Latin schools were in orders. To judge from the reference of a chronicle to a schoolmaster of Beverley in about A.D. 1000, a teacher was expected to be learned, of noble character, modest and skilful, careful in his teaching, and kindly and pleasant without lack of strictness. The Latin schoolmasters, although not, perhaps, the unimportant and unlearned teachers of vernacular reading to little children, had to be licensed by an ecclesiastical officer, generally the bishop or ordinary. A canon which was promulgated at Westminster in A.D. 1138 ordained 'That if schoolmasters hire out their schools to be conducted by others, they shall be liable to ecclesiastical punishment'. In this way it was sought to safeguard both orthodoxy and efficiency of teaching. The Church as an organization encouraged learning; but there is ample evidence that both before and after the foundation of universities, many ecclesiastics in the position to do so were prone to exact fees from candidates for licences to teach, contrary to the will of the Holy See. Between 1170 and 1172 the canon law plainly ordered 'That whatever fit and learned persons wish to keep schools of literature (*studia literarum*) shall be allowed to keep schools without any molestation or exaction, lest learning, which ought to be given freely to all, should henceforth seem to be exposed for sale at a price'.

One of the best illustrations of the desire of the medieval Church to foster learning is the decree of the fourth Lateran Council (1215), to the effect that there should be a schoolmaster, licensed by the bishop, in every cathedral. This applied to all Christendom, and while the custom of providing cathedral schools had been in existence for many centuries, henceforth there could be no question as to the bishop's canonical duty in the matter.

The medieval schools were not unprofitable. There is record of lawsuits at Beverley, Gloucester, and London for the exclusive right to teach in these respective centres. The old established schools resisted the attempts of newcomers to open schools which might draw away their paying pupils. About 1138 Henry of Blois attempted to cope with unlicensed teachers in London, commanding the Chapter of St. Paul's and Archdeacon William that after three warnings they should pronounce sentence of anathema on those who without due permission presume to lecture in London, apart from those who keep the schools of St. Mary-le-Bow and St. Martin-le-Grand, and, of course, St. Paul's. But generally speaking the bishops do not appear to have been niggardly in respect of the grant of licences to teach, for in the fourteenth century at least one Latin grammar-school existed in each considerable town. Disputes regarding the right to teach were frequently taken to the ecclesiastical courts, and appeals were sometimes forwarded to Rome.

The term 'free school' was frequently employed during the Middle Ages, and a difference of opinion exists as to its interpretation. On the one hand it is argued that this means a school giving free tuition, on the other hand that it is merely a synonym for a school of the liberal arts. Apart from the possibility that the term may not have been used consistently, there is a third possibility, namely, that a free school meant a school with free places. In many cases endowments provided for the free tuition of a limited number of pupils, others paying fees. At Bury St. Edmunds, for example, near the end of the twelfth century, Abbot Sampson bought a stone house in the town, assigning it for school purposes, so that poor clerks (or pupils) might be free of the rent which had formerly been exacted of each, irrespective of his ability to pay fees The Abbot also gave the schoolmaster a salary so that forty poor clerks might be free of all fees for instruction. Such a school would accept fee-paying pupils in addition to the privileged forty. There is even a fourth possible interpretation, that a free school simply meant a public school, from which none would be turned away.

It was only when Lollardry began to be appreciated as a serious menace that the ecclesiastical authorities of England commenced to endeavour earnestly to limit the number of Latin grammar-schools. Earlier attempts at restriction had been spasmodic, local, and temporary, having been made from the standpoint of vested interests, whereas the fear of Lollardry made limitation appear to have become necessary in the interests of orthodox faith.

In the middle of the fourteenth century the use of French in the grammar-schools of England was supplanted by the use of English as the language into which Latin was translated. Prior to the Norman Conquest the language employed had been Anglo-Saxon. From the Conquest to the middle of the fourteenth century the medium of instruction was Anglo-Saxon. In 1327 it was required that school pupils should construe their lessons in French; but after the first Plague of 1349 English became once for all, with Latin, the language of the schools. One important result seems to have been an increase in the number of Lollard schoolmasters, favoured by the number of empty schools as well as by the religious zeal of the sect, which defied the terrors of the plague. In this connexion it should be recalled that John Wyclif was successful for a time in making Oxford a centre of protestant influence; he even won the temporary approval of a number of bishops. Since among the functions of bishops was that of granting licences to schoolmasters, many of the Lollards had the opportunity of entering the schools under the patronage of the Church whose life and doctrine they aspired to reform.

The Lollards seems to have introduced their theological tenets into the curriculum of the schools; but in the reign of Henry IV (1401) an act forbade them to be teachers; while in 1408 appeared a set of constitutions drawn up by Archbishop Arundel which excluded all novel explanations of texts and all disputations about the faith and the sacraments from the schools. The provision for the censorship of school texts is interesting enough to be quoted in full, especially as it throws light not only upon the attitude of the Church to education but also upon the functions of the Universities and the method of publishing books prior to the invention of printing:

'Because a new path oftener misleads men than an old, we will and ordain that no book or treatise composed by John Wyclif, or by any other in his time, or since, or hereafter to be composed, be henceforth read in the schools, halls, inns, or other places whatsoever within our province aforesaid, and that none be taught according to such (book) unless it have been first examined, and upon examination unanimously approved by the University of Oxford or

Cambridge, or at least by 12 men chosen by the said universities, or by one of them under the discretion of us, or our successors; and then afterwards (the book be approved) expressly by us, or our successors, and delivered in the name, and by the authority of the universities, to be copied, and sold to such as desire, after it has been faithfully collated, at a just price, the original thenceforth remaining in some chest of the university forever. And if any one shall read book or treatise of this sort in the schools or elsewhere, contrary to the form above written, or shall teach according to it, let them be punished according as the quality of the fact shall require, as a sower of schism and a fautor of heresy.'

By this time, evidently, the universities no longer favoured Lollardry. The reaction succeeded to the extent of excluding from the schools their most zealous teachers, in bringing about the stagnation of research in the universities, and in seriously diminishing the number of schools.

B. *Attitude of the State*

There were times when the State was not minded to allow the Church to retain its exclusive rights over the schools. For example, in 1343, the Crown forbade the Court Christian to entertain a plea relative to the patronage of a grammar school, 'such pleas belonging especially to us and to no other in this Kingdom'. Edward III thus ordered the plea to be remitted to the King's Court.

In 1393–4 a petition to the Crown reveals the fact that the masters of three schools in London, St. Paul's, the Arches, and St. Martin's, had claimed the exclusive right to conduct schools in the city. These masters had taken proceedings against certain strangers, who kept rival schools, in the ecclesiastical courts; but the strangers had retaliated by bringing an action in the secular court. The petition of the old established schools was that the King should require the matter to be settled in the Court Christian. Evidently the strange masters were trying in a measure to win emancipation from the control of the Church. The petition was not answered by Richard II; and the Church would seem to have lost the day.

At other times, and particularly under fear of the possible consequences of Lollardry, the Crown proved more amenable to ecclesiastical influence. In 1446 King Henry VI gave his sanction to the limitation of the London grammar-schools to five. The fear of the Lollard movement had begun to react against freedom in education; for the change was the work of the Archbishop of Canterbury and the Bishop of

London. As an immediate consequence of this restriction, in 1447 four rectors of suburban parishes pointed out in a lugubrious petition 'the grete nombre of gramer scoles, that sometyme were in divers parties of this Realme, beside tho that were in London, and howe fewe ben in thise days'. They requested permission to open grammar-schools in their respective parishes; and the petition was granted subject to the consent of the Ordinary or the Archbishop of Canterbury for the time being.

A claim for trespass brought in 1410 by two masters of the Gloucester Grammar-School against another master who taught a rival school, was dismissed by the Chief Justice on the ground that the action could not be tried in the secular court. This appears to have been a test case. The Chief Justice pointed out that: 'If a man retain a master in his house to teach his children he damages the Common Master of the town. Yet I believe that he has no action.' To teach youth, it was pointed out by the bench, 'is a virtuous and charitable thing to do, helpful to the people, for which he cannot be punished by our law'.

Thus a common law right to teach was established, partly on this ground, and partly because there was no estate involved in the teaching of children. On the other hand, the right of the Church courts to take cognizance of such cases was not denied; and in general such matters were left to ecclesiastical jurisdiction. The State showed, however, its clear disinclination to co-operate with the Church in securing a monopoly of education for a few masters. It may be significant that the plaintiffs were not told that the ecclesiastical courts could help them; only that the secular courts could not and would not do so. Hankeford, Justice of the Common Pleas, in this case laid down the opinion that schools were not to be restrained from competition except with Universities and schools of ancient foundation.

In general, then, during the later Middle Ages the State tended to admit the authority of the Church over the schools, and to extend its help to education through the recognition of Benefit of Clergy; but with important reservations of its own power, and with the general desire, checked somewhat by fear of Lollardry, to encourage liberty of teaching. The facts that the Crown prohibited none from learning, and that the common law prevented none from teaching, were ignored by the Church; and according to De Montmorency the judgement on the Gloucester Grammar-School was not quoted in equity for three hundred years. Yet it is clear from the records of this case that education at the end of the Middle Ages was general, that many townspeople employed tutors for their children, and that other town children of the middle class were in the habit of attending the local grammar school.

C. *Attitude of the Aristocracy*

It will have been gathered that the general attitude of both Church and State in the Middle Ages was favourable to education. Nevertheless a conservative opposition was frequently manifested by the landholders. Even in Norman times there were some villeins wealthy enough and ambitious enough to send their sons to a Latin grammar-school. In such cases the boys might become parish priests, or possibly bailiffs upon manors, the accounts of which were kept in Latin. At the end of the twelfth century the chronicler Walter Map, or Mapes, complained that in his time the villeins were attempting to educate their ignoble and degenerate offspring in the liberal arts. This meant not an English, but a Latin education. At a later stage we hear of a petition of the Commons, who, it should be remembered, consisted essentially of knights of the shire, to the effect that no villein or neif should be allowed to send his children to school. This petition of 1391 was no doubt the result primarily of the shortage of labour which had been produced by visitations of the plague, and secondly by the desire to curb the revolutionary and Lollard ideas which were permeating the masses. The King, to his credit, rejected the petition. Not for the first time the Crown staunchly befriended the masses, who formed its natural ally against the barons.

Soon after this the villeins as a servile class disappeared. An early consequence was the educational emancipation of all ranks of society; and in 1406 the right of all, whether villein or freeman, to attend any school he pleased was formally established by Act of Parliament. 'Every man or woman, of what estate or condition that he be, shall be free to set their son or daughter to take learning at any manner school that pleaseth them within the Realme.'

D. *Benefit of Clergy*

The foregoing account of medieval educational policy would be incomplete without some mention of the practice of Benefit of Clergy, the most valuable effect of which was to set a premium upon learning. Benefit of Clergy, a practice dating in England from the days of Athelstan (about A.D. 926), was the recognition of letters as entitling an offender to be prosecuted in the ecclesiastical instead of in the civil courts. As the penalties in the former were much the lighter, the practice, while it may have debased the standards of ecclesiastical morality, undoubtedly constituted an incentive to learning. In Anglo-Saxon times education by the clergy already seems to have been paid for, as a statute of King Edgar (A.D. 960) enacts 'that no priest receive a scholar without the leave of the other by whom he was formerly retained'. The desire for continuity of instruction hardly explains the enactment; no doubt the right to fees was more potent in the promotion of legislation.

The practice of Benefit of Clergy meant that the greater the number of people who could read, the wider was the sway of the ecclesiastical courts. It was thus directly to the interest of the Church as a power in the world to encourage learning.

While Benefit of Clergy was at first co-extensive with the possession of holy orders, in the process of time it came to include all who could read, whether in holy orders or not. Learning was still, however, the recognized path to holy orders; and consequently to high preferment, however humble a man's origin might have been. A bishop who should have knowingly ordained an ignorant person was held to be guilty of deadly sin.

Even villeins might attain 'Clergie'; a process which the Commons attempted to defeat by the petition of 1391, which was practically vetoed by Richard II.

By an act of Henry VII (1488–9), while laymen of learning were still allowed to claim Benefit of Clergy on the first offence, yet in order that they might not be encouraged to crime by a sense of immunity from its legal consequences, they might be branded on the left thumb with an M or a T, according to whether the crime were a murder or other offence. This act deliberately aimed at the discouragement of crime committed 'upon trust of the privilege of the Church'. In 1531–2 a further step was taken towards the abolition of the criminal privileges of scholars. By an act of that year laymen and clergy in orders below sub-deacon were deprived of Benefit of Clergy altogether. Education, having become general, could no longer be privileged.

Strange to say, Benefit of Clergy was revived after the Reformation, perhaps because education had declined, as a result of the confiscation of many school endowments. In 1705, according to Blackstone:

'All women, all Peers of Parliament and Peeresses and all male Commoners who could read were discharged in all clergyable offences; the males absolutely if clerks in Holy Orders; and other Commoners, both male and female upon branding, and Peers and Peeresses without for the first offençe; yet all liable (except Peers and Peeresses), if the Judge saw occasion to imprisonment not exceeding a year. And those men who could not read if under the degree of peerage were hanged. Afterwards indeed it was considered that education and learning were no extenuation of guilt, but quite the reverse, and that if the punishment of death for simple felony was too severe for those who had been liberally instructed, it was *a fortiori* too severe for the ignorant also. And thereupon, by the same statute 5 Anne, c. 6, it was enacted that the Benefit of Clergy should be granted to all those who were entitled to ask it, without requiring them to read by way of additional merit.'

In fact, the privilege henceforth amounted to little, though it was not formally abolished until the reign of George IV (1826–7). The practice, never perhaps morally justifiable, had long been an anachronism.

VIII

THE RISE OF UNIVERSITIES

THE universities of Europe are a natural outgrowth of her schools. With the barbarian conquests, the great municipal schools of law and rhetoric which had flourished under the Roman Empire had lapsed; and from the sixth to the twelfth century no higher educational institutions existed in Europe than the cathedral schools and the monasteries. The body of knowledge available to students tended to shrink to the dimensions of such works as those of Capella, Cassiodorus, Orosius, Boethius, and Gregory the Great. At best, it might expand to little more than the limits of Isidore's unscientific encyclopaedia, the Etymologies. Only when a new and worthy body of knowledge became available, and when strong central Governments had restored a considerable degree of order to European countries, so that students and teachers might live and move in an atmosphere of relative security, were institutions of university rank restored.

The rise of the universities is the most notable intellectual phenomenon of the twelfth and thirteenth centuries. Well has the term 'twelfth-century renaissance' been applied to the movements in thought which agitated the period. Even the Italian renaissance of a later date reared no such mighty institutions as the universities for its enduring monument. But there could be no universities until the necessity existed of bringing them into being. They were not the device of popes, emperors, kings, or statesmen; but simply grew out of the exigencies of a situation which the older types of schools were powerless to satisfy. A new body of knowledge, having a marked professional value, and requiring for its mastery the protracted study of adult minds, under the guidance of eminent specialists, in the twelfth century began to make the university an indispensable institution.

The mass of new knowledge which caused universities to develop from lesser schools was related to several subjects, and had several more or less independent sources. Philosophy was stimulated not only by the controversy between realism and nominalism, in which Abelard so notably participated, but also by the recovery of the complete works of Aristotle, at first from Moorish sources, and afterwards directly from Constantinople. Theology was systematized in part as the result of the same controversy, and more completely as the fruit of the labours of Peter the Lombard, whose *Sententiae* appeared about 1145. The exercise of medicine received a notable impetus from Arabic studies. Civil law became a university discipline as the outcome of the researches and teachings of Irnerius, a monk of Bologna. The Church or Canon Law underwent a similar organization at the hands of another Bolognese monk, Gratian, whose collection of the decrees of the Councils and of the Popes was published as the *Decretum*. Even classical scholarship, although far from representing the main intellectual interest of the period, experienced a not inconsiderable revival, which centred about the great cathedral school at Chartres. Thus in philosophy, theology, medicine, Roman and ecclesiastical law, and literary classicism, there developed in the twelfth century a mass of material which could only be studied effectively by men of some maturity of intellect, under expert masters, and over a period of several years. Universities were the natural reaction to the pressure of this situation.

Let us consider the scholastic aspect of the twelfth-century revival in greater detail. The controversy between Realism and Nominalism, which began in the eleventh century with the polemic between Anselm and Roscellinus, divided the scholars of Christendom into two great camps, whose disputations are the beginning of the intellectual movement known as scholasticism. The place of Abelard in relation to this controversy has already been indicated. Unlike other schoolmen, he not only revealed many inconsistencies in the theological judgements of the early Christian fathers, but in his 'Yea and Nay' left the reader to find a solution for himself. In general, schoolmen attempted to rationalize not only their secular experience, but also their religious faith. A clear distinction, indeed, was drawn between philosophy and religion, between reason and revelation; and while every liberty was taken by the schoolmen in stating objections to articles of faith, they were expected to conclude by the triumphant vindication of the orthodox position. Yet, in many matters, it was the great schoolmen themselves who defined what is orthodox. In the thirteenth century the line of notable schoolmen included the Aristotelian Alexander of Hales, the encyclopaedist Vincent of Beauvais, the seraphic and mystical Bonaventura, the universal doctor—learned in Arabic commentaries—Albertus Magnus, the angelic Thomas Aquinas, and the subtle John Duns Scotus. The *Summa Theologiae* of Thomas Aquinas is still the standard of orthodoxy for the Roman Catholic Church.

As universities developed, the leadership of thought departed from the monasteries and fell to these freer, larger, and more international institutions. Most of the schoolmen were closely associated with the universities. The influence of the new orders in the Church, the Franciscan and Dominican friars, was intellectual as well as moral; and friars, once they had been permitted in the middle of the thirteenth century to occupy university chairs, tended to replace the monks as the leading scholars and teachers of the period. Albertus Magnus and Thomas Aquinas were Dominicans; Alexander of Hales, Bonaventura, Roger Bacon, Duns Scotus, and William of Occam Franciscans.

In essentials, both philosophical and theological scholasticism consisted of the systematization of speculation and faith, by the rigid application of the Aristotelian logic to these fields. The re-discovery of Aristotle was one of the main stimuli to the establishment of universities. Aristotle was strong meat to the Middle Ages; he needed breaking down into essences by such commentators as Averroes, in order that his theories might be assimilated. Arabic scholars had long possessed the Aristotelian writings, although generally in corrupt texts. In Spain the Moor Averroes had produced 'the great commentary', which, along with the bulk of Aristotle's writings, was rendered into Latin. The new Aristotle was eagerly studied; the old Aristotle, which Boethius had preserved in Latin form to Western Christendom, having always been cherished. In the early universities, however, the new Aristotelian philosophy encountered a strong conservative opposition. At Paris the reading of a number of Aristotle's works was prohibited. A papal committee was appointed to purge him of error. But gradually the schoolmen rehabilitated Aristotle; and according to Albertus Magnus, those who inveigh against him understand not what they are saying. By the middle of the thirteenth century the partial prohibitions had been abandoned.

Much has been written of the merits and demerits of scholasticism, regarded from an educational point of view. It must be admitted that the scholastic method, being essentially deductive, did little to promote the acquisition of new truth. Many students wasted their time in logical subtleties, making logic not the means, but the end, of their education. Only men of rare genius, like Roger Bacon and Albertus Magnus, were able to pile induction upon deduction and advance the cause of science; others became clever and subtle, precise in the use of terms, exact in classification, without doing more than to organize what was already a matter of common knowledge. Yet this in itself was much; new truth could be grafted more safely upon a perfected scholastic system, and upon a tradition of exact reason, than upon the heterogeneous mass of ideas which it was the task of the schoolmen to disentangle, arrange, and docket in convenient form. Modern science owes much of its system, and most of its terminology, to the schoolmen. Moreover, if there is any force at all in the theory of formal discipline, the intellect was never more keenly whetted than in the universities of the Middle Ages.

The name originally applied to such early universities as Bologna and Paris, was *studium generale*—literally a common school. In course of time the term *universitas*, meaning any corporation, came into use. Although the medieval universities of the twelfth and thirteenth centuries developed to some extent independently, they soon became interrelated, especially when the *ius ubique docendi*, or right of teaching everywhere, came to be more or less established as the privilege of graduates. Bologna and Paris were the first to become celebrated, together with Salerno, the last-named being essentially a State-controlled medical college.

As the European universities fell into two types—the southern, in which the initiative rested mainly with the students; and the northern which developed largely from the activities of gilds of masters—it is desirable that Bologna should be described as an example of the southern, and Paris as an illustration of the northern type. Of classical origin, the schools of Bologna came to supplant those of Ravenna in public reputation, on account of the researches of Irnerius into the Roman Imperial Law. A generation later the monk Gratian produced his *Decretum*, which at once became the standard ecclesiastical code. Emperors and popes awakened to the significance of the movement towards higher education which was becoming centred in Bologna. In 1158 the Emperor Frederick protected the students of Lombardy by charter. In 1189 a papal bull attempted to regulate the rents which were charged of students. The student body organized itself on the model of the gilds to which the Middle Ages were accustomed. The students governed themselves through their rector, at first himself a student. In vain did the masters, doctors, or professors attempt to resist their tyrannical rule. Even the city authorities were sometimes defeated when their disciplinary measures tended to antagonize the student body, whose most effective weapon was secession. If goaded to a sufficient extent it would leave the city for another of the neighbouring Lombard towns, and doubtless, as a rule, the threat was enough. Trade, population, and prestige depended upon its presence. Thus a secession from Bologna in 1321 was healed only on terms dictated by the students, namely that an offending magistrate should be publicly flogged, and that the city should erect a chapel for the university. The two university bodies which grew up side by side at Bologna, the one Italian, the other foreign, known respectively as *universitas citramontanorum* and *universitas ultramontanorum*, had coalesced by 1317. The university obtained many privileges, including that of holding its own courts. In 1411 we find councillors appointed by the university exercising not only civil, but criminal, jurisdiction over its members. Many matters, indeed, were controlled by the rector and a council, but for a long time the student body itself, excluding such as lived at other men's costs, remained the supreme authority, and met on occasion in congregation. A professor was required to swear obedience to the student rector. He might suffer *privatio* or expulsion. He might be fined for lateness at lectures or for skipping a chapter of the text which he was supposed to expound. If his lectures were ill attended he was fined by the city. Booksellers were carefully supervised, and might be penalized for errors in their books. Profits on second-hand books were regulated. Money was only to be lent by four authorized pawnbrokers, although it seems that professors sometimes entered this trade *sub rosa*. There were few residential colleges, and these, indeed, were merely licensed hostels.

The doctors, or professors, protected themselves, however, by a gild, perhaps older than that of the students; but living by fees, they had drifted into a subordinate position. Doctors gave the ordinary morning lectures; in the afternoon lectures, not indispensable but bearing on the course, might be given by certain approved scholars besides. Competition for eminent men led gradually to contracted salaries, at least as early as 1180. A century later there were in Bologna twenty-three doctors of law paid under contract. By this time the State had appointed governors, so that of the twenty-three, all but one were indirectly State nominees, while one had been appointed by the university itself. The State gradually deprived the student body of its powers, of which for a long time the Church had been the efficient protector.

Other changes also occurred during the latter part of the thirteenth century. The better-paid teaching positions were now restricted to citizens of Bologna. The professors to some extent even had their offices made hereditary. They also gave the degrees, although in 1219 the Pope required the consent of the Archdeacon to all promotions to degrees. In Paris the ecclesiastical control of the Chancellor had already been admitted. A bull of 1292 enabled the doctors of Bologna to teach throughout the world, and thus a new element was added to the accepted ecclesiastical hierarchy.

At Bologna medicine and arts arose later than law to the status of a separate *universitas*, although degrees in these branches were granted by the same archdeacon. In each instance the student body gradually lost the supreme power that it had once possessed. For this the superior intelligence of the staff, and the growing precision of the machinery of State and Church, must share the responsibility. In 1352, there was added a theological faculty, participating in certain of the privileges of the university, but not in all.

The universities of Italy, Spain, Pressburg, Cracow, and (in name, but not in fact) Upsala, followed the Bolognese type. Paris and the northern universities, however, had a somewhat different history, although all the early universities could look back to a common origin in the Cathedral schools.

On the Island of Paris stood the cathedral church of Notre Dame, whose chancellor claimed a monopoly of the grant of licences to teach. On the other hand, various monasteries tended to establish private schools, such as Abelard maintained on the hill at Ste Geneviève, across the Seine. Medieval abbeys seldom taught other than novices; but the wealth and population of Paris seem to have led to an expansion of the strictly monastic school into the common school type. Masters of monastic schools tended to found a sort of gild, with the object of establishing their independence of the Chancellor of Notre Dame. Their object was facilitated when a separate chancellor was appointed at Ste Geneviève. The union of these masters made another union necessary. Out of the guild of the masters who held certificates from the chancellor at Notre Dame, together perhaps with some masters otherwise empowered to teach, arose the University of Paris. Bologna, it will be remembered, arose otherwise, as a gild of students.

In order to receive a degree, a student was required to satisfy both the masters and the chancellor. The masters were concerned with the matter of his proficiency, and before recommending him for the degree required him to give a public lecture, called the *inceptio*, which betokened his entry into the privileges and duties of the seniors. The chancellor was concerned with his fees; moreover, he would refuse to grant a degree to a student sent up by unlicensed masters. In spite of Papal prohibitions, licences to teach seem to have been made a source of profit by chancellors and by the bishops whom they represented, and this accounts both for the jealousy with which the monopoly of licences was guarded, and the persistency with which the gild of masters sought its independence. The chancellor of the University of Paris was a governor, generally more or less at loggerheads with the university proper, or masters' gild, while the popes tended to befriend the rising cause of the masters. The masters, too, practised effective boycotts against colleagues licensed by the chancellor without their approval; and by the end of the thirteenth century the chancellor was obliged to confer degrees upon all students approved by the body of masters, while many of his powers were taken over by the rector of the faculty of arts, who became virtually the president of the university.

During the thirteenth century the tendency was for the influence of the monasteries to be superseded by that of the friars, while at the same time a renewed interest was being developed in scholarship and art. The rise of the universities was a natural growth, which fulfilled the needs arising from the new situation. In them the narrow limits of the monastic schools might be transcended, in them the enthusiasm of the friars could be utilized, in them the new knowledge might be attained and communicated. The university movement seems to have been a popular one, determined not by civil or ecclesiastical authorities, but by the desires of individuals. Not until about 1300 did popes and emperors realize the full significance of this new *imperium in imperio*, and require that no new university should be established without their charter. Of the first fourteen universities, only three were founded by the State, and only two by the Papacy. In A.D. 1200, indeed, Philip Augustus had given a charter to the scholars of Paris, but they did not then constitute a university in the true sense of the word. The need of charters, however, was emphasized, as the practice of sending students abroad for theological study, in order to return as teachers, became general. This plan was expressly established by a bull of 1219, and in 1292 even Bologna and Paris yielded to the extent of obtaining charters granting the *ius ubique docendi*—the right of graduates to teach anywhere. Even then, however, the Papal charter was not the last word, for several universities found means to exclude teachers who had graduated from other institutions, while Paris and Oxford re-examined each others' doctors. Meantime kings frequently granted charters to the universities situated within their own dominions. Down to 1400, there seem to have been eleven unchartered universities, sixteen with Papal charters, ten chartered by Kings or Emperors, and nine chartered by both civil and ecclesiastical authorities. By the year 1501, Europe had no fewer than seventy-nine universities.

The medieval universities remained under ecclesiastical control; but were less exclusively clerical than the old monastic and cathedral schools. Cities and monarchs shared in their foundation; and their government tended towards autonomy. Meanwhile the Church still held the monopoly of the licence to teach, and regulated the dress and mode of life of masters and pupils alike. The masters still held ecclesiastical offices, while the students enjoyed clerical privileges, and in most cases contemplated a clerical career.

The revival of learning in the twelfth century represents in some respects an anticipation of the fifteenth-century renaissance. At Chartres, classicism was a pervading influence, and the writings of John of Salisbury still remain to show the reality of its effect upon both the form and the content of medieval studies. On the other hand, Europe was not yet ripe for humanism. Learning had to be popularized before it could be intensified. St. Bernard and Abelard, antagonists as they were, both concentrated the efforts of their scholarship upon theology, not upon classicism. Abelard was almost the founder of scholasticism. The elements of the university curriculum in the Middle Ages may be defined as theology, Aristotle, civil and canon law, the seven liberal arts, and medicine. The focus of greatest interest was certainly the scholastic theology. Aquinas, who brought the system to its greatest perfection, captured the universities almost completely, although his contemporary, Roger Bacon, was able to perceive the weakness of the scholastic foundations, which lay in the imperfectly understood and often corrupt texts of Aristotle and the sacred writings. Aquinas triumphed, while Bacon was forgotten. Meanwhile a large republic of letters was evolved, inspired by a charitable and even by a democratic spirit. The tendency to equality of rich and poor students was marked; and in many cases the poor were even favoured. Great influence came to be wielded by university opinion, as instanced by the appeal of Henry VIII to the universities, and by the determination of doctrinal disputes by the University of Paris.

Lectures in the medieval universities began early. Latin grammar was a prerequisite to attendance, as the lectures were almost all delivered in Latin. It was found necessary, however, to establish grammar-schools within the universities themselves, in order that students might perfect their literary knowledge. Lectures were of two kinds, the ordinary, and the extraordinary or cursory, the latter being generally optional, varied, and free in method, and supplementary to the ordinary lectures. At first seven years may have been required for the mastership, as in the case of apprentices to a trade; but if so the term was gradually diminished to three or four years. At a certain point in his course the student would become a *baccalaureus*, a sort of literary journeyman. This involved a ceremony known as *determinatio*, or the leading and summary of a debate. At the end came the *inceptio*, which admitted a student to teach. The mastership or doctorate in arts was, in fact, originally a professional degree, qualifying for the teaching profession. To become a master in the profession of law, medicine, or theology, eight or ten years more might be required; but regulations were frequently evaded or suspended, and studies might be more nominal than real. Examinations may have been lax, and degrees subject to bribery, but evidence on these heads is to be accepted with caution. The value of the scholastic studies of the universities has often been underrated. Much freedom of thought and discussion was practised under the guise of hypothesis, and real achievement in science and medicine was made by numerous individual scholars, most of whom have been forgotten. The terminology and classifications of modern science and philosophy are, moreover, deeply indebted to medieval university studies. Never, perhaps, have the qualities of memory, exactness, and readiness of expression been as systematically and successfully developed as in the universities of the Middle Ages.

The organization of the universities presented a number of interesting features. Unlike many of the monastic schools, they were located in cities. Naturally, in such a cosmopolitan centre as Paris, the students grouped themselves according to nations, French, Norman, Picard, English, and after the hundred years war, German. The term faculty, of later origin, came to be applied to a department of study, such as arts, and especially to the organization of masters which controlled such a department.

In Arts, preliminary Latin was demanded for the baccalaureate. Most of the lectures were delivered in Latin. Advanced grammar was studied chiefly from Priscian. Aristotle's logic was required, and subsequently his metaphysics and ethics. The 'New Aristotle', which had been prohibited at Paris in 1215, was required by a later statute (1254).

With Aristotle, the great Moorish commentator, Averroes, was read. The art of rhetoric was displaced entirely by logic; but geometry and astronomy, founded on the Greek, with some Arabic influence superimposed, were not neglected in university courses.

Although the government rested in the first instance mainly with the students themselves, the rector at Paris and most other universities soon became a royal nominee. Student powers were gradually alienated, as the granting of charters and privileges tended to involve the imposition of various limitations. Ultimately university rule became strict, severe, and despotic, as in Spanish and English colleges at the end of the Middle Ages. There were various regulations against the practices of carrying arms and gambling.

The age of admission varied considerably; but by a statute of the University of Paris a 'determining' bachelor had to be at least fourteen. Entrance must, therefore, have been made even earlier. Many students held benefices, some mere boys being canons—these according to Rashdall not the least disorderly members of the student body, being secure in their privileges. Although so young, students enjoyed great liberty in the choice of studies, attending the lectures of several masters before finally selecting their courses. Frequently students would club together to form a Hall or Hospicium, one of themselves being principal. In the fifteenth century masters frequently became principals of such halls or hostels.

As to penalties, at first there was no university discipline except excommunication for grave offences. Gradually this condition gave place to a system of graduated fines. In the fifteenth century corporal punishment might be administered to young undergraduates; but it was generally reserved for such serious offences as homicide. Flogging was employed only by masters of grammar. During the fifteenth century, when the bonds of discipline were being tightened, efforts were made to compel students to live in licensed halls supervised by masters, to retire at 8 or 9 p.m., and to attend lectures and disputations. Yet drunkenness was even then scarcely regarded as an offence; and much looseness of living was condoned. There were some quaint penalties; thus at the Sorbonne a fellow who cruelly beat a servant had to provide a quart of good wine for his brother fellows.

The development of colleges, accompanied by foundations for the support of certain students, led in the sixteenth century to more stringent conditions being imposed. Poor students maintained at an endowed college were subject to rigid control. Sometimes the influence of monasticism is traceable, as when fasting, silence at certain hours, and walking two by two, are enjoined. As the college movement flourished especially in England, in that country more than elsewhere did flogging become a feature of college life. At Cardinal College, founded by Wolsey, it might be inflicted to the age of twenty. In some colleges *lupi* were appointed to inform against students who spoke except in Latin, unless on licensed occasions. Thus had the undergraduate sunk to the level of a schoolboy.

But it was not only, nor perhaps chiefly, the authorities that a medieval student had to fear. As a freshman, known as *beianus* (from *bec iaune*, i.e. yellow-beak or fledgling), he might be subjected to ceremonies of initiation both painful and costly. At first officially condemned, such ceremonies became at length authorized under official regulations.

The privileges of universities included the right of internal jurisdiction, of which many vestiges remain. The degree, or licence to teach, was a further privilege of great importance. Members of a university enjoyed convenient exemptions from taxation and from various contributions, and might be wholly or in part exempt from military service. These were privileges which had been granted by the later emperors of ancient Rome to distinguished teachers. At Paris the students could only be called upon for military service if an enemy came within five miles of the city walls.

The status of a scholar was that of clericus, that is to say, he adopted clerical dress, and was in orders, although he might not become ordained unless he were a theological student and desired to begin to preach. He enjoyed 'benefit of clergy'. His academic dress originated simply as clerical dress. The early statutes upon this subject were, in the main, sumptuary restrictions, as against wearing green or red boots, pointed shoes, trunkhose and puffed sleeves. The dress of masters, indeed, was regulated earlier than that of students. By one university statute the academic gown was to reach to the heels, 'at least when it is new!'

Since the earlier universities were essentially gilds, the master's degree was a sign that a student had completed his apprenticeship to the teaching profession. This degree was known sometimes as a doctorate, licentiateship, or professorship, according to the local usage. In Italy the doctorate of law gained a certain pre-eminence over the ordinary degree of master or doctor in arts. In Paris for some time a master of arts was required to devote a certain number of years to teaching, so that this was clearly regarded as a professional, rather than as a purely cultural, qualification. The baccalaureate merely indicated that a student had reached, as it were, the position of journeyman—not yet a master, but recognized as an aspirant for that rank. The baccalaureate marked the conclusion of the first stage of preparation for the mastership. Only in the fifteenth century did it develop into a separate degree.

At Oxford, something like a separate degree in pedagogy was established. During the fourteenth century the university had established a certain control over the town grammar-schools, the masters of which were licensed by the university authorities. In the sixteenth century the grammar masters, at their *inceptio*, or graduation, were invested with a palmer and a birch, instead of with a book like other masters of arts. The master so invested was expected to flog a boy before the school as part of the ceremony, being required to pay the Bedell a groat for the birch, and the boy a groat 'for his labour'. 'There is no reason', writes Rashdall, 'to believe that boys came to attend these inferior grammar-schools in the university towns except from the immediate neighbourhood.' To some extent this may have been true of Oxford, though not wholly, as there appear to have been more grammar-schools at Oxford in proportion to the population than in other towns. It can hardly be true of European university centres, whither many young boys, 'A B C shooters', flocked, along with other students, aiming at a grammar school-education as the preliminary to a professional career.

In the universities there grew up an educated public opinion, which gradually found the means to assert itself. Even in the lifetime of Abelard the point of view of the scholar had begun to be regarded with respect. To a certain degree university life was democratic. Considerable freedom of speculation was permitted, even in theology, so long as nobody attempted to preach heresy to the populace. In theology the judgement of the University of Paris became almost absolute, difficult points of doctrine being referred to it by the popes.

Sometimes the arbitration of other disputes was entrusted to universities, the most notable instance being the appeals made by Philip of France and Henry VIII in the matter of their respective divorces. Perhaps the chief part in the attempt to heal the great schism was played by the universities. They crystallized intellectual interests, and made libraries and teachers more accessible than they could ever be in monasteries. The University of Paris has the credit of securing the limitation of the activities of the Inquisition. Yet, nothwithstanding all these qualities, their methods and materials tended to be dry, formal, and ultra-scholastic. It remained for Francis Bacon to outline a university of another type, an experimental, inductive, and somewhat utilitarian institution, in his notable sketch of Solomon's House in the *New Atlantis*.

IX

THE VISION OF DANTE

IT is natural that the heroes of literary history should have been representative of the education of their period. Until recently a liberal education was considered to be the only education worth having, and no great writer, especially in the Middle Ages, has failed to reflect it in his work. The poetry and prose of Dante illustrate the widest scholarship, the noblest thought, the highest outlook possible in the long interval between the fall of the ancient Roman Empire and the end of the thirteenth century. In him medieval education may be said to have culminated. Born at Florence in 1265, Dante devoted his youth to poetry, study, and manly exercises; and seems to have fought as one of the Florentine cavalry in battle. The death of his beloved Beatrice in 1290 led the poet to collect the lyrics which he had written in her honour, with prose exquisitely interspersed, in the *Vita Nuova*, representing his own new life. Involved in politics and for a brief time a high magistrate in his native city, in 1302 Dante was banished with fifteen other citizens from Florence. His treatise *de Monarchia* expresses the conviction that the Roman Empire had extended by right, and that the Empire of later centuries was destined to become its truly Roman and Italian successor.

Having left his fellow-exiles, after vain attempts made in their company to secure a return to Florence, Dante set about two prose works, which remained unfinished, one on *Vernacular Eloquence*, the other, the *Convivio* or *Banquet* (1306–8), a treatise nominally in explanation of some of his own *Canzoni* or Odes, but in reality a popular exposition of his philosophy.

The utter failure of the Emperor Henry of Luxemburg to introduce unity into Italian politics, or idealism into Italian life, left Dante in complete disillusion and despair. Introspection led him to feel that he had been unfaithful to his new life, and to the memory of Beatrice. In the *Divina Commedia* he presents, as he tells us, 'man as by good or ill deserts, in the exercise of the freedom of his will, he becomes liable to the justice that rewards and punishes'. Throughout the appalling *Inferno*, throughout the wonderful conception of the *Purgatorio* and the transfiguration of all things but love in the *Paradiso*, throughout the whole *Divine Comedy* Dante reveals from stage to stage of his visionary journey the extent and limitations of the highest type of medieval education.

Escorted by Virgil, whom Beatrice has persuaded to be his guide, the poet comes first to Limbo, wherein are suspended without torment the shades of the great pagan writers of antiquity. To this abode of the virtuous heathen Virgil himself has been consigned. Here, in the first circle of Hell indeed, but in a serene air, are met Homer, Ovid, Horace, and Lucan. These hail Virgil as their master; and Dante himself is admitted as the sixth of the noble band. Virgil, whom Dante had hailed at the outset as the honour and light of all other poets, is now described as 'Lord of the highest song, who o'er the others like an eagle soars'. Ignorant of Greek, Dante and his contemporaries failed entirely to recognize how secondary and derivative are the merits of the *Aeneid*. Of Homer, Dante knew little but the name. Orpheus and Linus appear to have been regarded as historical poets.

Elsewhere in Limbo Dante recognizes Aristotle, whom he describes without naming as the 'Master', elsewhere as the 'Teacher', sometimes as the 'Philosopher', and in the *Convivio* simply as 'He'. There was no need to mention Aristotle by name to medieval scholars; he was the recognized fountain of secular science. Socrates and Plato are placed next in rank to the Stagirite; but of Plato, Dante knew only the *Timaeus* in a Latin translation. Through the *Consolations of Philosophy* of Boethius and the Patristic writings, many other Greek philosophers had become familiar by name and by an attenuated reputation to the Florentine's generation; thus he mentions Democritus, 'who sets the world at chance', Diogenes, Heraclitus, Empedocles, Anaxagoras, Thales, Zeno, and Dioscorides.

Among Greek mathematicians and astronomers are mentioned Euclid and Ptolemy; and among medical authorities Hippocrates and Galen, as well as the Moor Avicenna. Here, too, are seen Cicero and Seneca, representatives of Roman philosophy. There is an unexpected liberality in the placing of Mohammedans like Avicenna and Averroës, the great commentator who first had made Aristotle intelligible to the Middle Ages, nay, even the arch-foe of the Crusaders, the Sultan Saladin, in a relatively peaceful and honourable niche of the infernal regions.

Figures from Greek mythology, the Furies, Charon, Cerberus, the Minotaur, the Centaurs, and the like, are not wanting to the lower circles of Hell; but their allegorical character was clear to Dante's mind; and the Centaurs, for example, appear to typify the mercenary soldiers of Italian tyrants. A few scanty references are made to English and French history, very many to Italian, and some to German events and personages. Ancient history receives copious if uncritical attention. The boldness of Dante in placing certain of the popes in the Inferno is an illustration of the high degree of freedom that was allowed to educated men in the Middle Ages, so long as no popular heresy happened to be abroad. Dante sharply criticizes the avarice of eminent churchmen, but his theology is intended to be perfectly orthodox, although certain minor passages of his great epic did not pass unchallenged. The Donation of Constantine, a forgery of the early Middle Ages, according to which the Emperor Constantine withdrew to the west in order to leave the Pope supreme at Rome, was regarded by Dante as a genuine, though ill-advised, document. Aesop's fables were well known to the poet in their medieval, but not in their classical form.

Ulysses and Diomede undergo penal torture on account of their activities against Troy, the home of Aeneas, whom Dante seems to have regarded as the true and not merely as the legendary founder of Rome. At this point Virgil advises the Florentine to leave the talking to him, for 'they were Greeks'. Thus Dante appears to confess his personal ignorance of the Greek language. The whole episode of the visit to the Inferno springs primarily from the similar visit described in the *Aeneid*; but for the minor incidents Lucan, Livy, and Ovid, as well as Virgil, have been freely drawn upon.

In the lowest Hell, deep in the centre of the earth, the travellers come upon the devil, encased in an icy crust. His three heads have three mouths, which devour respectively Judas Iscariot, Brutus, and Cassius. The two Romans are regarded as arch-traitors to the Empire, as Judas was arch-traitor to the Church as well as to his Master. The journey is continued to the other side of the earth, which was well known to be a sphere, not to Dante only but to all educated people from ancient Greek times. Hence before emerging on the other side of the globe the poets reverse, end for end, so that they may reach in an upright position the antipodes.

What then lay at the antipodes? The general theory assumed the existence merely of ocean; but for the purposes of his allegory the poet imagines land whence the travellers again behold the stars, and whence later they recognize the *tremolar* of the open sea. After several adventures Dante, with Virgil, climbs the steep mountain of Purgatory where they behold how men are purged, terrace by terrace, of the seven deadly sins—pride, envy, anger, sloth, avarice, gluttony, and incontinence.

There is, apparently, in the writings of Dante a strange confusion of sacred with classical instances; yet, upon closer analysis, something like a pattern is found to have been woven into the web. The favourite device of the author is to couple one example from mythology with one from scripture or history.

Thus, for examples of chastity, on the last cornice of Purgatory, the Gospels and Ovid are quoted alternately; and this is only one of a hundred instances to be found, not only in the *Commedia*, but also in such prose works as the *Convivio*. Similarly, the terrestrial paradise which is reached by the cleansed souls after the expiration of their term in Purgatory, is not only the Garden of Eden, but the dream of ancient Greek philosophy. In Purgatory Dante beholds the Emperor Trajan, who, according to legend, had been delivered from hell by the prayers of St. Gregory the Great, on account of his act of justice to a poor widow.

In Florence Dante had known the two great painters, Cimabue and Giotto. He takes occasion to moralize upon the way in which Giotto's fame has eclipsed that of his master. The works of Dante, Petrarch, and Boccaccio in vernacular literature, and of Cimabue and Giotto in painting, are sufficient proof that there would have been an Italian Renaissance even without the classical revival which ultimately determined its direction.

To the intellectual subtleties of the Middle Ages Dante shows himself by no means indifferent. The poet is keenly exercised to reconcile free will with the sovereignty of the Creator. The primal bent is from Heaven; but there is freedom thereafter to choose good or ill, hence responsibility and judgement. Following Albertus Magnus, Dante recognizes in man a twofold principle, nature and the will.

Nature, as was generally held in those days, follows the stars; but the will is free, although, in the absence of resistance the will tends to be drawn by the stars and nature.

In general, Dante revels in scholastic logic, and in the *Convivio* his reasoning is highly syllogistic. His psychology recognizes separate faculties of apprehension, wisdom, &c.

The Middle Ages set high store upon the Christian imitators of Virgil—Sedulius, Juvencus, and Statius. Meeting the spirit of Statius,

Dante has the pleasure of introducing this Christian imitator of Virgil to his beloved model. Statius wishes to embrace Virgil, but the latter forbids it, both being shades. Statius replies:

> Now thou hast proved
> The force and ardour of the love I bear thee,
> When I forget we are but things of air,
> And, as a substance treat an empty shade.

When Virgil, having fulfilled his task of conducting Dante to the earthly paradise, returns to Limbo, the Florentine cannot stay his tears. Beatrice now descends from Heaven, rebukes Dante, and becomes his guide. The third section of the *Commedia*, that is to say the *Paradiso*, reveals at once the extent of Dante's astronomical knowledge and his wide reading both of the Latin fathers of the Christian Church and of the great medieval schoolmen. Together with Beatrice, Dante ascends to the Moon, for the purposes of his allegory regarded as a part of Heaven, although, in the various planets which partake of the Divine Vision, there is assumed to be a diversity of mansions and of degrees of glory. Hence the ascent is by way of Mercury, Venus, the Sun, Mars, Jupiter, and Saturn, to the stellar heaven in which the fixed stars were supposed to be set, thence to the *primum mobile* which moves all the rest by Divine grace, and ultimately to the peaceful empyrean, from which the earth is seen as a tiny point of light.

In the Sun the poet encountered a galaxy of great medieval teachers, Albertus Magnus, Thomas Aquinas, Gratian, Peter the Lombard, Orosius, Boethius, Isidore of Seville, the Venerable Bede, Buonaventura, Hugh of St. Victor, and many others, with whom are curiously placed Solomon and Dionysius the Areopagite, whose pseudo-authorship was accepted as genuine. Due honour is paid in various cantos to St. Francis, St. Dominic, and St. Bernard, and, finally, the great realities of the Trinity and of the union of Man with God are mystically revealed.

In the *Convivio* or *Banquet*, later known as the *Convito*, Dante apologizes at some length for his employment of the vernacular Italian in a commentary. Latin he admits to be both stable and incorruptible, of a higher virtue than the vernacular, of greater nobility and even of superior beauty. Yet since the odes are Italian the commentary should also be Italian; Latin would be sovereign rather than subject to the odes, would not readily follow every turn of feeling or expression, and would fail to reach many who could read the odes themselves.

In *De Vulgari Eloquentia*, it may be observed, Dante claims the greater nobility for the vernacular tongues, as against Latin. He is further moved to write the *Convivio* in Italian because of his burning love of his native tongue, his fear lest another should translate a Latin commentary into a discordant and clumsy vernacular form, and his desire to prove that no other vernacular exceeds in merit his own. There are some who depreciate Italian through thoughtless repetition; some as an excuse for their own incompetence; some from the vanity of those who, acquainted with foreign languages, therefore exalt them above their own; some from envy; some from poverty of patriotic spirit. Italian is the language in which the author's parents lived and loved, which led him up to Latin, which has been ever the object of his ambition, which has entered into his spiritual texture, and to which he is ardently devoted. Thus were the rights of vernacular languages vindicated as completely by Dante as, later, the inductive method by Francis Bacon.

Most of the work of Dante is allegorical. In his preference for this method of expression he is typically medieval, as well as typically poetical. In the *Convivio* he proceeds to explain the four senses in which a text may be commented upon—the literal or direct meaning; the allegorical, which hides truth under a beauteous fiction; the moral, which readers may note for their own behoof; and the anagogical, which finds a spiritual meaning above the sense. The song of the prophet states that 'When the people of Israel came out of Egypt, Judea was made holy and free'. This, anagogically or spiritually interpreted, implies that 'When the soul goeth forth out of sin, it is made holy and free in its power'.

Dante himself, like most allegorists, occasionally falls back upon mere intellectual ingenuity for his interpretations. This was, indeed, a general vice of medieval scholarship, in no way peculiar to the great Florentine.

Thus in not one but many respects Dante represents medieval thought. Before the Italian Renaissance had burst into flower he was devoted to the classics, inspired by the Christian fathers, and familiar with the scholastic philosophy. He was, indeed, acquainted with Greek literature only in fragmentary Latin translations, yet his knowledge, limited as it was by a deficiency which was soon to be regarded as fatal to genuine scholarship, ranged far and wide through the seven liberal arts. His acquaintance with astronomy, fundamentally fallacious as it may have been, exceeded that of many liberally educated men of the present day; and no artist will condemn his love of allegory, no poet his mystic soarings. It may be admitted that the turn of thought which the schoolmen of the Middle Ages had implanted in the universities, and which, revelling in the refined subtleties of the Aristotelian syllogism, provoked the impatience of many humanists of the fifteenth century, might easily be considered a blemish in so great a poet, were it not redeemed by the spacious and profound outlook and the ineluctable logic of a philosophic mind. Truly medieval is the pure chivalry of Dante's devotion to Beatrice, his determination to confer fame on her memory, and the identification of her personality with the principles of love and virtue. His political aspirations were founded upon a medieval idea of the divine right of both Church and Empire. Knowledge, he held with Aristotle, is the distinguishing perfection of the soul: 'All men by nature desire to know.'

But while the contemplative life exceeds in felicity the active, yet since heed must be given to the capacity of the learner, he may proceed by way of the moral rather than by the intellectual virtues, if so be that path is easier for him. But the whole universe is a cosmic dance of love; love binds its leaves into a single volume. Thus Dante may have been medieval; but he was himself a renaissance. He, among medieval writers, is best described by his own heroic line on Virgil:

Che sopra gli altri com' aquila vola!

A SELECT BIBLIOGRAPHY

A

Adamson: 'Education in Middle Ages' (Article in *The Legacy of the Middle Ages*, ed. C. Crump and E. Jacob).
Azarias (Brother) (Mullaney): Essays, Educational. (*Primary Education in Middle Ages*, *Mediaeval University Life*, &c.).
Cornish: *Chivalry* (Chap. III).
De Montmorency: *History of State Intervention in English Education* (Chap. 1).
Drane: *Christian Schools and Scholars.*
Gasquet: *English Monastic Life.*
Hazlitt, W.: *Schools, School Books and School Masters.*
Jessop: *Coming of the Friars* (Essay on Building of a University).
Laurie, S.: *Rise and Early Constitution of Universities.*
Leach: *Educational Charters.*
—— *Schools of Mediaeval England.*
Lyte: *History of University of Oxford.*
Maitland: *The Dark Ages.*
Mansbridge: *Older Universities of England* (Chaps. 1, 2, 3).
Mills: *History of Chivalry* (vol. i, Chap. 2).
Mullinger: *History of Cambridge University.*
Poole: *Illustrations of the History of Mediaeval Thought.*
Rait: *Life in a Mediaeval University.*
Rashdall: *Universities of Europe in the Middle Ages* (3 vols.).
Sandys: *History of Classical Scholarship.*
Taylor: *The Mediaeval Mind.*
Watson: *English Grammar Schools to 1660.*
West: *Alcuin and the Rise of Christian Schools.*

B

Abelson: *The Seven Liberal Arts.*
Adams: *Civilisation During the Middle Ages.*
Anderson: 'Development of Non-Professional Schools in Europe Before Renaissance' (*Ped. Sem.*, March and June, 1907).
Bartholomaeus Anglicus (ed. Steele).: *Mediaeval Lore.*
Batty: *Spirit and Influence of Chivalry.*
Clerval: *Les Écoles de Chartres.*
Compayré: *Abelard and the Origin of Universities.*
Coppée: *History of the Conquest of Spain by the Arab Moors.*
Coxe: *Ante-Nicene Fathers.*
Dante: *Convivio* (translated).
De Montmorency: 'Mediaeval Education of Women' (in *Journ. of Education*, vols. 31, 32.
De Wulf: *Philosophy and Civilisation in the Middle Ages.*
Draper: *Intellectual Development of Europe.*
Emerton: *Mediaeval Europe* (Chap. 13).
Farrar: *Lives of the Fathers.*

Gardiner: *English Girlhood at School.*
Gaskoin: *Alcuin, Life and Works.*
Gautier: *Chivalry.*
Gibbon: *Decline and Fall of the Roman Empire* (Chaps. 16–20, 37).
Hallam: *Europe in the Middle Ages.*
Harris, H. L.: *Thesis on Mediaeval Scholasticism.*
Haskins: *Life of Mediaeval Students as illustrated by their Letters.*
—— *Rise of Universities.*
Hatch: *Influence of Greek Ideas and Usages on the Christian Church.*
Hitchcock: *Clement of Alexandria.*
Hungerford: 'Rise of Arab Learning' (in *Atl. Monthly*, vol. lviii).
Lacroix: *Science and Literature in the Middle Ages.*
Lang: *Oxford* (Chaps. 2, 3).
Leach: 'Mediaeval Education of Women' (in *Journ. of Education*, vol. 32).
Lecky: *History of European Morals from Augustus to Charlemagne.*
MacCabe: *Abelard.*
—— *St. Augustine and His Age.*
Milman: *History of Early Christianity.*
—— *History of Latin Christianity.*
Monroe, P.: *Thomas Platter and the Educational Renaissance.*
Montalembert: *Monks of the West* (Bk. 18, Chap. IV).
Mullinger: Article on 'Schools' in Smith and Cheetham's *Dictionary of Christian Antiquities.*
—— *The Schools of Charles the Great.*
Munro, D. (editor of): *Mediaeval Student* (Trans. and Reprints from Original Sources).
Newman: *University Sketches* (ed. Sampson), Chaps. 13–16.
Norton: *Mediaeval Universities.*
Pace: 'St. Thomas Aquinas on Education' (Cath. Univ. *Bulletin*, July 1902).
Paetoy: *Arts Course in Mediaeval Universities.*
Painter, F.: *Great Pedagogical Essays* (Charlemagne, Rhabanus Maurus).
Parker: 'The Seven Liberal Arts' (*English Historical Review*, vol. v, 1910).
Parry: *Education in the Middle Ages.*
Paulsen: *German Universities.*
Putnam: *Books and Their Makers During the Middle Ages.*
Rickaby: *Scholasticism.*
Schaff and Wace: *Nicene and Post-Nicene Fathers.*
Stille: *Studies in Mediaeval History.*
Taylor: *Classical Heritage of the Middle Ages.*
Townsend: *Great Schoolmen of the Middle Ages.*
Vaughan: *St. Thomas of Aquin.*
Waddell: *The Wandering Scholars.*
Williams: *Education During the Middle Ages.*

BOOK IV

RENAISSANCE EDUCATIONAL THOUGHT

I

THE ITALIAN RENAISSANCE

THE Italian Renaissance is frequently treated as if it were an abrupt and new movement. Like the Mohammedan era, or the coronation of Charles the Great as Emperor of the West, it appeals to the historian as something sudden, portentous, unique. At this point he is constrained to begin a new chapter, perhaps even a new book. He takes leave of the Middle Ages and their manuscripts, and walks with surer tread the paths of the modern world. Here, if anywhere, he beholds a vision which captures his imagination. Here he perceives a natural boundary between the future and the past. He revels in the presence of things and events unknown to the Middle Ages, a new art and literature, the development of writing in the vernacular, the invention of printing, the extensive use of gunpowder, experimentation in politics, the recovery of a mass of ancient manuscripts, and the consciousness of a new geographical world. He even gives a date for the Renaissance, namely, 1453, the year of the fall of Constantinople. Unfortunately, this view of the Renaissance betrays a number of contradictions. Gunpowder, printing, and geographical discovery are associated more closely with other countries than with Italy. A more serious difficulty lies in the fact that extensive travel, the use of gunpowder, progress in art and vernacular literature—even the recovery of classical manuscripts—were features not unfamiliar to the medieval world. There is comparatively little historical evidence, moreover, that the fall of Constantinople exercised a profound influence upon the learning of the Renaissance. Above all, the events which are commonly regarded as responsible for a sudden dissipation of medieval traditions occurred at intervals of time so wide that it is almost doing violence to history to mention them together at all. The true Renaissance began in the twelfth century with Abelard, in some essentials the first modern-minded man. In reality, the Italian Renaissance ought not to be described as an event, but rather as a period of progress founded upon the important intellectual events of the twelfth and thirteenth centuries. The basis of its civilization, as revealed in the writing of Petrarch and Boccaccio, for instance, was still medieval. Medieval traditions and the products of medieval scholarship, so far from having been annihilated or replaced by the New Learning, have never ceased to exercise a profound influence upon the intellectual life of western Europe.

The educational significance of the Renaissance lies in the fact that it produced not the first, but the first large number of complete, rational individuals, the first crop of Abelards. That the Renaissance began in Italy may be attributed partly to the Italian genius, partly to the break-down of the feudal system in the Italian States. Traditions of despotism and oppression founded in medieval Italy by Frederick the Second and Ezzelino, and improved upon by a host of petty tyrants in the fourteenth century, had led to the partial demolition of feudalism and the establishment of centralized systems of government, the very tyranny and insecurity of which proved to be favourable to the development of individuality and enterprise. Intellectual, if not moral, giants were produced by the struggle for survival. Not only among the rulers, but also among their soldiers, officials, courtiers, and pensioners, talent became one of the essentials of success. Living only for his own gratification, the Italian tyrant cherished the poets, biographers, and artists in whose works he hoped to find a worldly immortality. From an equally personal motive he loved to found libraries and collections of objects of art. The despot of the fifteenth century, more refined in his methods than his predecessor of the fourteenth, not infrequently coupled the most audacious treachery and impiety with martial ability and intellectual culture. Vanity and inclination alike prompted him to be liberal towards art and study.

Under these circumstances, the pursuit of learning became more profitable than at any time since the ancient Roman Empire. Translations from the Greek into Latin were made to the order of noble patrons. In the middle of the fifteenth century, Alfonso the Great of Naples rewarded Poggio for his translation of the *Cyropedia* of Xenophon with five hundred gold pieces. At the more worthy court of the Dukes of Urbino were to be found a military school at which the scions of great houses were instructed, and also a library famous throughout Italy. The sincerity and patriotism of its ruling house attracted to Mantua the labours of Ariosto, Bembo, Bandello, and Tasso. On the other hand, although the necessary funds were provided by a system of confiscation, extortion, and torture, it was the boast of the Duke of Ferrara that the salary of the professors of the university was paid promptly to the date it was due. No wonder, under the circumstances, if Petrarch and other humanists were wont to sully their pages by the fulsome adulation of selfish if enlightened tyrants. A few proud scholars, following Dante, attempted to stem the tide of sycophantism. Boccaccio, indeed, went as far as the defence of tyrannicide; and an enthusiastic professor of Milan made a practical attempt of the sort in his city. On the whole, however, the revival of learning had little direct influence upon either political or private morality, unless to add refinement and impunity to the misdeeds of those in authority.

The beginnings of the modern intellectual atmosphere are to be sought, as has been pointed out, in the twelfth rather than in the fifteenth century. The Italian Renaissance, however, is a period at which intellectual processes were quickened by the development of local institutions, and even applied to new fields. Thus in Venice and Florence are found for the first time extensive applications of statistical science. Concerning Florence, trustworthy particulars are furnished by Villani. Out of an estimated population of about 90,000, from 8,000 to 10,000 are said to have been learning reading, from 1,000 to 1,200 arithmetic, and 600 logic and Latin grammar. The subjects of logic and Latin were offered in four schools of a distinctly secondary character, exclusive of the schools in which reading and arithmetic were taught. Arithmetic was practised in six schools only. From these figures the outstanding conclusion is that education, while still far less general among the lower than among the upper classes, was becoming more and more popular. Even in the Middle Ages, no doubt, Paris and Oxford had included an equally large proportion of learners, but their schools had, to a far greater extent than those of Florence, drawn their students from external sources. The University of Florence, however, was not founded until 1349, nor did it flourish as such, owing to the high cost of living. It was here, however, in 1396, that Chrysoloras filled the first chair of Greek in any Western university.

That the schools of Florence performed an important function in the making of her citizens is self-evident. To a moderate extent they may have contributed towards the tendency known as individualism. A critical element, which must not, however, be exaggerated, was making its way into the grammar-schools as it had done into the universities two centuries earlier. Just as the critical spirit had made a home in the universities through the renewed study of theology, philosophy, and law, it began to do so in the secondary schools through the renewed study of the classics. Although stifled in a measure by a new Ciceronianism which became as rigid and pedantic as the medieval text-books themselves, for some time the new learning tended to encourage genuine thought, that is to say, those original rational processes without which no system of education can be more than a conservative influence. What was true of Florence was more or less true of the other great Italian cities.

Thus education, while not alone, or even chiefly, responsible for the outcome, entered into partnership with the Italian temperament and the new conditions of civic life, the result being the production of large numbers of individuals of a type that may be regarded as essentially modern, conscious of themselves as entities apart from race, home, church, and other institutional forms. Such men, ceasing to think and to behave according to the uniform and generic standards dear to the past, were educated by the forces of uncertainty, change, conspiracy, and exile, as well as by the pursuit of learning, to rare heights and depths of original thought and conduct. At no period common, men of marked individuality appear in history chiefly during the age of Pericles, the Renaissance, and the nineteenth century, although the Middle Ages produced men who, had their lives and deeds been fated to lie near the epoch of printing, might have illustrated the complete development of personality almost as well as a Leon Battista Alberti or a Leonardo da Vinci.

The development of the individual produced vices as well as virtues. That failing of the ancients, the pursuit of fame, reappears in an exaggerated form in the Italy of the Renaissance. Dante did not escape its infection; Petrarch believed that he had it in his power to confer fame even on the most obscure. Even crime was welcomed by some as an avenue of escape from oblivion. Satire, epigram, and caricature were employed either as a means of self-assertion or as a weapon to be used against the arrogance of another. Aretino (1527–77), pensioned both by France and the Empire for the use of his caustic pen, is the literary ancestor of all blackmailing satirists. It is not to be supposed, however, that all the seekers after fame were unscrupulous, for not a few of the great figures of the Renaissance, like Rienzi, believed that in their own success was involved the good of the whole community.

To summarize, the principal factor in the Italian Renaissance was the Italian genius itself. The author of the best poems in the *Carmina Burana*, a witty and imaginative though gross collection of student songs, written in the Latin of the twelfth century, appears to have been an Italian. The works of Dante antedated the recovery not only of Greek but of many of the Latin classics. The second factor of importance was the political condition into which Italy had drifted. A multitude of self-made and self-seeking despots vied to aggrandize themselves, not only in the field of arms but also in the domain of literature. However disheartening to the few patriots who, like Dante, dreamed of the national unity of Italy, the political situation was entirely favourable to the spread of learning. There is little reason to doubt that without any other contributing cause the Italian genius and the political condition of the country would have sufficed to produce a Renaissance. Without the recovery of the Greek classics, however, which furnished precisely the nutriment needed by the Italian genius at this time, it is clear that the Renaissance must have been far other than it was. It must have been less universal, more local in its effects. For the classical literature of Greece and Rome was, in a way that nothing else could have been, the common heritage of all Europe; and a movement fed upon the revival of that literature could not long have remained Italian without becoming in a broad sense European.

In Italy the ancient world was not considered dead. A real local sentiment was aroused in the breasts of Petrarch and others by the sight of the ruins of Rome; though the importance of such influences must not be exaggerated, for it was still the practice to destroy the most precious relics of the past for the sake of making lime! In time the desecration was checked, but the literature of the ancient world has always exerted a greater influence than its architecture.

Books, then, were esteemed above buildings. Immense sums were devoted to the purchase of manuscripts or to having copies made from them. Pope Nicholas V paid 500 ducats and 1,000 gold florins, respectively, for Latin translations of Polybius and Strabo; and left a collection of from 5,000 to 9,000 volumes, which became the nucleus of the library of the Vatican. Driven from Rome in 1450, he would not leave his compilers and translators to the risk of pestilence, but took them with him to Fabriano, not, apparently, on general humanitarian grounds, but because their work seemed of paramount importance. Niccolo Niccoli, of Florence, having spent his whole fortune on books, was given unlimited credit by the Medici for the fulfilment of his purpose. Vast additions were made to the available stock of classical texts by the unflagging researches of Guarino and Poggio. Cardinal Bessarion, though a Greek, deposited a collection of 600 manuscripts of great value for security in Venice. Frederick of Montefeltro, a collector from boyhood, kept thirty or forty copyists constantly at work in the extension of the library of Urbino. Such copyists, or *scrittori*, few and unreliable in the fourteenth century, were far more numerous and better paid during the fifteenth, and disappeared but slowly in face of the new invention of printing.

Greek scholarship flourished in Italy during the fifteenth century, especially about 1500, when the living voice of a colony of Greek exiles was to be heard. The later development of Greek studies belongs to the Teutonic, rather than to the Italian Renaissance. Hebrew and Arabic were not neglected, and Pico della Mirandola perceived the merits alike of the Hebrew *Cabbalah* and *Talmud*, the commentaries of Moors like Averroës, and the works of the medieval schoolmen. Pico, however, who esteemed the mind above the tongue, the thought above the word, was in a minority, for the tide of fashion had set strongly in favour of the writings of classical antiquity.

There can be no doubt of the sincerity with which the writers of Italy paid homage to the greatness of the ancients. Dante himself, though Christianity remained foremost in his thoughts, maintained a constant parallelism between Christian and classical instances. Both Petrarch and Boccaccio pinned their literary reputation to their Latin writings; and Petrarch expressed the wish that his Italian poems might be blotted for ever from the memories of men. Like other leading scholars of the day, Petrarch and Boccaccio acted on the theory that the path to the revival of culture led not merely to the study, but also to the imitation of the classics. At a respectful distance, they vied with their models; and, in imitation of a custom attributed to the ancients, successful poets were crowned with a laurel wreath.

On the other hand, although the new learning gradually captured the imagination of Italy, its direct influence upon the schools and universities was but tardy and partial. Within these institutions the medieval traditions remained intact. During the thirteenth century the subjects of civil law, canon law, and medicine had been established in the universities on a firm basis; and the addition of chairs of philosophy, rhetoric, and astronomy came but gradually, while even at the height of the Renaissance chairs of Greek and Hebrew were not common. The influence of the Renaissance upon the Italian universities was exerted chiefly in three ways, firstly in an increase of keenness on the part of the learners, secondly in an increase of readiness on the part of the states and municipalities to assist educational institutions, and thirdly in an increase of competition among the various universities for the service of the most eminent professors. For education, while it still ran chiefly in the old channels, became more and more highly esteemed. A professor of Pisa, having accepted an appointment at Padua, was required to offer surety to the extent of 18,000 gold florins. Yet the tenure of professorships was usually brief. Appointments, unless renewed, might last only six months or a year; and many professors were merely unpaid volunteers. During a brief period, under Leo X, however, the University of Rome, called the Sapienza, was splendidly reorganized and manned with a full lecturing staff of eighty-eight.

The secondary or Latin schools of the Italian Renaissance remained very much as they had been for centuries, except that the new purist attitude caused them to emphasize the Ciceronian model more than hitherto, while the new researches by degrees furnished them with better texts. For some time, moreover, these schools had been conducted either by the municipality or by private individuals. The Church was no longer the principal agency in Italian secular education; it remained for the Reformation and the counter-Reformation to restore the full weight of religious influence in this field.

Two schools of a special character represent the highest achievement of the Italian Renaissance in the direction of educational experiment. Of these, one was conducted by Vittorino da Feltre (b. 1378, d. 1446) at Mantua, the other by Guarino of Verona (b. 1374, d. 1460) at Ferrara. Both were intended primarily for the children of princely houses, but in each case the enthusiasm and piety of the teacher led him to support a number of poor scholars in his own home. These court schools illustrate the fact that the nobility of Italy generally received their education from the humanists, or champions of the new learning. Both Vittorino and Guarino were profound scholars; but although the latter was an able and voluminous author, Vittorino, who published practically nothing, seems to have been the broader-minded man, and his school introduced several features which were new to secondary education.

As a student at Padua under masters as famous as Barzizza, the great Ciceronian scholar, Vergerius, the author of *De Ingenuis Moribus*, and Guarino, foremost of Italian students of Greek; as keeper of a boarding-house, or, to give it the more dignified Latin title, *contubernium*, for students, whom he also instructed in Latin and mathematics; as Professor of Rhetoric in Padua University following Barzizza (1422); and subsequently as a teacher of the New Learning in Venice, Vittorino da Feltre had attained such a reputation for letters, honour, and christian principle that his services were sought by the Marquis of Mantua for the direction of his proposed court school. 'I accept the post,' said Vittorino, 'on this understanding only, that you require from me nothing which shall be in any way unworthy of either of us.' The Casino or garden palace was given over by the Marquis Gonzaga to the purposes of a school. Here, amidst the most charming environment imaginable, were educated the children of the Marquis, including girls, as well as the children of foreign notables, and a group of talented sons of the poor who attended to the considerable number of seventy.

Three currents of thought mingled their influence in the school of Vittorino. These were Christianity, chivalry, and humanism, the compatibility of which within a single person is said to have been demonstrated in the life of the director himself.

(1) *Christianity.* Vittorino himself was accustomed to read devotional and religious books in the early morning, following which he scourged himself and went to church. His pupils, for their part, were required to attend church, to confess monthly, and to observe fast-days. Yet Vittorino was no externalist, no mere ritualist. All men, he held, are created unto a life of social duty. The rigidity of his conceptions of duty may be illustrated by the boldness with which he defended the refusal of a daughter of the ruling house to marry an unprincipled nobleman to whom her father desired to give her hand. Yet benevolence was mingled with his sternness. The ducal pension of 240 gold florins enjoyed by Vittorino was devoted by him in part to the support of poor scholars. No thought of self dimmed the great schoolmaster's devotion to his life-work. Though renowned as a scholar, out of humility he wrote little, and even destroyed the long-cherished poems of his youth. The unsullied purity of Vittorino's life contrasted sharply with the general reputation of contemporary humanists.

(2) *Chivalry.* If Vittorino himself had been less proficient in knightly exercises, in all probability the emphasis of Plato upon gymnastics would have determined him to make games and the practice of arms compulsory. Whatever the cause, whether the revival of Greek influence or the new courtly movement which formed a part of the Renaissance, and which finds its amplest expression in the *Courtier* of

Castiglione, Vittorino directed his attention to the health, exercises, and deportment of every youth under his charge. Even postures and gestures, as well as intonation and the management of the voice were thoroughly inculcated. The pupil was to be not only a Christian, but a Christian gentleman.

(3) *Humanism.* Himself a profound student, a collector as generous in distributing as he was ardent in acquiring books, Vittorino was recognized even by his contemporaries as one of the leaders of the humanistic movement. The method of his school was founded upon the canons laid down by Quintilian in his *Institutes*, the discovery of the full text of which by Poggio, at St. Gall, thrilled Barzizza, whose pupil Vittorino then was. The *Institutes* were supplemented by practices advocated in the *Republic* of Plato, such as the use of music for purposes of moral development, and by the precepts of Plutarch's treatise on education (translated by Guarino in 1411). No technical studies were countenanced; but in the classics the school more than held its own with the highest traditions of instruction in the universities. The literary curriculum consisted of a study of Greek and Roman authors, and was delegated to expert assistant teachers. The Greeks were studied chiefly from the standpoint of *eruditio*, or content value; the Latins mainly as literature. In the teaching of Greek two native Greek masters were employed. It is not to be forgotten that science, philosophy, mathematics, geography, and history, as well as literature, were still concealed within the covers of Latin and Greek texts, so that their pursuit necessarily involved the cult of the classical languages. Great emphasis was placed upon Latin prose composition, and upon the art of declamation, for the epistolary and oratorical use of Latin was of genuine diplomatic importance, even had not Quintilian and tradition been on its side. The full text of the *De Oratore* of Cicero, discovered in 1422 at Lodi, gave a new impetus to oratorical studies. In the meantime, history, in the absence of other available material, comprised little more than the reading of biographies such as the *Lives* of Plutarch.

Thus the atmosphere of the court school of Vittorino, model educational establishment of the Renaissance period, was at once humanistic, chivalric, and Christian. In any age such a school would be rare; in the semi-pagan Italian Renaissance its existence was a unique phenomenon. To it were sent the sons not only of princes but of scholars, the greatest of the day, sons of Guarino, Filelfo, Poggio. There was no need to proceed from Vittorino's school to a university where nothing more of humanism could be learned than at Mantua. Pupils remained with Vittorino even to the age of twenty-seven. Corrupt pupils were dismissed, corrupt assistants and servitors, if pains could secure that end, never employed. Music was taught, but limited to elevating harmonies. Methods of teaching were improved; for instance, letter-games for reading and spelling were invented for children aged four or five. Italian was not taught; Latin was the Roman tongue, and everything Roman seemed to the humanist eternal. In short, with the aid of Guarino, Vittorino da Feltre rescued the profession of teaching from contempt and gained for it a new public respect. He is the first modern schoolmaster worthy of the name.

By the end of the fifteenth century, humanism, if not a universal tradition throughout Italy, was at least supreme. Frederick of Urbino, greatest of the pupils of Vittorino, was himself the most learned scholar in his own learned court. In Florence, Cosimo and Lorenzo de Medici restored the Platonic philosophy to its old pre-eminence in the halls of wisdom. Pope Leo X and Alfonso the Great of Aragon, King of Naples, were among those who showed an incredible generosity towards the poets and historians. Nor was any court too insignificant to support at least one or two men of learning; and any prince ignorant of letters felt constrained to apologize for his deficiency. Orations and correspondence in elegant Latin were regarded as essential, even for the practical purposes of diplomacy. Popes and princes sought out Latin stylists to be their court officials; and the letters of Bembo and Sadoleto, the two great secretaries of Leo X, achieved permanent fame as models of epistolary Latin. Rhetorical display was expected at all important functions; and as a consequence the art of oratory was studied as it had not been since the days of Ausonius. Names, titles, ceremonies, all were latinized.

Latin essays and treatises on the Ciceronian model were numerous, but these are rarely of permanent value. The educational writings of Cardinal Sadoleto, for example, follow Quintilian closely. Latin histories like those of Poggio and Aretino were the worse for their bondage to the classical tradition. Inevitably, although this would not have been admitted by the humanists, the Latin of the age of Cicero was inadequate to describe the things and events of the Renaissance, even if the historians had not been encouraged by the example of Livy to regard history as a work of art in the execution of which accuracy might be treated as a secondary consideration.

After having reached the height of their influence during the pontificate of Leo X, the humanists fell upon evil days, heralded by the sack of Rome, but partly brought upon themselves by their arrogance and licentious living. Moreover, the Reformation was prejudicial to humanism. While but one church had existed in the West, a large amount of tolerance had been extended to both critical and creative thought; but from the days of Luther no compromise was felt to be possible. Henceforth men of learning were forced to take sides, and both critical and creative thought received a severe check from the growing power of two forces in Italy, Spain and the Inquisition. The defence of dogma took the place of the search for truth. Together with Ciceronianism, the whole tradition of knowledge for its own sake fell into disrepute. Neither the Reformation nor the counter-Reformation could be expected to be favourable to the humanistic movement as such, which, in spite of its artistic and literary achievements, was essentially worldly.

In the mean time, among the specific achievements of the Italian Renaissance in the field of education must be mentioned the conscious and deliberate creation of a new educational type, the courtier. In his book called the *Cortegiano*, Castiglione has drawn the outlines of this type with a completeness hitherto unknown. The guiding principle of the life of the courtier is to be not, as in feudal times, the service of his lord, but rather the standard of personal honour. In face, if necessary, of his lord's commands, he will decline unbecoming employment. He must be able to swim, run, ride, wrestle, leap, dance, play a musical instrument (in moderation), write poems, discuss literary subjects, use arms of all knightly sorts, and, of course, make love, all with dignity and grace. Most of this, it is true, had its place in the earlier chivalric education; but while the medieval standards had been feudal and religious, in short, social rather than personal, the aims of the *Cortegiano* are purely individual. He seeks nothing beyond his own honour and courtly perfection.

Not only in the Italian, but also in French, Spanish, and English versions, the *Book of the Courtier* was welcomed as fixing a standard of gentlemanly conduct. Ascham praised it, Spenser and Lyly made adaptations of it, and Elyot's *Governour* (1531) as well as *The Compleat Gentleman* of Peacham, and the book of the same title by Brathwait, who added also a *Compleat Gentlewoman*, were imitations of it. As Spenser expresses it, 'The Great Schoolmaistresse of all courtesy' is to be the 'court and royal citadell', and the courtier is no longer the man of prowess and devotion merely, but above all the realization of the Platonic ideal of harmonious and beautiful character. Castiglione himself (b. 1478, d. 1529) was no mean example of the courtier and ambassador, but perhaps his precepts were never so perfectly realized as in the personality of that accomplished Englishman, Sir Philip Sidney.

II

ERASMUS AND THE NORTHERN RENAISSANCE

WHILE the revival of classical studies in Italy had led not only to a narrow, imitative type of Latin culture known as Ciceronianism, but also to a measure of paganism and scepticism, it was otherwise across the Alps. There, under the influence of the stable Teutonic temperament, while the Italian level of culture was for a long time not even approached, there developed a tendency to utilize the new learning in the service of moral and social ends. This movement is associated chiefly with the names of Rudolph Agricola and Erasmus, although the Brethren of the Common Life, founded by Geert Groot (born at Deventer in 1340) had already made important advances in the same direction.

The advice of Rudolph Agricola (1444–85), whose personality caused him to be regarded as the typical figure of the Northern Revival, was whole-hearted: 'Regard as suspect all that you have been taught hitherto; ban and cast away as an imposture anything and everything that professes to be knowledge, unless its title can be vouched for by the evidence of the great writers of old.' Erasmus himself could effect no sharper break from medieval tradition.

Of Dutch birth, Agricola obtained his Bachelor's degree at Erfurt at the age of fourteen, and his Master's at Louvain three years later. His Italian studies began at Pavia in 1468; and his masters included Battista Guarino and Theodore Gaza. A scholar of varied accomplishments, he returned in 1479 to Holland, and in 1484 removed to Heidelberg. Great as were his attainments in Greek and Latin literature, his knowledge of French, German, Italian, music, and fine art was equally extraordinary for that age. His few writings include a treatise on logic and a short educational work, *de formando studio.* In the latter the classical writers are held to be the arbiters of educational worth, although, like Erasmus, Agricola maintained that knowledge should bear fruit in action, and that it must always subserve an ethical purpose. Agricola approached the incarnation of a German Leonardo da Vinci. His was indeed an extraordinary personality with a marvellous range of gifts; he could build an organ or draw a portrait, make an oration or edit a classical manuscript, teach or converse with singular charm.

Erasmus, who also called himself Desiderius as a Latin equivalent, was born at Rotterdam in 1466. He attended a private school at Gouda, and subsequently the Cathedral Choir School at Utrecht. Later, from nine years of age, he attended the large school of Alexander Hegius, himself a famous scholar, connected with the church at Deventer. Later again, perhaps from 1480 to 1482, he went to a school of the Brethren of Common Life at Bois-le-Duc. In 1483, influenced, he says, by the pressure of his guardian and of the monks, Erasmus entered an Augustinian monastery as a novice, being ordained priest in 1492. Erasmus was unfavourably impressed by the monastic schools. *Schola sit publica aut nulla* was his dictum.

At the age of eighteen Erasmus was already so far attached to the humanistic movement that he wrote an epitome of Laurentius Valla's *Elegantiae Linguae Latinae*, while the epistle *De Contemptu Mundi* written by him in 1486 shows that the monastic atmosphere was not quite as uncongenial at this time as his later utterances taken by themselves might indicate. In 1493, however, by the favour of the Bishop of Cambrai, Erasmus secured a dispensation from monastic residence, and proceeded to the University of Paris. Here his studies were chiefly classical, although theology was not neglected. The medieval theologians, however, were despised by the young scholar almost from the first. True theology, he came more and more to believe, was antemedieval; its climax having been reached in the works of St. Jerome.

At Paris Erasmus made several friendships with English students, one of whom was Lord Mountjoy, and secured a not too willing patroness to assist him after the humanistic fashion with money. Mountjoy took Erasmus in 1499 to England, where he met and made friends of More, Warham, and Colet. Colet would have retained his services at Oxford, but Erasmus never could brook the restraint of regular duties. In 1500 he was again studying Greek, 'without which', he declared, 'the amplest erudition in Latin is imperfect', at Paris. In 1502 we find him at Louvain, where he declined a proffered chair of Rhetoric; but Paris saw him again in 1505, and in the same year he revisited London, returning to the Continent in 1506 to travel with two pupils and their tutor in Italy. So buried was Erasmus in the civilization of the past that the natural beauties of northern Italian scenery and the magnificent art of the city of Florence were alike powerless to awaken his sensibilities.

Towards the end of 1507 Erasmus was received into the household of the great printer, Aldus Manutius, who was to do more than any other man to make Greek texts available in the West. From Venice the indefatigable scholar proceeded towards the close of 1508 to the University of Padua. On the opening day of March 1509, he arrived at Rome, where, though he had no eye for the contemporary labours of Raphael and Michael Angelo, he was shocked by the absence of a genuine Christian spirit among prominent ecclesiastics.

In 1509 the accession of Henry VIII drew Erasmus to England. He became Professor of Divinity, and probably taught Greek also, at Cambridge. In England the treatise *De Ratione Studii* was sent to Colet, while other works published during the five years spent in England included a treatise on Latin composition, a set of distiches, an oration to be recited by the pupils of St. Paul's, and a revised book of Latin syntax which still exists in a much modified form as the Eton Latin grammar. At no period was Erasmus more directly concerned with educational problems than while in England.

The departure of Erasmus from England in 1514 seems to have been due to his desire to publish his great edition of the Letters of Jerome and his text of the Greek Testament. No one was more convinced of the necessity of getting at original sources and exact texts. His wanderings for the next three years centre upon the great printing-establishment of Froben at Basle. The *Colloquies*, a series of dialogues intended to make Latin not only an interesting study but a vehicle for the discussion of current problems, appeared at Basle in 1516, and in a more perfect edition in 1523. The *Colloquies*, condemned as tending to unsettle the faith by the University of Paris, became the favourite text-book of schools in sympathy with the movement for religious reformation.

Though desirous of avoiding religious controversies, whether doctrinal or administrative in character, Erasmus was drawn into a polemic with Luther on the freedom of the will. Three strenuous years at Louvain (1519–22) were followed by a period of fruitful literary work at Basle (1522–9). Here in 1528 appeared the *Ciceronianus*, a satire upon merely imitative Latin. In this work it is pointed out that the Ciceronian thought himself lucky if he completed one fair-sized sentence in the exact style of Cicero as his night's work. In 1529 followed the excellent educational treatise *De Pueris Instituendis*.

The death of the printer Froben in 1527, and the spread of religious strife to Basle, were events that may have been responsible for the removal of Erasmus to a Catholic centre, Freiburg, in 1529. The change was not a success. In 1535 Basle was again the scholar's haven, and here Erasmus continued his work, pen in hand, though afflicted with disease, until his death on the 12th July, 1536.

To Erasmus the study of antiquity seemed the true path to social reform. In no way, he held, did humanism antagonize Christianity—witness the sympathy of Basil, Augustine, and Jerome for classical learning, although the admiration of each, especially of the two great Latin fathers, was strictly qualified. As to Latin, it should be a living language; hence it could not be merely imitative, merely Ciceronian. The latter attitude might indeed encourage paganism.

The study of the vernacular was unnecessary; Latin itself should be the spoken tongue of scholars. Latin, too, made a man a citizen of the world. Erasmus was never a nationalist, nor did he hesitate to disparage national folk-lore, traditions, and even history as expressed in the vernacular. The aim of all education, formally speaking, is the knowledge of Christ and His glory; but the path to this end is *eruditio*, not our modern erudition, but learning in use. The home or a small public school is the best educational institution and the classical literature the best educational instrument. Discipline must be kindly; the master is to remember that he was once a boy.

In his best treatise on education, entitled *De pueris statim ac liberaliter instituendis*, Erasmus argues that the education of boys should be commenced very early. 'A man ignorant of letters is no man at all.' It is in his immaturity while young, in his capacity for training, in his lack of fixed and definite instinctive acts, that man chiefly differs from the lower animals. Children are imitative; therefore easily spoiled by luxury or bad example. Even among the animals, nature needs to be reinforced by wise training. The three factors in education—nature, training, and practice—are all of them indispensable. Human nature as such implies firstly the capacity of being guided by reason; secondly, a difference in individual tastes and endowments. Instruction, it is generally held, should commence at seven years; but this dictum applies only to laborious studies. It is even better to take some slight risks to health than to defer instruction too long. Love, not fear, must be the master's instrument; though the schools, especially dame and monastic schools, are generally in an evil state. 'Teaching by beating is not a liberal education.'

'It is easier to outline the ideal schoolmaster than to find him in reality.' Let statesmen, however, see to it that a supply of suitable men is furnished; for this is a public duty not inferior to the maintenance of the army. The good master is sympathetic. 'Wholly wrong are those masters who expect their little pupils to act as though they were diminutive adults.' Pliny's warning is repeated: 'Remember that your pupil is but a youth still, and that you were once one yourself.'

Instruction begins with speech; but Latin speech is of course meant. The method to be adopted by a skilled teacher is illustrated by the use of a picture of a combat between an elephant and a dragon. A Latin 'picture talk' must have been quite entertaining. As the dragon is a classical beast, Erasmus takes his existence quite as seriously as that of the elephant. Such material seemed to him highly valuable, whereas it is a shame to think of 'the precious time and energy squandered in listening to ridiculous riddles, stories of dreams, of ghosts, witches, fairies, demons; to foolish tales drawn from popular annals; worthless, nay, mischievous stuff of the kind which is poured into children in their nursery days?' Yet why these materials are inferior to tales of dragons combating elephants is a problem which only a humanist could be expected to explain.

The method of teaching reading may be borrowed from Quintilian, who used ivory letters, and letters made of biscuit which may be eaten when learnt. 'In England I heard of a father who taught his boy to aim with bow and arrow at Greek or Roman letters painted on a target; a hit meant a cherry for the archer.' Yet games of chess, dice, &c., or mnemonic puzzles, are undesirable as involving more time in the learning than the subject itself. 'There is only one sound mnemonic art, and it has three rules: understand, arrange, repeat.' Emulation will be duly employed by wise teachers. The old plan of mere learning by rote must be abandoned. Erasmus expects to receive the familiar rejoinder: 'I had to learn Latin in this manner when I was a boy; what was good enough for me must do for him.'

III

THE EDUCATIONAL VIEWS OF MARTIN LUTHER

THE visit of Rudolph Agricola to Italy, about the year 1476, may be regarded as the signal for the German Renaissance. No fewer than nine universities, not necessarily devoted to the humanistic curriculum, were founded in Germany between 1456 and 1506. If anything were lacking in the northern mind, it was not intelligence. The great John Reuchlin, who visited Florence and Rome, is said to have moved a Greek teacher in Rome to exclaim, half in sorrow, half in admiration, that in him Greece had fled beyond the Alps! Neither did the Germans lack perseverance and determination. It was Reuchlin who gave ten gold pieces to a Jew for the elucidation of a difficult Hebrew phrase. As a student of the Hebrew writings, Reuchlin became their ardent defender when the proposal was made to destroy them. In the phrase of Ulrich von Hutten, he and Erasmus were 'the two eyes of Germany'.

The German Renaissance was a more sudden and a better defined movement than the Italian. Unlike the Renaissance in Italy, it followed a specific cue. Had there been no capture of Constantinople, there would still have been a new intellectual birth of Italy; but had the latter not occurred, would there have been a Renaissance in Germany? The northern scholars were fully conscious of the critical character of their age. 'Learning flourishes,' exclaimed Hutten, 'men's minds awaken, in such an age it is a delight to live!'

In Germany as in Italy, however, the universities long adhered to the old scholasticism. The Church and the Friars were determined not only to maintain the traditions of the past, but also to destroy the Hebrew writings which were beginning to attract the attention of the educated. Reuchlin, after many persecutions, was condemned in 1520 by the Pope. Humanism was already beginning to antagonize the hierarchy when a diversion was effected by the intervention of Martin Luther. The majority of the German scholars declined to throw in their lot with the rebellious monk. Reuchlin and Erasmus would not join him; but he secured the valuable support of Melanchthon and Hutten. The new issue, however, was neither humanism nor education in any form. It was Church administration and doctrine.

The education of Luther serves to illustrate the conditions of contemporary learning in the north. Driven from home by parental severity, at school he fared no better, having been beaten no fewer than fifteen times on a single morning. His names for schools are prisons, hells, purgatories; the school-children he deems martyrs. 'We learned', he declares, 'absolutely nothing.' Elsewhere the common-sense question is asked: 'Is it not a misery that a boy must study twenty years or more, for the sole purpose of learning as much bad Latin as will enable him to become a parson, and to read mass?'

The Latin school attended by Luther at Mansfeld had the usual simple but unattractive curriculum. *Donatus* was the grammatical text; in fact, Donatus was engraved on wooden blocks prior to the invention of movable types. *Cisio Janus*, a set of mnemonic verses designed to recall the ecclesiastical calendar, had to be learned by rote like *Donatus*. The character of these verses may be gathered from the initial phrase: *Cisio Janus Epy sibi vindicat.* Cisio stood for the Feast of the Circumcision, Janus for January, and Epy for Epiphany. *Donatus* and *Cisio Janus* were the backbone of the curriculum. True, Luther seems to have been taught to repeat also the Ten Commandments, Child's Creed, Paternoster, and certain hymns. The very nature of such a curriculum is sufficient to determine the method. It consisted of learning by rote, 'backing the book', and being thrashed for verbal errors.

An atmosphere of extreme severity seems to have surrounded the whole space of Luther's youth. On the one hand the popular and official belief in witchcraft and other superstitions impressed his imagination with an indelible stamp. On the other hand, at least as regards outward observances, he could not fail to become pious. 'When I was a boy,' he testifies, 'all games were forbidden, so that card-makers, pipers, and actors were not admitted to the sacrament, and those who had played games, or danced, or been present at shows and plays, made it a matter for confession.'

At the age of fourteen Luther was sent to a school, probably conducted by the Brethren of the Common Life, at Magdeburg. Here, according to the custom among poor scholars, he sang for bread before the doors of the citizens. In one instance he and his fellows ran from the gruff voice of a peasant, who in reality was bringing them food. The next year, 1498, saw him attending school under similar circumstances at Eisenach, where he found charitable friends who took him into their home. At the age of eighteen he proceeded to the University of Erfurt, essentially an orthodox and scholastic institution, yet at the time foremost among the German universities. At the university, his daily duty began with attendance at church. His motto, we are told, was 'Well prayed is more than half studied'. The remainder of the day was divided between lectures and the library. No Greek seems to have been taught as yet at the university; and even Latin attracted Luther not by the philological or literary merits so dear to the humanists, but by its human interest solely. Law attracted his attention for a short time, but on the 17th July 1505, he presented himself as a candidate for the novitiate at the Augustinian monastery at Erfurt. The resolve had been suddenly taken, having been due to a vow rashly made, and subsequently repented.

Through the discernment of the visiting Vicar, Luther was released from monastic confinement and was allowed liberty of study.

In the monastery he had devoted himself to the Bible and St. Augustine, although medieval theology was not neglected. Visions and temptations had troubled him, doubts and despair had encompassed his soul. Already, perhaps, he secretly challenged the infallibility of the Church as a visible organization.

In 1508 Luther was called to a chair of philosophy in the University of Wittenberg. This institution had been established but a few years, the funds having been provided out of church property by Imperial Charter and Papal agreement. We have some particulars of the condition of the university at this time. In 1507 Christopher Scheurl was chosen Rector. In his preface to a published list of lectures for 1507, he speaks of the mild climate and the kindly citizens of Wittenberg, of board to be had for the year for eight golden gulden, of degrees conferred without charge, of privileges similar to those of the older university towns, and of an alleged constellation of scholarly talent. Members of the university were forbidden to frequent taverns or to carry arms. There were seven professors in canon law, five in theology, three in Imperial law, four in Medicine, three in literature, and nine in philosophy, one of whom taught Scotus and one Aquinas. These figures make no allowance for the fact that the same professor is sometimes enumerated in connexion with two or three subjects. No history, Greek, Hebrew, or natural philosophy was taught.

For some reason Luther lectured for a time at Erfurt, returning, however, to Wittenberg, where he completed his Doctor's degree in 1512. In the meantime he went on a mission to Rome (1511–12).

The visit disillusioned him. While on his knees on the Santa Scala, praying his way to the top, he seemed to hear words that had already long been with him. 'The just shall live by faith.' These words became the tocsin of the Reformation.

Profoundly influenced by St. Augustine and by the anonymous *Theologia Germanica*, Luther taught theology at Wittenberg. In 1515 the *Letters of Obscure Men*, arising out of the Reuchlin controversy, convulsed Europe with laughter at the expense of the ecclesiastical dignitaries. The German mind was excited and stimulated; Germany was ready for the ninety-five theses. When he burned the papal bull of condemnation issued against him, Luther's self-education was complete. Henceforth he was not a learner but a teacher.

In spite of the vehement and intemperate language in which they are couched, Luther's letter *To the Mayors and Aldermen of all the Cities in Behalf of Christian Schools* (1524), and his *Sermon on the Duty of Sending Children to School* (1530) contain the outlines of a complete system of education.

1. Education is primarily a religious duty. Only by good Latin schools can preachers, schoolmasters, and professional men be duly provided. The decline of such schools is lamented. Yet religion, although the chief, is not the sole foundation of education. 'Were there neither soul, nor heaven, nor hell, it would still be necessary to have schools for the sake of affairs here below.'

2. Education should be provided for the sons and daughters of all, though for but two hours a day; and this requirement should be enforced by the magistrates. Moreover, boys of promise should be sought out for schooling by the state officials. Otherwise not only religion but industry and citizenship will suffer.

3. The schoolmaster's vocation is next to that of the preacher. 'If I were not a preacher, there is no other calling on earth I would have rather than that of schoolmaster. We must not consider how the world esteems it and rewards it, but how God looks upon it.'

4. Among subjects, Luther has a good word for Hebrew, Greek, Latin, and the vernacular, though the last is to be mastered less from books than by intercourse. Mathematics is a subject suited to the university stage of instruction. History, philosophy, dialectic, rhetoric, and music have their respective influences on the mind. 'Unless a schoolmaster sings I think little of him', says Luther quaintly. Together with music are grouped physical exercises; for since the days of ancient Greece the one suggests the other. Fencing, wrestling, and

the tournament seemed to Luther to promote the good proportion, health, and elasticity of the body.

5. As to methods, Luther was alive to the necessity of the knowledge and understanding of things before words, to the importance of the living speech in the study of language, and to the desirability of mildness in the discipline and training of the young.

IV

CALVINISTIC EDUCATION

PHILIP MELANCHTHON (1497–1560), the son of an armourer of Bretten, and a nephew of Reuchlin, became to the education of reformed Germany what his friend Luther was to its theology. A recognized master of almost all branches of learning, Melanchthon gave instruction in the classics, oratory, and history at the University of Tübingen, before being called to teach Greek at Wittenberg (1518). Hither he attracted students from many countries, refusing invitations to France and England. A founder and organizer of numerous reformed schools and even universities, a powerful champion of humanism, a prolific author of text-books, especially upon rhetoric, grammar, theology, and philosophy, Melanchthon deserved and won the proud title of *preceptor Germaniae*.

Even Melanchthon, however, scarcely exercised such a profound and permanent influence upon the protestant schools of Europe and America as John Calvin (1509–69). Calvin had received a sound training in grammar and the humanistic studies at Noyon, Paris, Orleans, and Bourges, before he experienced a sudden and, as he deemed, providential conversion in 1532 or 1533. Henceforth he was primarily a theologian. The famous *Institutes of the Christian Religion* came from his pen when he was only twenty-six years old.

By no means a mere recluse, Calvin elaborated a scheme of reformed government for the city of Geneva, in which no small part was played by education. In 1537 and 1538 the Reformer was instrumental in drawing up a curriculum for elementary schools. All children were to receive lessons in catechism on Sundays at noon. Neglect of this duty involved the parents in penalties to be exacted by the State. Children were also to receive religious instruction at home from their parents. During one hour daily psalms were to be sung in the schools. Latin grammar, study of the vernacular, arithmetic, and civic training were also thought worthy of a place in the curriculum. Collegiate and university institutions were established in such a way as to form a sort of training-school for protestants. The position of Geneva was such that the city became a natural centre for the reformers of Europe. So complete was the organization of Calvinistic education that it was copied to a certain extent in the *Ratio Studiorum* of the Jesuits.

Calvinistic education, indeed, spread far beyond the limited confines of Geneva. France, Holland, Scotland, England and her American colonies, all felt and in some ways profited by its influence. Unlike Luther, Calvin had appealed to reason; for instance, he was the first theologian to defend the taking of interest, prohibited though it seems to be in the Mosaic law (cf. Deut. xxiii. 19). This law, explained Calvin, was purely civil, therefore human in its source and local in its application. Calvin himself drew up a system of theology eminently reasonable if once the premisses be granted. Thus, through reading the *Institutes*, the Calvinists in America, France, and Scotland became lovers of strict argumentation, and consequently of learning. Among the first acts of the New England Puritans were the establishment of common schools and the foundation of Harvard. The tradition of Calvinism, too, was favourable to hard work; and gain was considered by no means an unlawful aim. Moreover, although the seventh day was kept with painful rigidity; ecclesiastical holidays were in general disregarded. On the other hand, in spite of his hardness and thrift, the Calvinist owned generosity to be a duty. The words of Calvin in his commentary on Deuteronomy deserve to become classical: 'I am master, but not tyrant; I am master, but it is on this condition that I be also brother; I am master, but there is a common master in heaven both for me and for those who are subject to me: we are all here like one family.'

Loving truth, the Calvinist believed that reason and education were paths to its attainment. Consequently, not only did the educational influence of Genevan thought permeate the Continent; but before Elizabeth's death Oxford and Cambridge had already surrendered to it. In 1578, Calvin's *Catechism* and *Institutes* were required of all Oxford undergraduates. Equally prompt was the victory of the new theology in European institutions such as Heidelberg, Utrecht, and the Huguenot Colleges in France, as well as in the Puritan universities of New England. Scotland attempted to rival Geneva by the establishment of a compulsory school system, which only fell short of completeness through lack of funds; and she actually laid the foundations of a religious and democratic system of education which has ever since been almost as accessible to the poor as to the rich.

Such qualities as industry, rigid exactness, moral training, conscientiousness, universality in the sense that the schools were for all rather than for the few, as well as a certain contentiousness and love of argumentation, may be enumerated as permanent characteristics of Calvinistic or Puritan education.

V

THE RENAISSANCE OF SCIENCE

THE ancients, in their quest of an encyclic education, neglected neither science nor philosophy. They had mathematicians, they had astronomers, they had physicists, they had physicians. Yet the typical character of panhellenic culture was the vivid representation of literary, speculative, and artistic interests. In the fifteenth-century Renaissance, the majority of the humanists concentrated their attention upon the mastery of classical Latin form; but, here and there, a new vision was applied to scientific data. The humanists, in the narrow sense of the word, were Ciceronian imitators. Among such may be mentioned Poggio, Bembo, and Sadoleto. But there were humanist reformers, and there were humanist scientists. Erasmus and More, if we may quote particular instances, employed their Greek and Latin studies in the service of social amelioration; while Copernicus, Galileo, and Francis Bacon gave a fresh impetus to science, and applied or upheld inductive methods of investigation, instead of the Aristotelian deductive logic.

If the Reformation movement is to be associated with the Renaissance, a fourth type of humanist appears, namely, the religious reformer. Martin Luther, like Melanchthon, Calvin, and Knox, illustrates the subordination of scholarship to faith; as, from another point of view, does the Jesuit order. The reformation led to bitter polemics. These only intensified the need and the desire for training in the ancient languages. An atmosphere of religious controversy, however, is not the most favourable to science. From a scientific standpoint, the most that can be said in its favour is that it failed to restrain the Copernican hypothesis, or to stem the current of inquiry into natural law.

It is unnecessary to argue that the underlying motive of scientific masters like Copernicus, Leonardo da Vinci and Galileo was the betterment of the human race. It was, in fact, simply the desire to know. This implies the aim of increasing man's mastery over his environment. Whether moral improvement must follow is problematical, and almost irrelevant. Thus the scientific humanist is not to be identified with the social, any more than with the verbal or with the religious humanist. Galileo, Erasmus, Poggio, and Melanchthon represent divergent types, yet all associated with the humanistic tradition in education.

In a dedicatory letter to his work on the *Revolutions of the Heavenly Bodies*, 1543, Copernicus apologized to the Pope for the publication of theories which were contrary to orthodoxy. He quotes the opinions of several of the ancients to the effect that the earth moves; and proceeds to indicate the inherent consistency of his own revolutionary conclusions:

'After I had then assumed the motions which I assign to the earth in the following work, I found, after careful investigation extending through years, that if the movements of the other planets were referred to the motion of the earth in its orbit and reckoned according to the revolution of each star, not only could their observed phenomena be logically explained, but also the succession of stars, and their size, and all their orbits, and the heavens themselves would present such a harmonious order that no single part could be changed without disarranging the others and the whole universe.'

But an hypothesis which had worked for more than a thousand years was not lightly to be shaken. The Ptolemaic theory which had so appealed to Dante, and to all the scientific minds of the Middle Ages, had come to be regarded as sacrosanct. In 1615 Galileo, the great professor of Pisa, who, apart from his own notable discoveries, had ardently supported the views of Copernicus, was condemned by the Inquisition; the Copernican theory being denounced as 'absurd in philosophy' and as 'directly contrary to Holy Scripture'. Galileo was forced to recant. The publication in 1632 of his *Dialogue on the Two Chief Systems of the World*, the Ptolemaic and the Copernican, was regarded as a fresh cause of offence. The form of the dialogue was not, as he may have anticipated, a sufficient protection for his lukewarmness on the Ptolemaic side; once more he was called to Rome by the Inquisition and forced to make a fresh recantation, the spirit of scientific inquiry being viewed with the gravest suspicion in high places, especially by metaphysicians trained in the application of Aristotle's *Organon.*

The idealization of the inductive method was the work of Francis Bacon. Practised by Aristotle, Roger Bacon, Galileo, and many others, this method found its philosophic exposition in the *Novum Organum*, by which Bacon meant the New or Inductive Logic. Turning with aversion from the hair-splitting of deductive controversy, he sought, and impelled others to seek, new and useful truth. In the words of Macaulay: 'He was not the maker of that road; he was not the discoverer of that road; he was not the person who first surveyed and mapped that road. But he was the person who first called public attention to an inexhaustible mine of wealth, which had been utterly neglected, and which was accessible by that road alone. By doing so, he caused that road, which had previously been trodden only by peasants and higglers, to be frequented by a higher class of travellers.'

Of his *Essays* and of the encyclopaedic *Instauratio* it is less necessary to speak than of the ideal which he advanced for the reconstruction of university research. This is the theme of the brilliant *New Atlantis*, an imaginary land situated in Pacific seas, supposed to have been inhabited by a civilized people, miraculously converted by St. Bartholomew. Its incorruptible officials decline to be twice paid. Solomon's house, the 'very eye of the kingdom', had been established for some nineteen hundred years, 'the noblest foundation, as we think, that ever was upon the earth and the lanthorn of this kingdom'. The richest jewel in the possession of the father of Solomon's House is presented to his visitors. Strange that it should have consisted of the narration of the true state of the institution! In a logical order, worthy of Bacon's aversion, a medieval schoolman, the narrative proceeds from the end of the foundation to its means and instruments, thence to the several employments and functions to which its fellows are assigned, and finally to a brief consideration of the rites and ordinances which it observes.

What, then, is the end, the fundamental aim, of Solomon's House? It consists, in fact, of the knowledge of cause and effect. The secret motions of things are investigated, to 'the enlarging of the bounds of human empire, to the effecting of all things possible'. The materials—the very complete and modern materials—which Solomon's House provides for the purposes of its inductive activities, include excavations, mines, and high towers. Hermits who choose to prolong their lives in lonely places are instructed in what it is useful to observe. Further riches include cataracts, streams, salt and fresh lakes, engines, wells, fountains, great and spacious laboratories, chambers of health, baths, orchards, gardens, parks and enclosures for beasts and birds, breweries, bakehouses, kitchens, dispensatories or shops of medicine, mechanical workshops, furnaces, perspective houses for experiment with light and radiation, sound-houses, perfume-houses, engine-houses, precious stones, crystals, fossils, a mathematical house, and houses of deceit of the senses.

The functions of the several fellows are thus divided: there are twelve merchants of light, to collect the materials of knowledge, such as books and patterns of experiments, from other parts; there are three depredators, to gather experiments from all books; there are three mystery men, to collect the experiments used in the mechanical arts, and in studies and practices not generally recognized as arts; there are three pioneers or miners, to try new experiments; there are three compilers, to tabulate the work of all the foregoing; there are three dowry men, or benefactors, to draw conclusions of practical benefit from the experiments of their colleagues; there are three lamps to consider the labours already done, and to direct out of these labours a series of experiments of a higher light; there are three inoculators to execute and report upon the experiments thus directed; finally, there are three interpreters of nature, to raise the discoveries of other members of the college into greater observations, axioms, and aphorisms.

Beneath the surface of such elaborate regulations the solicitude of Bacon for the systematic collection of knowledge and for its extension by means of experiment and induction is clearly to be discerned. Solomon's House is a vast school of science, its foundation is research, its typical activity experiment; its method is inductive, its aim the extension of human power. Novices and apprentices are trained in readiness to replace each older generation of scientists. Nor does the college scruple to determine what inventions may be published, what concealed; some inventions are to be hidden even from the State, and many from the multitude. There is an esoteric as well as an exoteric body of knowledge.

Let us pass to ordinances. There are means of celebrating successful discoveries, and of perpetuating the memory of great inventors. There is a gallery for the 'patterns and samples of all manner of the more rare and excellent inventions'. There is another gallery for the statues of the most celebrated discoverer, of whom Columbus alone is indicated by name, although the inventors of ships, gunpowder, and music are mentioned as types of those to whom the statues are raised. Local inventors receive in addition liberal and honourable rewards. The hymns, services, and forms of prayer practised at Solomon's House receive a somewhat perfunctory attention.

This Research University, moreover, exists wholly for the public advantage. For the publication of profitable inventions and the announcement of what Bacon calls 'natural divinations' of diseases, plagues, pests, famine, earthquakes, inundations, comets, temperature, and divers other things, and for counsel to the people how to meet and remedy such dangers and disasters, regular circuits are made from town to town on behalf of the College.

Is there any modern institution, may we ask, as nobly and magnificently provided? The modern type of university, it is true, has much in common with Solomon's House. Yet it is with difficulty that we realize how dramatically opposite was that grand conception from the universities of Bacon's time. They still relied upon the dialectical method which had been inherited from ancient Greece.

'Had Plato lived to finish the *Critias*,' writes Macaulay, 'a comparison between that noble fiction and the *New Atlantis* would probably have furnished us with still more striking instances. It is amusing to think with what horror he would have seen such an institution as Solomon's House rising in his republic; with what vehemence he would have ordered the brew houses, the perfume houses, and the dispensatories to be pulled down; and with what inexorable rigour he would have driven beyond the frontier all the Fellows of the College, Merchants of Light, and Depredators, Lamps, and Pioneers.'

VI

THE JESUITS AND THEIR SCHOOLS

Ignatius of Loyola and the Society of Jesus

IGNATIUS, born in 1491 at the castle of Loyola in the Basque provinces of Spain, was educated after the Spanish custom at the house of a nobleman and in due course became an officer in the army. Wounded in 1521 at Pampeluna, during convalescence he was influenced so profoundly by the study of the *Lives of the Saints* that he retired to a life of prayer and meditation, out of which grew the *Book of Exercises*, which has been aptly described as a 'little manual of practical asceticism'. The object of converting the Moslems led Ignatius to the Holy Land (1523), but being compelled to leave Jerusalem he devoted himself to study, learning Latin among little boys at Pampeluna, and studying subsequently at the Spanish universities, and finally at the University of Paris, where he attained the Master's degree. At Paris his force of character attracted to his side a number of distinguished and earnest students. In 1534 the group of friends took vows of poverty, chastity, and service in the Holy Land. Unable to fulfil the last of these vows, they drew up a constitution for a new religious order which received the papal sanction in 1540. The new order, known as the Society of Jesus, was to consist of neither monks nor friars, but of clerks regular. Ignatius was its first General. The military terminology employed at the outset, for Ignatius had spoken of a Company or Regiment rather than of a Society, has been thought to favour the view that the primary object of the Jesuits was to combat Protestantism. In fact, however, in the minds of the first enthusiasts, the main enemy was not Protestantism, but Mohammedanism. The members of the Order soon adopted the abbreviated name of Jesuits, given them at first by their enemies. For some time the Jesuits were sent to Catholic and to pagan countries, and only to Protestant countries at the request of the Pope; or, as in the case of Germany, at the instance of the Imperial authorities. Protestantism, naturally, soon became included among the enemies of the Society, which was essentially an order of service. The zeal and utter self-effacement of the Jesuits made them the principal agents of the great Catholic movement known as the Counter-Reformation. Ignatius died in 1556, and was canonized in 1622; but his spirit and energy were not unworthily reproduced by successive Generals of the Society that he had originated.

While it must not be imagined that education was the principal aim of the Society of Jesus, the claims of the young were considered from the very moment of its origin. The papal authorization of the institute of 1540 states as its object: 'The progress of souls in good life and knowledge of religion; the propagation of faith by public preaching, the Spiritual Exercises and works of charity, and particularly the instruction of youth and ignorant persons in the Christian religion.' The general aim of the Order, indeed, cannot be better expressed than by its motto: *Omnia ad Majorem Gloriam Dei*, abbreviated O.A.M.D.G., 'All for the Greater Glory of God'. Yet this, after all, tells us little; the same motto might have been taken by any Protestant school of the period. In practice, the aim of the Society was to defend the Church against its enemies. As a result, the educational aims of the Jesuits were naturally conservative. Pupils were to assimilate and to reproduce the approved elements of knowledge; they were even, contrary to the statements of some historians, encouraged to originality and reflection. It goes without saying that they were not permitted to challenge orthodox positions or to pass moral judgements which might be contrary to accepted teachings; for, after all, the main object of the Jesuit schools was not philanthropy, but the increase of the influence of the Church.

The Jesuit Constitutions contain ten parts, of which the first and longest has to do with education. In the final vow taken by a Jesuit he undertakes to have 'a particular concern for the education of boys'. Although the Jesuit schools are still of considerable importance, the great work of the Society, the work of educating most of the best minds of Europe, belongs to the seventeenth and early eighteenth centuries. During this period the Jesuits conducted education on a more systematic plan than can be discerned in the whole preceding range of European history. Each Jesuit, in the course of his long preparation, which lasted about eighteen years in all, gave several years wholly to teaching, his scholarly studies being suspended, even his religious exercises being shortened, during the time he served as a schoolmaster.

The Jesuit schools were supported by specific endowments, and until the inroads made by various potentates upon Jesuit property made such a policy impossible, they accepted no fees in return for instruction given. Even in the lifetime of Ignatius, colleges had been founded in Italy, Spain, Portugal, France, and Germany; while shortly before the suppression of the Society in 1773 there were, besides a number of institutions of higher learning, 669 Jesuit colleges in which some 200,000 students were enrolled. The losses of the Jesuits during the period of suppression (1773–1814) may never, perhaps, be recovered; but some hundreds of Jesuit colleges are in operation at the present time, of which a very large proportion are located in the British Empire, and in the United States. Sydney, for example, has two Jesuit colleges.

The distinguishing mark of the Jesuit schools in the period of their greatest influence was system. Nothing was left to chance, and little to individuality, although clauses, now far more comprehensive than formerly, were gradually introduced to admit of the modification of school organization in accordance with local needs. Administration was wholly centralized; one result being the rise of a system of secondary schools with a far more uniform curriculum, more exact methods, and more definite standards than those of the old fashioned grammar-schools.

The plan of Jesuit education was completed by one of the successors of Ignatius, General Aquaviva, under whom appeared the famous *Ratio atque Institutio Studiorum Societatis Jesu*, better known as the *Ratio Studiorum*. This is the first example in the history of Western education of a system of instruction devised in the modern manner as a result of the protracted deliberations of committees of experts. The work was essentially international. France, Spain, Portugal, Austria, Germany, and Italy each furnished a schoolman to examine plans of study, works on education, and the testimonies of practical Jesuit teachers. After a year spent in such work, the committee presented a report which was submitted to at least five men of experience in each province. A second scheme, published in 1591, was the result. This scheme was submitted to practical tests in the schools for a period of years; so that the *Ratio Studiorum*, issued in 1599, was produced by a painstaking and scientific procedure which might well furnish a model for all subsequent educational plans. Chief among the documents which seem to have influenced the Jesuit committee was the famous course of studies drawn up by Johannes Sturm for his gymnasium at Strassburg.

Two courses of study were drawn up, the *studia superiora et inferiora*; the *superiora* being taught only in the larger schools. In the town schools pupils began usually at about ten and were 'absolved' at about sixteen. The pupils might be either interns, that is to say, in training for the Order, or externs, attending merely as pupils. There was little or no tendency to favour the scholar of exalted rank above his meaner fellow. In the *studia inferiora* were comprised five or six classes, including, in the lower or grammar department, Infima, Media, and Suprema, and sometimes a fourth class; and in the upper school Humanitas and Rhetorica. Each class except Rhetorica, which required two years, was normally 'absolved' in one year.

The curriculum was humanistic; it consisted essentially of religion, Latin, and Greek. Latin had still a practical value, and no other language might be spoken by pupils of the upper school save on holidays. Other subjects, called accessories, were taught incidentally to literature.

Thoroughness was the dominant note in the Jesuit method. To the Jesuits belongs the honour of the first effective attempt to train teachers. Pedagogical seminaries were founded, and each teacher had a professional manual to consult for his guidance in the field.

The Jesuits made an important advance in the method of teaching the classics. Hitherto the text-book had been the central element in the process, whereas in the Jesuit schools the central element was the teacher. The *prelectio*, which meant for the lower classes an oral explanatory lesson, and for the upper classes a lecture (cf. German *Vorlesung*), is described as 'the typical form of Jesuit teaching'. Written exercises were required daily of the pupils. While the master corrected these, going over each exercise together with its author and with his appointed *aemulus* or rival, chosen boys who had already repeated their grammar heard the others say their lessons. Memorization was required not only of grammar but also of Latin conversations designed to help the boys in their duty of speaking no other language.

It was thoroughly understood by the Jesuits that motivation is the secret of successful teaching. Intrinsic interest, alas, was missing from the subject-matter of instruction; but there are other springs of work besides intrinsic interest. Of these, emulation is the most conveniently manipulated. Thus rivalry between individual pupils, sections of a class, whole classes, and in some cases even different schools was erected into an elaborate system. No doubt the rivalry was overdone; no doubt also it produced the desired results.

As to punishments, they were softened if not minimized. The

business of the Jesuit teacher was to win firstly the respect, and secondly the affection of his pupils, in order that his influence over them might be the greater. Rivalry was employed, therefore, in the promotion of discipline, and if the system of *aemuli* sometimes involved espionage, at least it tended to diminish offences, and to lessen the severity as well as the frequency of punishment. Offences were published weekly. Sometimes an offender was required to sit upon a separate form and to perform extra tasks until he should have found another more worthy of such a distinction. Prize-giving was managed better than at present. Frequently a class was divided into a number of groups, such that the members of each group had about the same ability, a prize being awarded to the best pupil in each group. We are told that in their teaching the Jesuits resorted to hundreds of devices, chiefly for the promotion of emulation. The individual pupil was studied, and a separate book kept to record his progress, mainly lest he might be overtasked or repelled by the work he was expected to do.

Such, indeed, was the superiority of the Jesuit schools that, even at a time when the echoes of religious strife still lingered, numbers of Protestant children were sent to learn of the Jesuits. The school hours were two and a half in the morning, and as much in the afternoon, with a whole holiday each week in summer and a half day in winter. Bacon, Ranke, and Grotius were generous enough to admire the success of the Jesuits in education. Voltaire and Lamarck were pupils of Jesuit schools whose lives go to show that individuality was not suppressed. More congenial to their teachers must have been the celebrity attained by other eminent pupils: the poets Calderon, Tasso, Goldoni, Molière; the eloquent Bossuet; the jurist Pothier; the scientists and historians Galileo, Cassini, Réaumur, Buffon, Lalande, Descartes, Muratori, and Du Cange.

The misconception that the modern Jesuit schools are still under the *Ratio Studiorum* of Aquaviva has been dispelled by Robert Swickerath in the *Cyclopedia of Education* (Monroe), vol. iii, p. 538. In the revised *Ratio Studiorum* of 1832, while Latin and Greek continued to be emphasized, it was provided that more attention and time should be given to the vernacular, and to history, science, and mathematics. Some of the modern Jesuit colleges have been expanded into universities conferring degrees in other faculties than arts. In 1906 the General Congregation of the Society decreed the complete abandonment of the portions of the *Ratio Studiorum* relating to the *material and arrangement* of the course of study in Jesuit Schools.

Judged by the ends they held in view, the Jesuit schools were profoundly successful, even according to the testimony of their bitterest foes; the ultimate cause of this success being, no doubt, that the teachers worked for no personal gain or reputation, but solely for what they conceived to be the greater glory of God.

VII

THE ENCYCLOPAEDIA OF ALSTED

JOHANN HEINRICH ALSTED, a theologian of the Reformed Church, the author of a vast body of theological, philosophical, and pedagogical works, and the master who, in many directions, exerted a profound influence upon the famous educator Comenius, was born in 1588 at Herborn, in Nassau. His father, a minister and teacher, devoted himself to his education until, at the age of fourteen, he was enrolled on the books of the gymnasium of his native town. This was at the time a famous school, having more than one hundred and fifty pupils. Its curriculum was devoted primarily to religious instruction and the study of the ancient languages, without neglecting arithmetic, music, and the mother tongue. Graduating as an accomplished Latinist, well-versed also in philosophy and theology, Alsted proceeded upon one of those academic journeys which were at the time regarded as the indispensable coping-stone to the education of a cultured scholar. Before returning home he had listened to the distinguished teachers of the day at Marburg, Frankfurt, Heidelberg, Strassburg, and Basle. Alsted now became a teacher in the High School at Herborn, where his amazing literary activity soon rendered his name illustrious throughout Germany, and procured for him the rank of extraordinary professor of philosophy. The youth of all the lands in which the reformed religion had taken root flocked to hear him, among others being Comenius, who owed to the youthful professor his first impulse towards didactic studies. In 1615 Alsted was promoted to be ordinary professor, and in 1618 was summoned to the Dordrechter Synod, at which the orthodox reformed theology won a signal victory over Arminianism.

In 1619 Alsted was appointed professor of theology. At this time the storms of the Thirty Years War devastated the land of Nassau, bringing plague and fire in their train. Knowing that the school at Herborn could never be maintained in the face of these disasters, in 1629 Alsted reluctantly obeyed a call to the conduct of a new academy at Stuhl-Weiszenburg. Here he continued to produce work upon work, and in spite of his untimely death on the 9th November 1638, he is ranked as one of the most prolific writers of any age.

Alsted was one of that noble-spirited band in whom the culture of antiquity, which had been made available by the scholars of the Renaissance, was happily united with the intense moral earnestness of the Reformation. Few had drunk more deeply at the springs of classical learning; few were more zealous in doctrinal disputation or more fervent in religious faith. Education was to Alsted at once a branch of human civilization and a handmaid of Divine truth. His *Universal Encyclopaedia*, in two folio volumes, published at Herborn in 1630, the most famous work of his pen, and an undertaking that has scarcely a parallel in the history of literature, includes a treatment of education which is not merely of interest as an illustration of the theory, but also of the practice of German education in that day. It is obvious that his books upon education, at least, were written with genuine love for the work and not in any perfunctory spirit. Alsted's Nassau writings include no fewer than one hundred and twenty volumes, several of which run to more than a thousand pages.

No one, not even Comenius, has left such an accurate account of the German schools of the seventeenth century as Alsted. Several years ago, having been fortunate enough to obtain a copy of his Latin *Encyclopaedia*, the present writer ventured to translate those parts of that monumental work which deal with education, partly in full, partly in an abridged form. The translation was published in a limited edition under the title of *A Neglected Educator—Johann Heinrich Alsted*. The most vital parts of Alsted's picture of the schools of his period are reproduced below. From them may be gathered precisely how both the vernacular and the classical schools were conducted.

'In lower or vernacular schools, be they rural or urban, or for boys or for girls, the teacher must be clad with patience like a corselet, and with humility and wisdom, and must teach the elements of piety, good conduct, and the reading and writing of the mother tongue. Girls are to be sent to the vernacular schools; but only those boys who will apply themselves to the mechanical arts. Boys whose parents are in such a station that they may hope for a more fruitful intellectual culture, ought to be sent not into the vernacular but into the Latin schools. The reason of this rule is that the time and effort spent in reading and writing the mother tongue is better devoted to reading and writing Latin. But there are these objections: 1. It often happens that inept minds are cut off from the more advanced studies. If, then, they have stayed a long time in Latin schools, and have afterwards been forced to leave, they will not even know how to read and write the mother tongue. 2. There is much profit in the legitimate reading and writing of the vernacular. The reply to the first objection is that there ought to be a selection of minds, to avoid what the fables tell us. A wolf sent to school could not be induced to say *a*; and when asked the reason for his refusal, replied that it was so that he would not have to say *b*. He was ordered to enunciate *pa* and *ter*. Asked what *p* and *a* made, he said *pa*; what *t*, *e*, and *r* made, *ter*; but when he was told to join together *pa* and *ter*, he said *agnus*. The answer to the second objection is that there is much truth in it, assuredly; yet all this can be easily learned almost in play, partly through the institution of the home, and partly through the connexion of the vernacular with the Latin tongue. Anyone who likes may dissent from me in this; I am only suggesting the plan which I should like to have followed by those whom I wish to be the best educated.

'In rural vernacular schools, boys and girls should be separated in different classes; in cities the schools for boys and girls should be distinct. In villages there are not enough children, nor is there wealth enough to have distinct schools for boys and girls. But boys and girls must be separated in different classes, because they will be petulant and naughty if they are seated promiscuously. But parish clerks may be put in charge of village schools if they are equal to the work. This has the advantage that the villagers will not be burdened with the payment of a salary; for the clerk has a salary, whatever it may be in each case, and a bonus may be added from the revenues of the church according to the wise opinion of Wilhelmus Zepperus. This was maintained in view of the decree of the Council of Constantinople VI, that presbyters teaching in rural districts or villages should take no fees from their pupils.

'As a rule girls will not learn Latin, because it is not only useless to them, but a great disadvantage, whether you look at the time that they uselessly pass in poring over it or the various opportunities and inducements to sinfulness which often arise from it. But noble women may learn it as an accomplishment.

'Children of five, that is to say, children beginning the fifth year, should be sent to the vernacular school; for when they have finished the fourth year the brain is strengthened and the voice articulated, and these are the needful foundations for what is prescribed in these schools.

'The mode of instruction in the vernacular schools depends on the following principles: 1. All the pupils should have copies of the same text. 2. No books are to be read at home except those which are explained at school. 3. The teacher should divide the book into fixed lessons, so that the pupil may know how soon he can finish his task. 4. Every passage should be read aloud by the teacher in a clear voice. 5. In repeating, one pupil should correct the other. 6. The teacher should win the attention of new pupils by small rewards. 7. The boys should attend the school four hours in the day, not more; and in the morning they should train their memory by learning off partly the elements of the Christian religion, partly notable texts of scripture and moral maxims, especially in rhyme. But in the afternoon they should learn to reproduce in written symbols, and to give an account of the acts of the whole day. 8. In reproducing, the fundamental letters mentioned already in the Grammar ought to come first; because he who can make them aright will easily learn the others. Speaking generally, this observation is exceedingly necessary in the case of all languages.'

In a subsequent chapter Alsted discusses the more dignified theme of classical or Latin schools. The following translation of his analysis may be of interest to students of the period.

'In intermediate and in higher schools there is the same sort of instruction, but a diversity of privileges. Here, then, we shall speak at the same time of the instruction given in the classical and in the public schools.

'Classical schools, which are presided over by a pedagogarch, or Rector of pedagogy, are those in which the minds of the pupils are imbued with a full knowledge of Latin and Greek, together with Music, Arithmetic, and a taste for Logic.

'Some of these subjects are general, others special.

'There are three general subjects in all classes. 1. Exercises of piety. 2. Composition, at least to the extent of accounts of the events of the day. 3. Relaxation of the mind.

'Special subjects are those belonging to each individual class as follows.

'In all there should be six classes, of which the three lower are called grammar, and the remaining three humanities. The latter are so called because they approach more adequately to the humane arts.

'In the lowest grammar class there is a double function to be discharged, in addition to those exercises of piety which, as we have said, ought to be common to all classes. The one concerns the alphabet, so that all the prerequisites for reading and writing Latin may be taught; the other the paradigms, so that the inflexions of nouns and the analogues or regular forms of verbs and also words belonging to the nomenclature of verse may be learned.

'In the second grammar class, which may be called the middle grade, the principles of etymology and syntax may be offered, together with Terence; and here, too, there should be grammatical variation, a copy of all the forms of grammatical composition. Here, also, should be taught the prerequisites for reading and writing Greek, and for inflecting irregular nouns and verbs. Lastly, a beginning should be made with music.

'In the highest grammar grade the application of the principles of Latin grammar in prose should be taught; both in analysis, though of Terence only, and in the beginning of exercises of composition, so that something may be translated each day from the vernacular into Latin, and again from Latin to the vernacular. Here, also, the principles of Greek grammar are to be set forth; and the elements of arithmetic, in addition to training in music.

'In the lowest "humanities" class, the elements of Latin rhetoric and poetry should be set forth; and the use of the Greek grammar may be demonstrated analytically in Demosthenes and Homer, and synthetically by exercises in Greek composition. Arithmetic and music should be more fully devloped in this class and the two following.

'In the middle "humanities" class, rhetorical and poetical exercises in Latin should flourish. The application of principles should be shown in the letters and easier orations of Cicero, and in the easier odes of Horace. Also the application of rhetoric and poetics should be made in Demosthenes and Homer.

'In the highest "humanities" class, the elements of logic are to be taught, the orations of Cicero and Demosthenes explained, and declamations written, together with various forms of verse, both in Latin and Greek, but especially in Latin.

'And indeed, this arrangement of classes is found almost everywhere.'

It must not be supposed that Alsted's discussion of schools is always prosaic. The subject lay, indeed, very near his heart, and it is fitting to conclude this introduction to his work by quoting a passage in which he gives full play to his eloquence and conviction, expressing an attitude in psychology and ethics in the highest degree characteristic of his time.

'Men are by nature like a *tabula rasa*, on which nothing is written, and on which anything you please may be inscribed. Therefore, O ye schools, inscribe the characters of piety and humanity! Man is by nature like a white line which can be given any colour. Tinge that white line with the vivid hue of honour! Men when first born into the light of day are like stones on which you may fashion any sort of figure. Ye schools, have therefore well-skilled sculptors, to remodel man, and remodel him as a progressive revelation of the image of God! Shatter gigantic audacity, restrain Cyclopean cruelty, discipline the Epicurean life. Ye are the stores and markets of useful learning, the seminaries of the Church, the armouries of the State, the nurseries of the family, the factories of piety, the mistresses of humanity, the fountains of honour, the sources of utility, the sinews of character and learning, the gardens of the Graces, and, in one word, the *Cornucopiae* of every kind of happiness. Happy the churches with which these homes of piety are allied! Happy the States in which these marts of Justices are opened wide! Happy this century of ours, when infinite advantages flow as it were from the locks of Apollo out of schools innumerable!'

A SELECT BIBLIOGRAPHY

A

Acton: *Cambridge History*, vol. i.—The Renaissance.
Ascham: *Scholemaster* (ed. Mayor).
Browning, O.: *Educational Theories* (Chap. 3).
Burckhardt: *The Civilization of the Renaissance in Italy.*
Campagnac and Forbes: *Sadoleto on Education.*
Castiglione: *The Courtier* (trans. Opdycke).
Elyot: *The Boke named the Gouvenour* (edited Croft).
Jebb: *Erasmus.*
—— *Humanism in Education.*
Kerr: *Scottish Education, Schools and Universities.*
Laurie: *Development of Educational Opinion Since the Renaissance.*
Leach: *Educational Charters.*
Lupton: *Life of John Colet.*
Lyte: *History of the University of Oxford.*
Montmorency: *History of State Intervention in English Education.*
Mulcaster: *Positions* (edited Quick).
Mullinger: *History of Cambridge University.*
Pater: *The Renaissance.*
Pattison, M.: *Essays.*
Paulsen: *German Education, Past and Present*, Bk. II.
Quick: *Educational Reformers* (Chap. 1.—The Renaissance).
Sandys: *Harvard Lectures on the Revival of Learning.*
Seebohm: *Oxford Reformers* (Chaps. I–VI).
Symonds: *Renaissance in Italy. The Revival of Learning.*
Watson: *Beginnings of Teaching of Modern Subjects in England.*
—— *English Grammar Schools to 1660.*
—— *Juan Luis Vives and the Renaissance Education of Women.*
—— *Tudor School Boy Life.*
—— *Vives on Education.*
Woodward: *Desiderius Erasmus, concerning the Aim of Education.*
—— In *Cambridge History of English Literature*—'English Universities, Schools and Scholarship in the Sixteenth Century'.
—— *Studies in Education During the Renaissance.*
—— *Vittorino da Feltre and other Humanist Educators.*

B

Adams: *Civilisation During the Middle Ages* (Chap. 15).
Allen: *The Age of Erasmus.*
Andrews: *Institutes of History* (Chap. 8).
Barnard: *German Teachers and Educators.*
—— 'Peter Ramus' (in *American Journal of Educ.*, vol. 30).
—— 'Renaissance in Italy' (from *Bernard's Journal*, vol. vii).
Beard: *Hibbert Lectures.*
Bevan: *Hellenism and Christianity.*
Blades: *William Caxton.*

Creighton: *The Early Renaissance in England.*
Drane: *Christian Schools and Scholars* (Chap. II).
Draper, J.: *History of the Intellectual Development of Europe* (vol. ii, Chap. 6).
Drummond: *Erasmus.*
Ducoudray: *History of Modern Civilisation* (Chaps. 9 and 10).
Duff: *Early Printed Books.*
Einstein: *The Italian Renaissance in England.*
Emerton: *Mediaeval Europe* (Chap. 13).
Field: *Introduction to the Study of the Renaissance.*
Grant: *History of the University of Edinburgh.*
Graves: *Peter Ramus and the Educational Renaissance of the Fifteenth Century.*
Guizot: *History of Civilisation* (vol. i, Chaps. 11 and 12).
Hamlyn: *Universities of Europe at Period of Reformation.*
Hazlitt: *Schools, School Books and School Masters.*
Jannsen: *History of the German People at the Close of Middle Ages.*
Keane: *The Evolution of Geography.*
La Croix: *Arts in the Middle Ages and at the Period of the Renaissance.*
Laurie: 'The Renaissance and the School' (in *School Review*, vol. iii).
Leach: *English Schools at the Reformation.*
Loomes: *Mediaeval Hellenism.*
Mark: *Educational Theories in England* (Chap. 2).
Michelet: *La Renaissance.*
Monroe, P.: *Thomas Platter and the Educational Renaissance of the Sixteenth Century.*
Oliphant: *Makers of Florence.*
—— *Makers of Venice.*
Owen: *Skeptics of the Italian Renaissance.*
Painter: *Great Pedagogical Essays*—Ascham.
Palgrave: 'The Oxford Movement in the Fifteenth Century' (in *Nineteenth Century*, vol. 28).
Pastor: *History of the Popes.*
Putnam: *Books and Their Makers* (vol. i, pp. 317–47).
Quick: *Educational Reformers*—Ascham.
Robbins: *Teachers in Germany in the Sixteenth Century.*
Robinson and Rolfe: *Petrarch* (Chaps. 1 and 2).
Rusk: *Doctrines of Great Educators.*
Russell: *German Higher Schools* (Chap. 2).
Scaife: *Florentine Life During the Renaissance.*
Schaff: 'The Renaissance and the Reformation' (in the *Evangelical Alliance for the United States*—Document 30).
Sedgwick: *Italy in the Thirteenth Century.*
Seignobos: *History of Mediaeval Civilisation.*
Stille: *Studies in the Mediaeval History* (Chap. 13).
Stowe: *English Grammar Schools in the Age of Queen Elizabeth.*
Tanner: *The Renaissance and the Reformation.*
Thurber: 'Vittorino da Feltre' (in *School Review*, vol. vii).
Walsh: *The Thirteenth, Greatest of Centuries.*
Whitcomb: *Source Book of the Renaissance* (vol. ii).
Williams: *History of Modern Education.*

BOOK V

SOME ASPECTS OF MODERN EDUCATIONAL THOUGHT

I

THE DIDACTIC METHODS OF COMENIUS

ON the 28th of March 1592 there was born at Nivnitz, in Moravia, the most enlightened educational theorist of the seventeenth century, John Amos Comenius. An Austro-Slav and member of the Moravian brethren, his life was full of the troubles common to his people and religion. Having lost his parents while still a child, Comenius was sent by his guardians to a folk-school, and at the late age of sixteen proceeded to a Latin school. At twenty he was a student under Alsted at Herborn in Nassau. Having begun Latin so late, he was able to see how bad were the traditional methods of teaching it. 'Ten years', he writes, 'are given to the study of the Latin tongue, and after all the result is disappointing.' Travel was by this time a recognized necessity for a scholar, and Comenius was enabled to spend some time at Amsterdam and at Heidelberg.

Before entering the ministry, Comenius served as Rector of the Moravian school at Prerau. As a pastor, he still retained the superintendence of a school, and having married, enjoyed two or three years of happiness, terminated only too abruptly by the Thirty Years War. His property and books were destroyed by the Spaniards. His temporary refuge became unsafe. He lost wife and child in 1622. Henceforth he wandered about the country, conducting his ministerial offices in secret. In the midst of adversity he still was able to think and even to write on education, to him what Gregory Nazianzen had called it, the art of arts.

At length flight became necessary. Comenius found protection at Lesna in Poland, whence he addressed Ratich and others on the subject of education, and completed the *Great Didactic*. In 1632 he was made bishop of the now scattered Moravians.

At the instance of Samuel Hartlib, whose whole life centred on projects of social reform, Comenius visited England, arriving on the 22nd of September 1641. An official invitation was extended him by the Long Parliament, and but for the Irish rebellion and the impending civil war, much might have been done towards the establishment of a college of sciences. At length a friend and patron of learning in Sweden, Ludovic de Geer, persuaded Comenius to go thither, full of ambitious projects for the reorganization of knowledge. The upshot was that the reformer was supported for six years by de Geer while he laboured upon didactic treatises at Elbing in Prussia. Comenius had not intended to forsake science for text-books, and frequently regretted that he had done so. Subsequently he was asked to re-organize education in Transylvania. Here practical experiments were made under his direction; but Comenius seems to have felt that by 1654 his work in Hungary was finished. He left the country in that year for Lesna, but calamity followed him, for in 1656 the town was destroyed, and with it his library and cherished manuscripts.

Finally the son of his old patron de Geer drew Comenius to Amsterdam. Here his didactic works were published in four folio volumes; and here he died on the 15th November 1671, at the ripe age of seventy-nine. The tribute of von Raumer is justifiable:

'Comenius is a grand and venerable figure of sorrow. Wandering, persecuted, and homeless, during the terrible and desolating Thirty Years War, he yet never despaired; but with enduring truth, and strong in faith, he laboured unweariedly to prepare youth by a better education for a better future. Suspended from the ministry, as he himself tells us, and an exile, he had become an Apostle *ad gentes minutulas—Christianam iuventutem*; and certainly he laboured for them with a zeal and love worthy of the chief of the Apostles.'

It is interesting to notice the debt of Comenius to several of his precursors. In Alsted he must have found a truly congenial spirit. The older teacher had the same religious enthusiasm, the same pansophic conception and the same educational aspirations as his more famous pupil. In the field of method, indeed, Alsted had suggested nothing as novel as the devices of Ratke, although his principles were decidedly sounder. The views of Ratke made a profound impression upon Comenius, who vainly endeavoured to conduct a correspondence with one who claimed to hold the secret of an easy path to languages. The work of Francis Bacon, with his pansophic outlook and his inductive method, had an even greater influence on Comenius than that of Ratke. Turning from Vives and Campanella, while acknowledging his debt to each, Comenius found in Bacon the inspiration for which he yearned. Here was true wisdom to be found. Comenius invented no new curriculum; but was content to retain the best of the classical writers. To this extent he was under the influence of the Renaissance. On the other hand, he seems to have preferred epitomes to original texts; and he certainly thought little of the humanistic motive by comparison with the religious. Further, he sought knowledge in the world of sense; whereas the humanists either concerned themselves with language alone, or at best with ideas obtained through the medium of language. Comenius, then, was no humanist; though his revolt was not immediately perceived as such, even by himself.

At heart Comenius believed that education could regenerate society. He did indeed write text-books; but his main interest lay not in these but in the reorganization of social knowledge and in the promotion of piety and virtue, as understood by his branch of the reformed religion. From infancy, he maintained, children are to be trained in godliness, always according to their capacity and by mild means. Such an education, united with the elements of all the sciences, might renew the kingdom of God upon earth. With this vision was coupled another, that of the unity of all the protestant states of Europe. Thus the writings of Comenius are tinged with a glowing fervour which added much to his contemporary influence.

Nor was Comenius unconscious of his mission as the first great sense-realist. Vives and Campanella, and especially Francis Bacon, had cleared the path to nature, and Comenius followed it. He abandoned the educational tradition of a thousand years, that the natural sciences should be studied incidentally to the classics. 'For', asks Comenius, 'do *we* not dwell in the garden of Nature as well as the ancients? Why should we not use our eyes, ears, and noses as well as they? And why should we need other teachers than these our senses to learn to know the works of Nature? Why, say I, should we not, instead of these dead books, lay open the living book of Nature, in which there is much more to contemplate than any one person can ever relate, and the contemplation of which brings much more of pleasure, as well as of profit?' Yet Comenius went too far in hoping that all things might be taught, at least in their elements, to all pupils. He was probably mistaken in the assumption that a thorough knowledge of nature is identical with wisdom.

Broad gaps are to be found in the knowledge of every man, however well taught he may be. Comenius reflected that this ought not to be so. If, he thought, each scientist knew something of all fields of knowledge, and if each made himself acquainted with what others are doing, then gaps and fallacies would disappear. All would know everything, at least in its elements. The essentials of universal education were a universal or pansophic method, and a college to work out such a method in its details. This ideal had been projected by Bacon, in the *New Atlantis*, and was shared by Milton and Locke, by Alsted and Diderot. Not only did Comenius write a number of treatises on pansophism; he also attempted to apply the pansophic method in the schools. For example, in his description of the school of infancy he shows that a child under six is already a student of all the sciences. The elements of metaphysics are learned in the terms something, nothing, is, is not, so, otherwise, where, when, like, unlike, &c. The beginning of physics is the recognition of water, earth, fire, rain, snow, ice, stone, iron, tree, grass, bird, ox, &c., and the parts of the body. The knowledge of light, darkness, and colours is rudimentary optics. The recognition of the sun, moon, and stars, with their rising and setting, is elementary astronomy. In this way Comenius goes on to establish the foundation of the whole gamut of the sciences in the period of infancy. Naturally, as he comes towards years of maturity the pansophic scheme becomes less satisfactory. It is clear to us now, though it was not to Comenius, that never again can there be an Aristotle; never again can one mind encompass the sum of human knowledge. Our universities try to represent knowledge not as individual, but as social; not as a completed system but as a body of related contributions.

In the *Great Didactic*, Comenius gave to the world the most elaborate, and at the same time the soundest system of general method that had ever seen the light of publication. Strange to say, the nominal basis of the whole is fallacious. The argument is based on natural analogies which are easily overthrown or confronted by counter-analogies. It is evident, however, that if the nominal basis of the method is natural, the real basis is in human experience. The methods have been first studied and tested, and afterwards forced into the form of alleged natural laws. This does not mean that Comenius was not in earnest in saying that to teach and learn surely we must first find the *modus operandi* of Nature, and accommodate ourselves to that. Had he said human nature, indeed, there would be found few to disagree with him.

According to the *Great Didactic*, method should proceed *certo* or quickly, *facile* or easily, and *solide* or thoroughly. Without following the details of the syncretic or anagogical method of Comenius, let us notice his main precepts. Above all, since knowledge comes through the senses, actual objects should be presented first, or when these are not procurable, pictures as like them as possible. Other principles of importance are fitness of time; fitness of pupil; preparation of material; one thing at a time; movement from within outwards, from general to special, step by step and perseveringly; avoidance of contraries; early beginnings; preparation of mind; movement from the easy to the difficult, not burdensomely but slowly, spontaneously, and with reference to present use; uniformity; due care for real advantage; no important omission; a solid and deep basis; accurate and articulated distinctions; continuity and correlation of studies; psychological arrangement and continual exercises.

The principal aim of the secondary schools of the day was to teach Latin, and in his *Novissima Linguarum Methodus* Comenius applied his general methods with important results. It was admitted by the thoughtful that progress in Latin was all too small for the time and pains bestowed upon it. Comenius pointed out three evils in the current methods. Firstly, Latin was taught abstractly; *necessitas* was learned before necessity was intelligible to the learner. Secondly, formal grammar, though quite incomprehensible to young pupils, was taught from the first. Thirdly, impossible leaps were attempted; a pupil proceeded directly from formal grammar to the *Eclogues* of Virgil.

To overcome these evils a number of methods had been attempted. Some, like Montaigne, had advocated conversation. Ascham had preferred a system of double translation. Melanchthon, however, had insisted on grammar. Caselius advocated much reading of authors and numerous written exercises. Ratich began with an author such as Terence, intelligible to boys. He introduced grammar only at the third reading, and then only incidentally. Lubinus advocated the use of pictures with descriptive Latin sentences. An Irish Jesuit at Salamanca printed a book containing Latin words in complete sentences, with a Spanish translation, and without repetitions. The last plan appealed to Comenius, and in 1631 appeared a similar but improved book of his own, the *Janua Linguae Latinae Reserata*, which was widely welcomed and translated into a number of languages. This book was afterwards supplemented by a *Vestibulum*, intended to precede it, and an *Atrium*, intended to complete it. The three were to lead up to the *Palatium*, or Palace of authors.

A better and still more popular text-book than any of these was the famous *Orbis Pictus*, or 'The World Illustrated'. This book contained a series of engravings, together with a description of them in both Latin and German. Comenius also wrote other texts, including a dreary school drama in Latin, and a text-book in Latin-Greek. The faults of attempting too much, and avoiding the repetition of words, limit the positive value of these books; but they represented not only an advance upon the printed materials of the time, but even an improvement upon many of the text-books now in use in the majority of classical schools.

II

LOCKE'S 'THOUGHTS CONCERNING EDUCATION'

AS an educationist, John Locke represents the best English tendencies of his time. Born near Bristol in 1632, he was the son of an eminent jurist, and received the scholastic education of the day at Westminster School and subsequently at Oxford. Turning away from scholasticism to the philosophy of Descartes, he interested himself in medical and scientific pursuits. Driven into exile under Charles II, Locke used to correspond at some length upon educational subjects, and after his return to England the letters were edited and published. They were concerned exclusively with a matter of which he had practical knowledge, the rearing and education of boys of the upper classes under the conditions of English tutelage. For a time Locke himself had acted as tutor to the son of the great statesman Shaftesbury.

Although indebted to Quintilian and to the other precursors, Locke had a mind cast in the modern mould, liberal in views, common-sense in outlook. His *Some Thoughts concerning Education* begins with an endorsement of the classical theory: 'A sound mind in a sound body is a short but full description of a happy state in this world.' In estimating the power of education he went farther than Erasmus, and almost as far as Helvetius, who claimed that education can do everything. 'I imagine', writes Locke, 'the minds of children as easily turned this or that way, as water itself.' With regard to the body he adds: 'Our bodies will endure anything that from the beginning they are accustomed to.' Too sound and cautious to be always the adherent of any one abstract theory, Locke was nevertheless a disciplinarian who regarded education as essentially a process of training. To him it was less the content than the form of education that matters. The process of 'filling the mind' is the logical antithesis of his procedure, which was not to fill but to shape the mind. Locke held, however, that the essential principle of education is to effect all changes by slow degrees.

Locke's theory of bodily training is somewhat ascetic. His regimen includes bathing in cold, even ice-cold water, swimming, life in the open air, exposure to the sun, even without a hat, absence of strait-lacing and pinching by clothes, simple food, with meat but once a day, avoidance of spice or too much salt, spare diet, small beer (but never wine or strong drink), and then only after eating, little fruit and that well ripened, early rising and early retiring, abundance of sleep but to be gradually reduced to eight hours, hard beds made in different ways, as little use of medical drugs as possible, with reliance rather upon regular habit than upon medicine for the maintenance of good digestion and of general health. While some of his views appear drastic, for example the wearing of thin and leaky boots, and the practice of taking meals at irregular hours, a certain common sense precludes extremes, so that he would avoid the sudden chills that may arise from resting on the damp ground after exercise, or the reduction of sleep to an unreasonable degree.

'As the strength of the body lies chiefly in being able to endure hardships, so also does that of the mind.' Discipline should begin early, the great mistake is in the neglect of beginnings. Such also had been the view of Erasmus. People humour and indulge children; and later are surprised to find them perverse and unruly. Rousseau, who read and criticized Locke, enlarged upon this dictum, which had been expressed both by Erasmus and by the ancient Roman satirists. The young must indeed have desires and appetites, but must develop the power to govern and rule them. Too often they learn to be vain and proud of clothes, to use lies and equivocation, to regard eating and drinking as the main purposes of life, and to consider luxury as a good. 'The principle of virtue and excellency lies in a power of denying ourselves the satisfaction of our own desires, where reason does not authorize them.' Children, in fact, are not to have what pleases them; but what is thought fit for them. Locke has little of the confidence which Rousseau and Froebel were to manifest in the principles of child nature. 'Fear and awe ought to give you the first power over their minds, and love and friendship in riper years to hold it.' But surely the transition is both difficult and, in a measure, unnecessary.

Together with almost every serious educational thinker, Locke condemns the abuse of corporal punishment. 'Great severity of punishment does very little good, nay, great harm in education; and I believe it will be found that, *ceteris paribus*, those children who have been most chastised, seldom make the best men.' Awe is useful only to procure ready obedience; the spirit must not be abased and broken, for low spirits seldom attain to anything. The rod teaches children to govern their actions merely according to sensual pleasure or pain, and breeds an aversion to learning. 'A slavish discipline makes a slavish temper.' Sensual rewards such as apples or sugar-plums, or monetary rewards, are equally undesirable.

Yet rewards and punishments are necessary, though they are commonly of the wrong kind. They may be such as to change the external act; but not the inward appetite. Esteem and disgrace are preferable. Praise and coldness must be skilfully employed, and should have other agreeable or disagreeable concomitants. Difficulties may arise through the folly of servants. It is true that reputation is not the true principle of virtue; yet it lies nearest to the sense of duty, which is the true principle. In general, praise ought to be administered in public, blame in private.

Locke had very little conception of the great educational significance that lies in childish play. It is, however, a thing to be tolerated. 'Innocent folly, playing and childish actions are to be left perfectly free and unrestrained, so far as they can consist with the respect due to those that are present.' There is much misapplied and unnecessary correction. Few rules should be laid down, and those fixed rather by repetition and practice than by punishment for infractions. The individual must be studied. 'He therefore that is about children should well study their natures and aptitudes, and see by often trials what turns they easily take, and what becomes them.' It would seem that children's minds are no longer as easily dirigible as water.

The treatment of affectation is reminiscent of Castigilone. Plain, rough nature is better than affectation, which is an acquired fault, due to mistaken education, and to be remedied by practice under supervision until it shall give place to habitual, becoming ease.

Manners may be learned better from example than by precept. Dancing is to be commenced as early as possible, since it promotes not only grace of bearing, but manliness of thought. This no doubt was peculiarly true of the stately dances of the period. Lack of outward civility, however, matters little, provided that the inward will be civil. Time will cure minor faults, if only the veneration of parents and teachers, with respect and goodwill towards others, be implanted in the youthful mind. Even carelessness, when unaccompanied by pride or ill nature, may very well be tolerated. Children imitate their company, as the chameleon takes on itself the colour of surrounding objects. Consequently, care is necessary lest the character of children be marred by the flattery of idle or vicious servants. Children should be much in the company of their parents. Lest this condition induce constraint, let them have every liberty except to do wrong; but let them never accept gifts and favours from other than a parent's hand. No influence is as great as that of company.

'Virtue is harder to be got than a knowledge of the world, and if lost in a young man, is seldom recovered.' Before a boy leaves his father's house, the principles and practice of virtue and good breeding should be implanted in him. Locke prefers a tutor to a school. The latter produces pertness and confidence among boys; but the home-taught boy is more companionable in the society of grown men. It may be observed that Locke never rises beyond the conception that education is a preparation for life; he fails to see it as a part of life as well worth while as any other, hence to be regarded somewhat as an end in itself. The parent, as Juvenal and others had indicated, must himself reverence his son, by setting a careful and good example in his own conduct.

There is no wiser advice in the *Thoughts concerning Education* than to study children's inclinations, to avoid setting learning as a task, to induce the children to ask their tutor to teach them. The rod then has little place. Frequent chiding will be equally unnecessary. Locke holds, perhaps inconsistently, that beating is the punishment for stubbornness, whatever the number of blows a victory may cost. He admits indeed that blows do great harm unless the mind be reached and bent. Cannot this be done in a more economical way? He is wrong in regarding blows as the corrective of a faulty attitude of will, nor is there much grace in the proviso that the beating should be done by another than the parent, and not immediately after the offence.

Locke, however, gladly returns to his main thesis. The true way of dealing with children is to reason with them. This theory was soon to be challenged by Rousseau. The reasoning must of course be obvious. Beating is the fashion of the schools; but why should it be needed for Latin and Greek, when it is seldom applied for other subjects? Milder methods should be thoroughly tried. Surely, if a few beatings do not succeed, where is the sense of continuing the practice?

From earliest childhood, let the boy at whatever care or cost have a good governor or tutor, who is to be treated respectfully by the parents, although not permitted to use corporal punishment without the latter's consent. Locke is not of Plato's opinion, that children should know only what is good. Send not the boy into the world without a compass; let him learn of its evils, without taking evil to himself. The tutor should know the world. As soon as possible, moreover, the father should treat his son as a man. Commands and captious logic will be discarded for friendly talk.

Young children love dominion, whether to have their own way, or to possess objects. Satisfy all wants of nature; but not wants of fancy, except as to recreation, which is 'as necessary as labour or food'. Children may indeed be permitted to surfeit themselves with recreation, but not with useful pursuits, for which it is desirable that an appetite should remain. Listen not to trivial complaints. Teach children to vie in liberality, not in selfishness. Crying is to be discouraged; but its various sources should be discriminated. The constant appeal is to common sense.

Avoid sudden frights, which produce timorousness. Gradually and carefully accustom the young to objects which they fear. Inure children gently and in good humour to suffer some degree of pain without complaint—a modified Lacedaemonian theory. If signs of cruelty appear the contrary usage should be taught. Mischief not due to ill nature may be passed over; ill-natured mischief must be watched and early remedied. Curiosity, being an appetite after knowledge, should be encouraged, and children's questions deserve to be seriously answered. Children should no more be deluded than a stranger who makes inquiries of his way. Some questions by children are novel and stimulating. Mere pertness is less desirable than the tendency to reason about things which come in their way, which is commonly but unfairly stigmatized as inquisitiveness. Listlessness is far more serious; but a child who is merely listless about learning, while otherwise active, may be readily cured. First the mischief may be explained to him; failing improvement he may be shamed on account of his laziness; this remedy also failing, he should be required to play, and not be permitted to learn, until his appetite be sated. If listlessness be general, work upon the strongest desire you can find in his disposition, until a more general foresight and desire shall have been cultivated. Manual work may be the means of leading up to intellectual occupation. Children love freedom, therefore let their lessons be free. They hate to be idle, therefore satiate them with useless activities until they come to prefer those that are useful. Require a boy to whip his top so many hours a day, and let him look forward to his book as a recreation when the task is done. This device, it may be objected, is indirect and highly artificial—what boy would not see through it? Children should be allowed to use but one plaything at a time; and so far as possible should make all the playthings themselves. Thus will they be taught 'moderation in their desires, application, industry, thought, contrivance, and good husbandry'.

The child's first lie should be wondered at as a monstrous thing; the second should bring sharp displeasure. If premeditated lies continue, they should be treated as obstinacy, by blows. Excuses should be met by shame rather than by roughness; but full confession should bring immunity, that this practice may be encouraged.

The essentials in the education of a gentleman's son are (1) virtue, (2) wisdom, (3) breeding, (4) learning. Locke does not contemplate universal education, or suggest a system of education for the masses; but most of his precepts apply generally. It was at a later stage of his career that he interested himself in a project for workhouse schools.

(1) A true notion of God should be early implanted, and a plain form of morning and evening prayer adopted; but no thoughts of other spirits, no unintelligible notions, need be introduced. Children should not hear of goblins or bugbears. Naturally, they will fear the dark no more than the light. It is, however, doubtful, Locke notwithstanding, whether children do not instinctively fear the dark. It only remains to cultivate truth and good nature.

(2) Cunning, being only the ape of wisdom, should be discouraged. 'To accustom a child to have true notions of things, and not to be satisfied till he has them; to raise his mind to great and worthy thoughts, and to keep him at a distance from falsehood and cunning, which has always a broad mixture of falsehood in it, is the fittest preparation of a child for wisdom.'

(3) The essentials of good breeding are 'not to think meanly of ourselves, and not to think meanly of others'. Sheepish bashfulness can only be cured by variety and change of company, 'and that of persons above us'. Young people must abstain from roughness, contempt or want of respect, from censoriousness, raillery, contradiction, captiousness or ceremoniousness. They should avoid interruption, magisterial correction, wrangling and warmth of dispute. 'The tincture of company sinks deeper than the outside.'

(4) Learning is a secondary matter; indeed Latin and Greek may be had at 'a great deal cheaper rate of pains and time, and be learned almost in playing'. 'I have always had a fancy that learning might be made a play and recreation to children.' Locke describes, somewhat after the manner of Quintilian and Erasmus, but perhaps in a more practical way, how children may play themselves into reading and

spelling. Aesop's *Fables* and *Reynard the Fox* are suitable primers for reading. Reading should be suited to the child's capacity and notions, hence the promiscuous reading of the Bible as a primer is educationally unsound, although some part may be read to advantage.

Writing seasonably follows the ability to read. Positions of pen, paper, and body must be practised. Tracing with black ink upon a large hand engraven in red ink is recommended. Exercises on fair paper follow.

Drawing follows the art of writing. Logically and historically one may comment, drawing takes the precedence. So much should be learned of perspective and drawing as to enable the pupil 'to represent tolerably on paper anything he sees, except faces'. Do not harass the boy who has no talent for drawing. *Nil invita Minerva.* Shorthand is recommended, without being essential.

'As soon as he can speak English, 'tis time for him to learn some other language.' French is proposed before Latin, because it is taught, as Latin indeed should be taught, as a living language. 'Latin I look upon as absolutely necessary to a gentleman.' On the other hand, the custom of teaching Latin to boys who are to engage in trade, and who will never use, but will speedily forget it, is deprecated strongly. Grammar-school methods are bad; the boy should 'have Latin, as English has been, without the perplexity of rules, talked to him'. If the direct method be used, the boy will learn so much more readily that he may at the same time master some part of geography, astronomy, chronology, anatomy, history, and even geometry. Locke speaks with some admiration, although to-day little would be felt, for a young gentleman 'bred something after this way, able to demonstrate several propositions in Euclid before he was thirteen'.

Next to conversation, Locke recommends the writing of a literal English translation of a simple Latin work, such as one of Aesop's fables, in one line, with the corresponding Latin words just above it in another line. This the pupil reads over and over, using it also as a copy in writing. The plan, which indeed had been employed by the Anglo-Saxon Ælfric before the Norman Conquest, necessitates learning a certain minimum of grammar. It is better to help a boy straightway than to waste time by bidding him to find out the correct form for himself. The latter may be a controversial question; but as regards language Locke is to a great extent right. Rebukes and corrections distract a child from his lesson. 'The great skill of a teacher is to get and keep the attention of his scholar.' Boys who are reading Latin authors should be permitted the use of translations; for rote learning is the necessary method of mastering language. Who does not speak English by rote?

'If grammar ought to be taught at any time, it must be to one who can speak the language already.' Latin themes and verses are practically useless and on the whole ridiculous. Learning long passages *memoriter* is of no advantage at all. Memory may be exercised in more profitable ways, as by learning wise sentences.

Geography should be confined at first to a study of the natural parts of the globe. Upon this method Rousseau greatly improved. As to arithmetic, 'a man cannot have too much of it, nor too perfectly'. It is the first sort of abstract reasoning to which the mind is commonly accustomed, and is of general use.

The materials of higher education are briefly reviewed. Astronomy should include a knowledge of the constellations of the hemisphere, followed by an account of the Copernican system and the situation and distances of the planets from the sun. In geometry, the first six books of Euclid are enough; beyond this a man may go himself, if he so please. Geography and chronology, the latter implying a review of the whole course of time, are vital to history. 'As nothing teaches, so nothing delights more than history.' Ethics may be taught by practice rather than by precept, until the youth is of an age to appreciate Cicero, *de officiis*. Subsequently the young man should read Grotius or Puffendorf upon Civil Law; and should study the English constitutions, history and statutes.

Rhetoric and logic are to be had in the shortest systems that can be found; since the arts of speaking and reasoning well are not attained by the study of rules, but by careful practice.

Style may be practised by setting children to tell a story, and by correcting the 'most remarkable fault they are guilty of in their way of putting together'. When they can tell the tales well, it is time for them to write them. Letter writing is so necessary that it must be practised; Cicero's letters being the best pattern whether for business or for conversation. English should be studied and laboured upon more critically than either Latin, Greek, or any other language.

Natural philosophy deals with spirits and bodies. Concerning the former, a good history of the Bible is to be desired. Concerning bodies, books like those of Boyle, concerned with observations and experiments, are preferable to those containing merely speculative systems. There exist few such admirable treatises on Natural Philosophy as that of Newton upon the planetary system.

'No man can pass for a scholar that is ignorant of the Greek tongue.' Greek, however, is not necessary to a gentleman as such. Meanwhile, the pupil should study the adaptation of method to subject; for example, the order of time is suited to history, while progression from one place to the next is the order of nature, and of the mind's own activity.

Dancing is of value to promote a graceful carriage; but to music is attributed the last place among accomplishments. Fencing and 'riding the great horse' are looked upon as essential to breeding; but the former exercise is deprecated in so far as it may be conducive to quarrelling.

'I would have him learn a trade, a manual trade'—even two or three, but one particularly. Gardening and joinery are especially desirable, giving valuable skill and ample exercise. Recreation consists not in idleness, but in change of occupation. Play itself indicates 'that men cannot be perfectly idle'. Moreover all gentlemen are advised to learn merchants' accounts.

The period of travel, with which education is commonly concluded, should come either while one is still under tutelage, or else when of mature age. Yet it is commonly ordered otherwise. Locke points out that his treatise is intended for those who prefer to consult their own reason in the education of their children, rather than to rely wholly upon established custom.

In general Locke emphasizes discipline. The disciplinary theory of education has found expression in all periods of conscious civilization. It is, essentially, the theory that it does not matter so much what one learns, as how one learns; and further, that in learning any one thing there is developed a general capacity which tends to apply itself to widely different matters. While these views are to be found in the most ancient of European writers, they did not become the very foundation of schooling until the seventeenth century. At that time several causes contributed to the supremacy of the disciplinary conception of education, especially in the secondary schools.

1. The humanists had emphasized not only the form, but also the practical value of the classical writings. Soon, however, the question of practical value took a new turn. Translations of the classics made a knowledge of the originals less necessary than in the Renaissance period to the making of an educated man. The content and form of vernacular writings had come to equal and almost to surpass those of the classics. French was beginning to supplant Latin as an international language. The humanists, therefore, deprived of their

strongest argument for a purely classical education, looked about for another. They found it ready to hand in the theory of formal discipline. Latin and Greek, if no longer essential to knowledge, might still be the best instruments for the training of the mind.

2. Scholastic inertia tended to perpetuate the reign of the classics. Schoolmasters had studied little else themselves; for other fields they possessed no suitable implements, no stock of perfected methods, no established course of study. This argument, however weak in logic, was potent in practice.

3. Moreover the disciplinary theory of education harmonized with the current theories of religion and psychology. The religious conception of the natural depravity of man and the psychological theory of innate faculties alike suggested that the process of training the young is more important than the knowledge content which they may acquire.

4. Nor was the theory of education as discipline out of harmony with the prevalent social ideals. The classics not only provided a mental training for the leaders, but also established a clear differentiation between the upper classes and the masses. Locke's theory of hardening, derived from classical authorities, may be regarded as a special application of education through discipline. In the time of Locke the qualities of orderliness and soldierly obedience were still of the highest social significance.

5. The practical success of many of the classical schools, notably those of the Jesuits, supplemented these theoretical considerations by the argument *ad experientiam*. As the history of British India proved, men trained in Latin grammar were by no means inefficient in the arts of war and government.

6. It was sometimes maintained that even if learning the ancient languages is a task disagreeable to boyhood, so much the better. One cannot begin too soon to thwart the appetites. Only by doing disagreeable things is the power to do such things perfected. In more recent times the rejoinder has been made that life provides enough opportunities for such an exercise without the manufacture of unnecessary occasions; and further, that more work, not less, is likely to be produced when interest supplements effort.

In the *Conduct of the Understanding* Locke emphasized the part played by the 'perception of the intellect' in the process of constructing complex ideas out of the raw material which has been furnished to the mind by the senses. The educational process should consist mainly in the discipline of the perception of the intellect. Similarly there should be a discipline of the body, of the feelings, and of the social activities. The great aim is the formation of good habits; and the development of the *reason* at the expense of the *appetites*. The acquisition of knowledge is a secondary matter, and may be trusted, within limits, to look after itself.

III

THE 'ÉMILE' OF ROUSSEAU

'EVERYTHING is good as it comes from the hands of the Author of Nature; but everything degenerates in the hands of man.' Thus runs the fundamental thesis of the Swiss reformer Rousseau (1712–78), author of that strange eighteenth-century charter of educational liberties, *Émile* (1762). Man, he maintained, mutilates everything; changes everything according to his own fancy. As plants are formed by cultivation, so men are formed by education. This education is derived from Nature, from men, or from things. Nature is independent of ourselves, things are partly independent, but the human element, that is to say, the tutor, is mainly in our own power to provide. Nature, we are informed, is nothing but habit. It should be observed that when Rousseau speaks of Nature, he generally, although not consistently, implies inborn faculty. He is not far wrong in regarding Nature, for purposes of education, as equivalent to inborn habit.

We cannot, he maintains, fashion a man and a citizen at the same time. Frequently our primitive dispositions are opposed to social institutions. The latter tend to make people unnatural, leading them astray from their absolute, primitive humanity. In practice, the process of education may be either public or private. Public education may be seen in an ideal form in Plato's *Republic*; it does not exist in reality. How can there be a civic training where no country exists? We cannot regard as a system of public instruction 'those ridiculous establishments called colleges'. Domestic or private education, which implies training a man for himself solely, is idle without a study of the natural man.

In order to form a natural man, the chief necessity is to prevent anything from being done. For many years education must be negative, and instruction must be banished. 'To live is the trade I wish to teach him.'

'Civilized man is born, lives and dies in a state of slavery. At his birth he is stitched in swaddling-clothes; at his death he is nailed in his coffin; and as long as he preserves the human form he is fettered by our institutions.' Let him alone. The old idea that a nurse moulds the child's head to a better form is ridiculous. Nature does not coddle.

According to Rousseau, experience shows that there are more deaths among children delicately reared than among others. Hardening is recommended, even if it should involve some degree of risk. We command, or obey, or punish a child, and thus implant evil passions in him. There is weight in the comment that after having taken the trouble to make him bad, we complain of finding him such.

The father is the best guardian of his son, but claims that he is too busy. Rousseau therefore proposes to provide the boy with a tutor, himself. Preferably the tutor should be a young man; the child loves youth, and another child, if he could have the necessary wisdom, would make the best tutor of all. 'Children sometimes flatter old people, but they never love them.'

Education begins before birth; and is a continuous process. There should be but one tutor who should have charge of the boy for about twenty-five years. The tutor will be, however, a governor rather than a preceptor; but these two functions are really inseparable. 'The master ought not to give precepts, but should cause his pupil to find them.' Émile may honour his parents, but he is to obey his tutor alone.

It is assumed that Émile is healthy; you cannot teach any one to live whose only care is not to die. 'The most useful part of medicine is hygiene.' Even when physicians cure the body, they destroy courage. This part of the discussion mostly follows Plato, *Republic*, iv. Cities are condemned as the graves of the human species. John Locke's theory of hardening by bathing in water of different temperatures is approved. The use of swaddling-clothes is condemned. In education, experience precedes lessons. More knowledge is gained from experience than from scholarship; but such knowledge is commonly taken for granted, and is scarcely realized.

In general, the child should not be allowed to contract fixed habits. When he can distinguish objects, choose those which are to be presented to him. The suggestion of Locke is followed, that he should be gradually accustomed to ugly objects, so that he may not grow to regard them with fear. In this way ugly faces, firearms, and other formidable things will lose their terrors. If the child should cry, remove the cause of his discomfort. With Locke, Rousseau mistrusts the company of servants. Outbursts of petulance and anger are provoked not by things, but by restraint imposed by the will of others. Children of the upper classes suffer the most from restrictions, and are seldom as robust or as independent as children of the common people. 'The first tears of children are prayers, and unless we are on our guard they will soon become orders.' Do not encourage a child to complain or to command either people or things; hence if he wants an object, it is better to carry him to it than to give it to him.

The moral comments of Rousseau are always interesting, if not invariably convincing. 'When Hobbes called a rogue a robust child, he said a thing absolutely contradictory. All wickedness comes from weakness. He who can do everything does nothing bad.' At this point Dr. Payne, in his translation of the *Émile*, ironically remarks: 'Nero and Charles V, for example!' Yet such tyrants as these were not omnipotent, and it ought to be sufficiently clear that the reference is to the Almighty, since our author adds: 'Of all the attributes of the omnipotent Divinity, goodness is the one which we can spare from his conception with the greatest difficulty.'

According to Rousseau, reason alone can teach us to know good from evil. He rightly points out that before the age of reason there is no morality in our actions; but what then is the age of reason? Children are able to reason about matters lying wholly within their own experience at a very early age, certainly long before twelve, the age of reason which Rousseau appears to have in mind. Yet the educational application made by the reformer may be sound; the child is destructive not because he is bad but because he is active. In this element of activity the weakness of a child differs fundamentally from the weakness of old age. Since the child is at the same time weak and active, he looks to others for aid in his undertakings. It is necessary for him to learn, however, to limit his desires to his powers to satisfy them, and to exact less from other people. Parents and teachers are far from realizing this. In practice, the child's every wish and slightest muttering is met more than half-way. We should anticipate his real needs; but pay no heed to his crying. We should not stun his ear with many words; but let him hear few, distinct articulations. The children of the peasantry are better trained in these respects than those of the upper classes. Doubtless country people may articulate too strongly and roughly; but this is preferable to the affected speech of the city. The advice of Rousseau is to limit the vocabulary of the child, that he may not possess more words than he has ideas. It is doubtful, however, whether in practice the child ever has enough words to express adequately his mental operations.

Hitherto the discussion has concerned itself with infancy; but attention is now turned to the period from five to twelve years. Speaking must now replace crying. If not answered until he stops, Émile will soon utter but one cry. The tutor will remain unmoved by minor hurts or accidents; Émile must learn to suffer, and with reasonable discretion on the tutor's part he can do himself little harm.

Rousseau vigorously condemns what he calls the pedantic mania for instruction. To teach a child to walk, for example, does no good; but may do harm. Let him play freely out of doors. As he grows in power and knowledge, he should be treated as a moral being. Be humane; do not sacrifice his present to a future which he may never live to reach. This idea represents a most important departure from the theories of the past; and Rousseau does not fail to drive it home with vehemence and effect.

'Keep the child dependent upon things alone, and you will have followed the order of nature in his education.' If his actions must be checked, let the opposition come from natural obstacles or punishments, not from any arbitrary force. Rousseau is undoubtedly right in the view that much obedience is needlessly demanded; and much control needlessly exerted. Yet it is probable that, notwithstanding his contention, children should be trained to obey the proper authorities implicitly. It is no doubt the duty of these authorities to respect natural laws. Thus a child should not be compelled to keep still when he desires to move, nor to move when he desires to remain quiet. Tears and entreaties should not be encouraged; and should not be allowed to prevail where words do not. The tutor should not be prodigal in refusals, but should never recall them. The imperiousness of children when veiled in polite terms may become worse than vulgar rudeness.

Avoid excess either of severity or indulgence. Man's nature requires small evils; that it may appreciate great blessings. He who has not suffered knows neither tenderness nor pity.

One cannot, if one would, give a child everything that he desires. The habit of domineering brings only rebuffs; let it not be encouraged in the young, to whom it is peculiarly unsuitable, since they are so helpless. On the other hand, the child should have liberty, lest he become timorous. Émile should not do anything from obedience; but everything from necessity. Do not tell him to obey, or to do his duty, until the age of reason is reached. Locke is deemed to be wrong in advocating reasoning with children. Let the child simply act from force of circumstances. Situations can be manipulated in such a way as to produce the desired results.

'Nature would have children be children before being men.' This is perhaps Rousseau's most practical suggestion towards educational reform. Insistence on obedience means force and threats on the one part, insincerity and evasion on the other. 'Treat your pupil according to his age.' Let him realize the force of necessity, but not that of authority. Substitute well-regulated liberty for the ordinary educational instruments—'emulation, jealousy, envy, vanity, covetousness, and debasing fear'.

Rousseau assumes that morality depends upon experience; and that there is no innate sense of right and wrong. He therefore condemns punishment, or insistence upon apology, on the ground that a child is a non-moral being. Village children, although often needlessly thwarted, are freer than little gentlemen, and are better to be trusted when the opportunity for licence occurs.

The most useful and important rule of education is not to gain time, but to lose it. 'They must do nothing with their soul until it has all its faculties.' The rejoinder is that the mind cannot be trained *in vacuo*. Rousseau does not really want this; but only that the mind should ripen naturally and without being forced. 'The first education, then, ought to be purely negative.' This generalization leads up to the cynical maxim: 'Take the very reverse of the current practice, and you will almost always do right.' Hence the tutor must hasten slowly. Let him exercise the pupil's body, his organs, his senses and his powers, but keep his soul lying fallow as long as he possibly can. By watching, too, the tutor will learn the particular genius of the child; and will thus learn how to treat him. 'The physician who is in too great haste, kills.'

The tutor must himself become a man, must gain respect and love, not by money or gifts but by opening his heart. The village will contain fewer attractive forms of vice, and will offer a better opportunity for the control of Émile's environment than the city. Long streams of conversation by teachers are not apprehended, and are distorted by the child's mind. If the headstrong child does mischief, let him suffer the natural consequences. If he break a window, let him feel the inconvenience of the weather, if he break it again, put him in a room without windows. It is, however, more than doubtful whether such a plan could be universally adopted without inhumanity; but perhaps wherever it can, it is best. Falsehood will involve no other punishment but to be disbelieved. Under the system proposed, Rousseau believes, Émile will be unlikely to lie; since lies will not be suggested to him by questions as to his conduct; nor will he feel dependent upon the wills and judgements of others. As Morley has pointed out, the independence is only apparent; but of this fact Rousseau was well aware.

If you want a child to be liberal, teach him to give away things which are dear to him. Locke is criticized for the view that children should be taught that the most liberal are the best rewarded. 'This is to make a child liberal in appearance; but avaricious in fact.'

Apparent stupidity is sometimes a sign of a strong mind, as in the case of the younger Cato. For this reason the teacher should respect childhood, not judging it hastily either for good or for evil. Allow time for nature to act. 'You are alarmed at seeing him consume his early years in doing nothing! Really! Is it nothing to be happy? Is it nothing to jump, play, and run, all the day long?' Rousseau suggests that the Greeks and Romans wasted time in this sense; and were none the worse for it. It may easily happen that the apparent ease with which children learn may become their undoing. They retain words rather than ideas. No doubt in the eighteenth century this was the peculiar danger of the Latin schools. Since children retain sounds, forms, and sensations, but rarely ideas, they have no real memory. It may be urged that this is an exaggeration; children have the type of memory which is proper to childhood. Strictly speaking, indeed, they cannot retain sensations as such; whereas they do retain a great number of ideas, although they naturally have a less abstract kind of memory than adults. It is a gross libel upon the child mind to affirm, as does Rousseau, that all their knowledge is in sensation, nothing having penetrated to the understanding. Moreover, although it may be true that children's knowledge is easily confounded, this is partly because the teacher's prestige makes them ready to take seriously even a trivial or foolish remark which comes from such a quarter; and partly because they are aware of the relative limitation of their own knowledge.

Rousseau perceives that children reason well enough about things which they know; and is right in supposing that we misunderstand the limits of their knowledge, and too often expect reason without laying a foundation for it in experience. This principle, that sense experience should wherever possible precede reason, is fundamental. It was even truer in Rousseau's day than in our own, that 'All the premature studies of these unfortunates relate to objects entirely foreign to their minds.' Had the modern kindergarten existed, Rousseau might consistently have praised it; as it was he anticipated many of Froebel's theories. Education in his day was much as he described it: 'Words, words, nothing but words.'

A vigorous condemnation of verbalism leads up to the criticism of languages, which according to Rousseau have no place among primary studies. Children, he aptly remarks, may use five or six vocabularies, but they have only one language. They are instructed chiefly in dead languages, the remains of which are imitated. When they claim to speak these languages there is none to contradict them. Moreover, 'Representative signs are of no account without the idea of the things represented.' Hence geography and history are taught before they are intelligible. The child's mind is plastic; but should not be misused by engraving upon it the names of kings, dates in history, terms in heraldry, astronomy, and geography. Let Émile remember what he sees and hears. Is there any reason, however, one may ask, why what he hears should not include such of the material above indicated as can be related to his interests, or as may be indispensable to his intellectual progress. 'Émile shall never learn anything by heart.' This dictum represents a pardonable reaction against the practice of the eighteenth-century schools. 'All children are made to learn the fables of La Fontaine, but there is not one of them who understands them.' Children retrieve the wrong moral, if any, from fables; in the story of the fox and the crow, they despise the crow, but admire the fox.

'Reading is the scourge of infancy, and almost the sole occupation which we know how to give them.' In the twentieth century this is doubly untrue; but Rousseau had in mind the school texts of his own generation. Books suited to children scarcely existed. 'At the age of twelve, Émile will hardly know what a book is.' Before reaching ten, however, he will doubtless be able to read and write, because he will have found these arts of present use, and will have desired to master them. 'Present interest is the grand motive power, the only one which leads with certainty to great results.'

Émile will feel himself free, but it would appear that the freedom is to be merely one of appearance, having no reality in it. 'Let him always fancy that he is the master, but let it always be yourself that really governs.' Everything lies in the tutor's hands without the pupil's knowledge.

According to Rousseau, the caprice of children never results from nature, but from bad training. Let the tutor take notice of the beginnings. 'Our first teachers of philosophy are our feet, our hands, and our eyes.' Children are clad too warmly; Locke is said to contradict himself when he makes reservations concerning the exposure of children to extremes of temperature, or to dampness. The child should be inured to such experiences, and to interruptions of sleep, so that he may gradually rise above the law of nature to which at first he is subject. 'In general, a life of endurance, once converted into habit, multiplies our agreeable sensations, while a life of ease prepares for a countless number of unpleasant sensations.' Émile must be familiarized with perils, properly graduated and shared by his tutor.

Rousseau's discussion of the education of the senses is of the greatest importance, because of its influence upon subsequent educational practice. His fundamental principle is expressed in a single sentence; 'To exercise the senses is not merely to make use of them, but it is to learn how to judge by them; and it is also, so to speak, to learn how to feel, for we neither know how to touch, nor to see, nor to hear, save as we have been taught.'

Fear of the dark, attributed by Locke and others to the nursery tales of goblins and the like, is perceived by Rousseau to have a natural cause. Yet this natural cause is probably not, as Rousseau would have it, ignorance, but instinct. Therefore the advice to play games in the dark, and to take timid children into dark places, is of questionable value. It is clear, however, that darkness may be utilized in training the senses of touch and hearing. Rousseau perceives that surprises are the wrong method to cure timidity. Thus Émile is to be protected against unforeseen accidents; and broken glass will be removed from the track of his little feet.

The boy will practise jumping, climbing, balancing. 'I would make him the rival of a roe-buck rather than the dancer of the opera.' Many occasions will arise to interest him in measurement, such as the following: 'I would make a swing between these two trees; will a rope twelve feet long answer the purpose?' A detailed description is given of how an indolent young nobleman was induced to run races, and to judge distances, without being aware of the intention of his tutor, or of the operation of any other will than his own. All this takes time, but we must, in instructing children, know how to lose time in order to gain it.

The plan of teaching drawing which Rousseau advocated has some elements in common with our present practice. He writes: 'Children, who are great imitators, all try their hand at drawing. I would have my pupil cultivate this art, not exactly for the art itself, but for rendering the eye accurate and the hand flexible; and, in general, it is of very little consequence that he understands such and such an exercise, provided he acquire the perspicacity of sense, and the correct habit of body, which are gained from that exercise. I shall take great care, therefore, not to give him a drawing-master who will give him only imitations to imitate, and will make him draw only from drawings. He shall have no master but Nature, and no models but objects.' The tutor is to begin as awkwardly as the pupil. But does Rousseau imagine that an intelligent pupil can be deceived into believing the tutor to be his equal in unskilfulness? Probably not; he merely insists that the tutor shall descend to the pupil's level, a sound principle within reasonable limits. The better the drawings the plainer should be the frames, so that Émile may aspire to ideals of simplicity and modesty.

The treatment of geometry in the *Émile* was revolutionary in its day; and is now admitted to be sound for young children, if inadequate to that rational mastery of the art which may be expected of more advanced students. Figures will be mechanically drawn, measured, and superimposed, the pupil making his own deductions, instead of learning the demonstration that has been offered by another.

Children are not, as is erroneously supposed, inept in manly exercises. Let them have rackets, balls and court suited to their age and strength, and they may play tennis well. Rousseau points out further that while childish feats of intellect are unreal, on the other hand childish gymnastic performances are what they purport to be. Premature progress of the body is thus less to be dreaded than precocity of mind. It is doubtful, however, whether the former may not sometimes be as undesirable as the latter, for, as Aristotle pointed out, scarcely any cases were on record of Olympic victors winning prizes both as boys and as men.

In speech Émile will avoid declamation, in singing he will practise no theatrical music. He should learn music by ear, always singing to the harpsicord; and from the outset will compose simple phrases of his own. He will be rewarded for simple physical feats, such as winning a race, by cakes or other concrete gifts; but should not be stimulated to a noble deed by a merely corporeal reward. He will not become a glutton; he may easily be interested in other pursuits than eating; any such tendency, moreover, will naturally disappear at adolescence, when all food is agreeable to the palate, and when other interests prevail.

Thus has Émile been educated from the age of five to twelve. He has grown quite naturally, as a child should grow; but now his period of labour, of study, and instruction begins—the most precious period of his whole life.

At this point indeed it may be observed that Rousseau draws an unjustifiably sharp line between the period from five to twelve years, during which the faculties are ripening; and the period from twelve to fifteen years, during which they are to be exercised in intellectual labour. He assumes that the mind shall first be given a form, and afterwards a content. Such a separation is both illogical and impracticable; but if it be assumed, as it should be, that Rousseau has heightened the contrast merely to give a sharper point to his suggested reforms, there is less to be said in criticism of his theory. The critics of Rousseau commonly fail to perceive that his sweeping epigrams are not intended to be taken with literal exactness. How many wise maxims could survive so rigorous a test?

The remainder of Rousseau's argument may be briefly summarized. From twelve to fifteen Émile is in possession of a surplus of faculties and powers, beyond what are needed to satisfy his moderate desires. He is now, apparently, to make up for the time that has been lost, though well lost, during his childhood. He begins the study of geography by observing and recording the rising and the setting of the sun. He maps the locality in which he lives. He learns gradually to give continuous attention to the same subject. He becomes interested in electricity and magnetism by observing the tricks of a juggler at the village fair. He proceeds in science by making discoveries in situations prepared for him. Simpler phenomena gradually lead to higher generalizations. He finds the need of understanding the compass by being lost in the forest. He begins to ask the use of everything; and is at no time repelled by discursive explanations. He still confines his attention to what he sees. He reads only one book, *Robinson Crusoe*, which shows in a wonderful way how one natural need after another is satisfied. He enters workshops and takes part in the work which happens to be going on. He knows no laws except necessity; he has still to study mankind. For the present he attends chiefly to agriculture, forge work, and carpentry, in that order of importance. He develops the habits of inquiry, resourcefulness, and foresight. He learns the simpler uses of money, but not its abuses. He picks up much information by conversing at table about the objects which are utilized. He understands exchange and economic interdependence. In fact, he knows the universal laws which govern human society, of which, however, he is still but a spectator. He learns also a trade, not an accomplishment, but preferably the trade of a cabinet maker. Thus mind and body are exercised in conjunction. His habits are now formed for the best; his knowledge is purely physical, and may amount to little, but it is his own.

After fifteen is the age for Émile's moral and religious education. He must now perfect his reason, and must study mankind. His rising passions are not fed by needless information; but his questions are answered simply and truly. He is already affectionate, if not conventional. He beholds the simple life of the country rather than the exotic practice of the city. He learns that man is naturally good but socially depraved. If necessary he may be permitted to become the victim of confidence men or sharpers. He should be instructed by fables rather than by rebukes. Interest him in good deeds rather than in the abstract apprehension of the virtues. He loves the poor, and tries to reconcile quarrels among his social inferiors. His beneficence must above all be put into action. As yet he knows nothing of religion; even now, according to the Swiss reformer, it may be too early to teach him about his soul; it is necessary that he should rise from the study of Nature to the search for its Author. The critical moment must come at last, when instead of being protected by his ignorance he must seek protection in his reason. It will be time for him to learn about individuals, and he will need a companion, whom he should love before beholding. This also is the period for Émile to read good books. His fitting companion is Sophie, a girl possessing a love, happiness, and innocence equal to his own. Sophie is not to be brought up in Paris, but in a kind of conventual retreat, wholly irreconcilable with the theory of education according to nature, and therefore inconsistent with our writer's own fundamental principles. In fact, the account of Sophie's education is almost oriental in its advocacy of seclusion, and negates the standards of liberty which have been so carefully safeguarded for Émile.

IV

REVOLUTIONARY THEORIES OF HIGHER EDUCATION

THE Encyclopaedists and Rousseau were at one in criticizing the existing order of things, but they did so from very different standpoints. For Rousseau, civilization was an evil; but because it was a necessary evil, there might be a kind of negative function for education to fulfil, even in the protection of the individual from social temptations. The Encyclopaedists, on the other hand, attacked existing conventions not as contravening nature but as contrary to reason. They heartily believed in civilization as such. 'I venture to affirm', writes Diderot, 'that purity of morals has followed the advance of clothing from the skin of the beast to the robe of silk.' [1] Especially did they believe in the value of positive educational instruction. 'The glory of literature is the foundation of all other glories.' [2]

The most influential and celebrated of the contributions of the Encyclopaedists to a theory of education is the 'Plan for a Russian University' drawn up by Diderot (1713–84) in response to the invitation of Catherine of Russia (1776). Diderot begins by a general statement of the importance of civilization in general and literature in particular. He finds that earlier writers had seen well enough the vices of the times, but not how to remedy them by education. Above all they had neglected the sciences, and the need of their enfranchisement. Again, they had been too preoccupied (Diderot speaks only of French writers) with ecclesiastical ends.

'Rollin, the celebrated Rollin, has no other aim but to make priests or monks, poets or orators; that is the aim! . . . But what is the (true) aim?—Eagle of the University of Paris, let me tell you, it is to give the sovereign zealous and faithful subjects, to the Empire serviceable citizens; to society educated, honorable, and even lovable individuals; to the family good husbands and good fathers; to the republic of letters certain men of good judgment, and to religion edifying, enlightened, and peaceable ministers.' [3]

What is a university? Diderot answers:

'A University is a school whose door is open without distinction to all the youth of a nation, and where masters salaried by the State initiate them into

[1] 'Plan d'une Université pour le Gouvernement de Russie.' *Œuvres*, Bruxelles, 1829, vi, p. 182. [2] Ibid. [3] Ibid., p. 184.

the elementary knowledge of all the sciences.'[1] It should be open without distinction, because 'the number of cottages and other individual residences being to that of palaces in the relation of ten thousand to one, the betting is a thousand to one that genius, talents, and virtue will spring rather from a cottage than a palace.'[2]

Diderot finds that the order of the curriculum depends on capacity and use. That comes first which is suitable and needful for all, in whatever state of society they be; then, as some drop out, comes that which has a utility a little less general, but such as is suited to those who remain.[3] Diderot draws the logical conclusion, venturesome enough in his day, that the knowledge of Greek and Latin, as concerning only the few, should be postponed to near the end of the university course.[4] The university course of instruction, according to Diderot, is simply a continuation of the elementary curriculum.[5] This, he adds, will not make men superficial; it will make them or tend to make them in time profound.[6]

Diderot would establish preliminary requirements. At home or in the private schools (*petites écoles*) the child should have learned to read, write, and spell his mother tongue 'courageously', and to know the rudiments of arithmetic. Not age, but understanding, should regulate admission.[7]

Again, Diderot would divide the ideal university into four faculties, arts, medicine, jurisprudence, and theology. The arts course will be the most general or universal. In arts, then, there will be three parallel courses.[8]

'The first course, divided in eight classes, comprehends the mathematical sciences, the natural sciences, the logical sciences, and rhetoric. The second course, divided in two classes, comprises the first principles of metaphysic, morality, natural and revealed religion, history, geography, the first principles of economic science. The third course is only composed of one class where drawing and the principles of architecture are taught.'

To these courses Diderot would add various other courses of training, but that he feels the hopelessness of the attempt in the face of all custom and tradition. That he even mentions them in connexion with a university is sufficiently remarkable.

'It is not customary in universities to teach music, dancing, fencing, riding, or swimming. If these accomplishments, which distinguish *le galant homme*, the

[1] Ibid., p. 185. [2] Ibid. [3] Ibid., p. 188. [4] Ibid., p. 187.
[5] Ibid., p. 193. [6] Ibid. [7] Ibid., p. 196. [8] Ibid., p. 197.

man of the world, from the pedant, have so little importance in our eyes that they are never introduced into any public institution, it is doubtless one of the consequences of the inveterate defect of our monkish education.' [1]

It is not, however, in the direction of fashionable accomplishments alone that the university curriculum suggested by Diderot has its revolutionary side.

'I have yielded ridiculously to custom, and I must have been strangely swayed by routine, not to include the school of agriculture and of commerce, the two most important pursuits of society; the art which gives bread, wine, nourishment; which furnishes the primary requisites to every industry, to the consummation, to the traffic between citizen and citizen, and to the exchanges from society to society.'

In the scheme of Diderot as above outlined there will be noticed the following tendencies which, through Jefferson, Chevalier, Quesnay, and others who were instrumental in carrying French ideas across the Atlantic, came to modify profoundly the American theory of a university education.

(1) A confidence in humanity in which the influence of Rousseau is discernible.
(2) A confidence in civilization which contrasts with the views of Rousseau.
(3) A confidence in the moral power of education.
(4) An unprecedented stress upon the sciences, without depreciation of literary culture.
(5) A desire for the complete emancipation of the intellect from all external control.
(6) A lively mistrust of ecclesiastical interference.
(7) The wish for a state system of education.
(8) The widening of the curriculum.
(9) The democratic principle of the education of talent wherever found.
(10) The notion of parallel courses, leading naturally to a principle of freedom in the student's election of studies.

What was the existing condition of the university organization which Diderot thus proposed to reform? It seems probable that the origin of the University of Paris as a school of theology and perhaps medicine may be referred to the time of Charlemagne, and may date

[1] 'Plan d'une Université pour le Gouvernement de Russie.' *Œuvres*, Bruxelles, 1829, vi, p. 197.

[2] Ibid., p. 198.

about A.D. 800. Students who flocked to the university became by the twelfth century divided into nations. The four *nations* of France, England, Picardy, and Normandy united during the fourteenth century into a faculty of arts. The first organized faculty was theology (1259), and theology with medicine and law gradually aggrandized themselves at the expense of the nations, who still, however, having four votes against three, controlled the office of Rector of the university. From the thirteenth to the eighteenth century there went steadily on a process of endowment of colleges, which gave places of retirement to the students and stability to the university.

Especially during the earlier period of its existence, the University of Paris was mainly under the control of the secular clergy. The regular orders only gained a footing with the establishment of the faculties. The vigour of the mendicant friars, in the face of many restrictions, soon gave them a powerful hold on the university. At a later period the Jesuits after a long struggle succeeded in founding colleges and lecturing in the Sorbonne, but were expelled by Henry IV. During the seventeenth and eighteenth centuries the university suffered no vital changes, down to its dissolution in 1792.

Apparently, the French Revolution made as sharp a break in education as in the social, political, and religious order. In each of these departments the eighteenth century had witnessed an admirable speculative advance, especially in the writings of the encyclopaedists, but changes in theory had had no visible effect upon the stagnancy of concrete institutions. But with the revolution France, or rather Paris, tried to make a new world without using the material of the old. The first thing was to tear down what had already been built up. Yet, as might have been expected, when the University of Paris destroyed in 1792 was replaced in 1808 by the University of France, there were not lacking evidences of a material continuity. It was proved by the abortive attempts at an entirely new scheme of education, made under the Republic in 1795 and again in 1802, that an absolute break with old educational habits was impracticable.

Never did theory pure and simple have so clear a field as in the earlier years of the French revolution. All that was old seemed bad; all that was new, good. One result of the new way of thinking was a certain amount of temporary unpracticality, but another was an unprecedented stimulus to constructive thought. The abortive efforts at an ideal educational system made by the Convention in 1795, and by the National Assembly in 1802, take on a new importance when one recollects that they were intended to embody the best thought of the encyclopaedists, and that they filled the air with an enthusiasm for education that was soon reproduced in the bosom of American patriots.

In each of the attempts mentioned there may be noticed a tendency characteristic of the encyclopaedists towards a preoccupation with higher rather than with primary education. Other common features are secularity, a broader curriculum, a scientific bent, and a graded eliminating system from the primary school to the university, involving centralization.

According to the plan of 1795, there were to be three orders of schools, primary schools for each canton, a central school for each department, and certain special schools in which were to be taught astronomy, geometry and mathematics, natural history, medicine, the veterinary art, economy, antiquities, political science, painting, sculpture, architecture, and music. The primary schools were to teach the first principles of republican morals, as well as the inevitable arithmetic, reading, and writing. The central school was to include three grades or classes, of which the first was to consist of pupils not younger than twelve years, the second of pupils of not less than fourteen years, and the third of pupils of at least sixteen years. The curriculum of the first class was to include drawing, natural history, and languages ancient and modern; that of the second, natural philosophy, mathematics, and practical chemistry; that of the third, the fine arts, general grammar, history, and legislation. In the whole range of this curriculum the most interesting factor is probably the teaching of civics in the primary schools. It is an index of the liberal and patriotic, if secular and political motive which functioned prominently in French revolutionary thought.

The scheme of 1795 was ill executed; and in 1802 a new system was adopted by the National Assembly. It had been drawn up by Fourcroy, Roederer, and Regnaud. Its principal feature was the substitution of *lyceums* for the central schools. There were to be primary schools, secondary schools, *lycées*, and special schools. The primary schools were under municipal control, but not free, except that poor scholars to the number of one fifth of the total number of pupils might be admitted free. Secondary schools were placed under the supervision of departmental prefects, and not even private schools might be established save by permission of the government.

In the secondary schools were taught Latin, French, and the

elements of geography, history, and mathematics. In the lyceums were taught Greek, Latin, rhetoric, logic, and morals, and the principles of mathematics and of physical science. Each district having a tribunal of appeal had at the least one lyceum, and to each lyceum there were at the least eight professors. At its own expense the State maintained a total of 6,400 pupils in the lyceums and secondary schools, of whom 2,400 were sons of deserving government employees in the army or elsewhere, while the remainder were chosen by examination from the secondary schools, limited only by a population basis for each department. There were also paying boarders and day scholars in the lyceums. Each lyceum was administered by a council of three nominated by the first consul. The first consul also nominated three superintendents or inspectors to visit each lyceum yearly. One or more special schools were attached to each lyceum. Very little attention was paid to primary education. Although the government supported the lyceums, the support of the elementary schools remained dependent on the people.

The law of Napoleon in 1806, creating an Imperial University which was to embrace the whole educational system of the country, has been the basis of all the efforts made at various times during the nineteenth century to promote education in France. The law was put into operation in 1808, and little more than the title of the system was changed under the Bourbons and Louis Philippe. The title *University* is used in no connexion with any special college or set of colleges, but rather indicates the totality of the institutions for imparting education in France.

The weak aspect of the Imperial University Scheme was the comparative inefficiency of primary education, which was only set upon a satisfactory footing by the efforts of M. Guizot in 1834. So far as higher education is concerned, it may be sufficient to add to what has already been said of the tendencies in French education a brief account of the plan of administration of the university, as it was conducted early in the nineteenth century.

The minister for public instruction was president of the university, and authority was centred primarily in his hands together with a council of six. The affairs of the university were administered in two sections, professional and administrative, each of which had its president. The professional section comprised four *bureaux*, the administrative section three.

The Council of Public Instruction already mentioned was aided by a board of inspectors-general having very wide powers, which extended over the whole interior economy of the academies and even of the primary schools. There were twelve inspectors-general, and they divided the institutions among them. The local divisions of main importance were termed academies. Each academy was governed by a rector, was chosen for five years, eligible for re-election, and selected from among the principal office-bearers of the university. Each rector was assisted by a council of two inspectors, acting like the inspectors-general but on a smaller scale. This council, with the rector, superintended the establishments of education throughout the departments embraced within the academy.

Normal schools to train primary teachers were established under the law of Napoleon in 1808, but by 1830 only three were in existence.

There were private *pensions* and institutions which gave a college education, and also colleges supported by many of the communes, which were, however, only compelled to support primary schools. In each academy there was also at least one royal college, supported almost entirely by the government. There were some three hundred communal and fifty royal colleges in the thirties. Of academies there were twenty-six, each covering from two departments upward.

It was, perhaps, rather what was thought and said in France upon educational reform, than what was actually embodied in French institutions, that secured the admiration and imitation of American reformers such as Jefferson. For while something was achieved in France it was natural that speculation should outrun achievement. Accordingly such a document as the report of Condorcet to the National Assembly in 1792 may give a more satisfactory idea of the tendencies in French education that may have influenced America than even the actual history of the 'University of France'.

Condorcet begins with a general statement of the aims of instruction which harmonizes well with the revolutionary thought, and with the preamble of the American Declaration of Independence.

'To offer to all the individuals of the human race the means of providing for their needs, to assure their well-being, to recognize and exercise their rights, to understand and to fulfil their duties.

'To assure, to each of them, the opportunity to perfect his industry, to render himself capable of social functions, to which he has the right to be called, to develop the whole extent of the talents which he has received from nature; and thereby to establish, among all citizens, an equality of fact, and to render real the political equality recognized by the law.

'Such should be the first aim of a national instruction; and from this point of view, it is, for the government, an obligation of justice.

'To direct education in such a way that the perfection of the arts may increase the enjoyment of the generality of the citizens, and the comfort of those who cultivate them; that a greater number of men may become capable of well fulfilling the functions necessary to society, and that progress, always increasing light, may open up an inexhaustible force of help in our needs, of remedy in our misfortunes, of means of individual help and common prosperity.

'To cultivate in short, in each generation, the physical, intellectual, and moral faculties, and, thereby, to contribute to the general and gradual perfection of the human race, the final end towards which every social institution ought to be directed.

'Such ought again to be the aim of instruction, and it is, for the government, an obligation imposed by the common interest of society, and by that of the whole of humanity.'

From the general field of education Condorcet would separate the 'distribution and organization of the establishments of public instruction'. For differences of opinion as to scope need not hinder the needful preliminary step of the establishment and organization of institutions. These are planned under the following principles.

1. Instruction should be universal, so that none may say that in his ignorance he has felt 'not the will of nature, but the injustice of society'.[1]
2. 'It should, in its different degrees, embrace the entire system of human knowledge.'[2]
3. 'No public power ought to have the authority, or even the credit, of preventing the development of new truths, the teaching of theories contrary to its particular policy or its momentary interests.'[2]

Five degrees of instruction are distinguished:

1. Primary schools.
2. Secondary schools.
3. Institutes.
4. Lyceums.
5. The National Society of Sciences and Arts.

In the suggested curricula Condorcet places deliberate emphasis on the substitution of scientific for classical study.

The primary schools are to teach what is needful for all citizens to

[1] Condorcet, *Rapport*, &c., p. 4. [2] Ibid., p. 5.

know, including the elements of civics, such as may fit them for the position of municipal officer, or of juryman. The secondary schools are to carry on education so far as may fulfil the needs of the middle walks of life. They will have a three years' course, while the primary school course is to last four years. The institutes are to fit for public functions and the perfecting of industries. In them there is to be an option of courses to some extent. 'In the institutes, instruction will be divided into several courses, in order that the students may be able to attend two or more of them at the same time, according to their talents and their progress.' [1] The lyceums are to embrace the arts and sciences in all their branches. Finally the national society of sciences and arts is to form a board of control and a sort of republic of specialists.

In this report, which foretells so much of modern educational reform, historians may without difficulty recognize the educational manifesto of democracy, humanism, science, enlightenment, and freedom.

[1] Condorcet, *Rapport*, &c., p. 65.

V

PESTALOZZI AND SENSE-PERCEPTION

ROUSSEAU stood by no means alone in his desire for educational change. Diderot and the Encyclopaedists, for example, aimed at a cultural education of the pansophic type. If England had given the first stimulus to reform, through Bacon, Hobbes, and Locke, it remained for the Swiss through Rousseau, the French through Diderot, the Germans through Lessing and Herder to maintain and carry forward her educational, philosophical, and literary traditions. Rousseau had expressed a democratic and romantic confidence in the original nature of man and especially in human feeling. Notwithstanding the inconsistencies of his thought, few leaders have inspired more followers. Most of these, indeed, found it necessary to qualify his exaggerated and dogmatic opinions, however desirous of progress they might remain. This was the experience of Germans like Lessing and Herder. *The Education of the Human Race*, a short but inspiring treatise of Lessing, takes a broad view; social experience, regarded as a whole or in large fragments, is a divine training meted out to mankind. The Germans of the 'Enlightenment' applied the principles of nature and reason to many departments of life, especially to philosophy, art, and literature. This movement percolated gradually to the schools.

The Pietist movement which, on its educational side, was closely associated with Francke (1663–1727), although Lutheran in character, was to contribute towards scientific education. The Pietists reacted against the 'little popes' who tended to dominate German Protestantism; true religion, they contended, is a matter of the heart. Francke succeeded in establishing an educational foundation at Halle; and this became the centre of Pietist influence. In the Pietist schools more than one-half of the time was devoted to religion. One of Francke's institutions at Halle was the first *Realschule*, established for scientific instead of for classical discipline; a school indeed widely different from the modern *Realschulen*, but nevertheless their pioneer.

It is unnecessary to state that the Pietist movement stands outside the naturalistic impulse which Rousseau had communicated to European thought. The direct heirs of the imaginary tutor of Émile were the Philanthropinists. These Friends of Humanity introduced great enthusiasm, much artifice, and a little chicanery into their attempts to realize a natural education and natural methods of teaching. The 'Philanthropinum' of Basedow was opened at Dessau in 1774. Although this school endured only until 1793, its novel features attracted widespread attention. Utility was the aim; but the method was learning through things, not words. Natural religion replaced the catechism in the Philanthropinist schools. Outdoor occupation tended to simplify the problem of government. If not as non-existent as Rousseau desired, at least discipline was gentle, privileges being granted to the boys according to an intricate system of numerical marks.

It remained for Heinrich Pestalozzi, born at Zurich in 1746 (d. 1827), to attract universal attention to the value and methods of popular education. From early youth Pestalozzi was associated with ideas of political reform, and even of revolution, in Switzerland. He was an active member of the Helvetic Society, which aimed at civic freedom such as Rousseau had suggested in his *Social Contract.* Reared in an atmosphere of poverty, self-sacrifice, and idealism, Pestalozzi turned his attention to the Church and afterwards to Law; but his first active experiment in earning a living was in farming. In this he failed, even though wool-spinning was added to his agricultural activities. Converting his farm at Neuhof into an industrial school, he lived as a beggar among beggars, but although aided by philanthropic contributions this venture ultimately lapsed. The strength of Pestalozzi lay not in organization or administration, but in vision and enthusiasm. Finding a precarious means of support in literature, he produced an important work in 1781, *Leonard and Gertrude.* In this work many of the ideas of Rousseau were improved, corrected, and adapted to the conditions of family life. Yet it could not be said that as yet Pestalozzi had founded any educational system. Later, influenced by the personal encouragement of the philosopher Fichte, he wrote a philosophical treatise which failed of its intended effect, entitled *Enquiries into the Course of Nature in the development of the Human Race.*

Called in 1798 to the charge of an orphanage at Stanz, whither the French army had carried fire and massacre, Pestalozzi devoted himself to his duties in the face of unimaginable difficulties. He was now beginning to understand how human powers develop of their own impulse according to certain laws. The orphanage having been resumed for purposes of a military hospital, he next received a teaching appointment at Burgdorf. Here the definite design shaped itself, to reduce instruction to a psychologically ordered sequence.

In 1800, aided by other enthusiasts, Pestalozzi established an Institute of his own. In the following year, *How Gertrude Teaches her Children*, the most valuable, the most interesting and the least obscure of his educational writings, was published and met with immediate success. For a brief period the reformer's Institute was accorded a measure of national support. He attempted to work out an A B C of observation and of number, in order that elementary instruction might be genuinely founded upon a trained power of sense-perception. The catechetical and Socratic methods of Campe, Salzmann, and other philanthropinists were definitely discarded in the light of this doctrine of Anschauung.

In 1804, political changes unfavourable to Pestalozzi compelled him to abandon his Institute at Burgdorf. After a brief period of association with Fellenberg, the head of a notable industrial school in which manual work played the most considerable part, Pestalozzi established himself at Yverdun, where with the assistance of talented colleagues he was able to demonstrate to an astonished world a system of elementary education so novel, so attractive, and so inspiring that observers from many countries flocked to behold the miracle.

Beneath the surface, however, the Institute at Yverdun was rent by dissensions, which ultimately brought about its ruin. In 1825 it was closed; and the last years of Pestalozzi, to his death in 1827, were embittered by both recrimination and litigation. Yet his work was done; he had not only lived for social betterment, but had shown a new path along which it was to be reached. Both Herbart and Froebel had witnessed and appreciated his efforts. The former was to establish a vastly improved method of primary, the latter of infant, education. They were to provide means for the realization of Pestalozzi's ideals, how the young mind can be trained to help itself, how the inner nature can be improved, how men can be taught to be men. 'He is not a man whose inner powers are undeveloped.'

Pestalozzi's system remained imperfect. He never found himself able to give a logical account of it; and to this defect many of the divisions among his followers were due. Yet some advantage accrued even from its vagueness. Men were compelled to interpret his principles for themselves; and although many criticized their leader, there was none to deny his power of inspiration. Nor could there logically be any rigid Pestalozzianism, as there came to be a rigid Froebelianism and a rigid Herbartianism. It was open to everybody to place upon

Pestalozzi his own interpretation; and, under these circumstances, the influence of the Swiss reformer's object teaching and number teaching radiated throughout both Europe and America.

Holding with Herder that language is a natural rather than a conventional product, Pestalozzi set great store upon names. In this way a new kind of verbalism came to be promoted, even at the expense of the principle of sense-perception. Names were learned so that objects might be connected with them at a later stage, being held in the memory like nets in readiness to catch future experiences. For the purpose of developing their powers, young children were exercised in spelling unmeaning words. Thus the principle of development of faculties was abused for want of reconciliation with the principle of sense before names.

According to Pestalozzi, the inner powers to be developed fall into three groups, the intellectual, the practical or technical, and the moral. Within the last group the religious sense is included. Development is from within, but the inner powers must be used. Objects must be apprehended separately and distinctly, until all vagueness gives place to clearness. Definition should follow a process of observation, comparison, and the abstraction of what is essential from what is contingent or accidental. The gains of sense-perception are held fast by words. Finding that children differed in their rates of development, Pestalozzi organized his classes so that each followed the same subject at the same time, in order that pupils might be advanced according to their respective capacity for progress. 'The nature of the child must determine all the details of his education.'

All steps in education should be graduated, almost imperceptibly, so that the child may grow after the manner of a plant. Continuity should be unbroken. The *Mother's Book*, which appeared in 1803, is only in part the work of Pestalozzi; but its object was to explain to mothers how children may be taught language without a breach of continuity, and in close connexion with sense-perception. The exercises in this book begin by the systematic naming, classification, and description of the parts of the body. Unfortunately, a number of absurdities were allowed to creep into the work. At no time was Pestalozzi able to apply his principles with the consistency of a Froebel, or with the logic of a Herbart; yet without his enthusiastic stimulus the achievements of neither might have been possible.

In harmony with the tradition which had been established by

Rousseau, Pestalozzi would do nothing without the co-operation of the child. 'Let the child use his chalk or pencil freely, assisted and occasionally stimulated by his teacher, but do not force him into directions which do not appeal to him. He will finally become sensible of the need for greater accuracy. At that moment methodical training may properly begin.' Only when the child feels the need of assistance should assistance be extended to him. There should be no mechanical exercises without intellectual stimulus. Interference may be fatal to spontaneity. These principles apply particularly to the development of practical power in physical exercises, music, and manual training.

While the fundamental principle in intellectual education is sense-perception, and in practical education the exercise of inner powers, in moral education it lies in 'subordinating the demands of our intellectual and practical capacities to the higher demands of morality and religion'. Pestalozzi distinguishes between the natural man, guided by his inclinations, the social man, guided by law, and the moral man, guided by principle. The child's dependence upon his mother is the means which leads him towards dependence upon God. The school should continue the life of the family, not replace it. Love and kindness, without any appeal to such easily excited motives as fear or love of praise, will promote purity of feeling and discipline of will. The teacher should cultivate a sense of duty, so that exertion comes to be regarded as neither avoidable nor an evil. Ethical systems are not for the comprehension of childhood; but 'the boy should have an inner feeling for what ought to be, and he should be conscious of moral power'.

While the system of Pestalozzi suffered both from the unintelligent and mechanical applications of others, and from its own inconsistencies and imperfections, it profoundly influenced the elementary schools of Switzerland, Germany, and other countries. It introduced new purposes, methods, and technique. It convinced teachers that the education of the young could be founded not only in theory, but in practice, on a basis of sense-perception.

VI

THE EDUCATIONAL THEORY OF HERBART

JOHANN HEINRICH HERBART, one of the most noted philosophers, psychologists, and educational theorists, was born in 1776 at Oldenburg. As a boy he was talented and precocious, as a mature student scholarly, critical, and constructive. At an early stage he reacted against the idealistic philosophy of Fichte. According to Fichte, mind is the constitutive principle in all things; but Herbart agreed with Kant in maintaining that reality is not ultimately a mental construction. Kant had held that there are real and permanent, although unknowable, things-in-themselves which cannot be regarded as mental constructions of any kind. Because of his postulation of these reals, Herbart is regarded as the founder of the modern school of philosophical realism. Among unchangeable and unknowable reals he included the human soul. While, from his point of view, the soul can have no faculties whatever, it does, like other reals, tend to preserve itself, and this activity towards self-preservation gives rise to appearances which are termed ideas or presentations. These ideas have no ultimate reality, so that from the standpoint of Herbart the mind as we know it belongs to the world of phenomena or appearances, while the soul, which cannot be known, must be regarded as a permanent existence or entity.

The self-preservations of the metaphysical soul appear to have a cumulative effect. Each new presentation or idea is influenced by the preceding presentations or ideas which persist as mental phenomena. Thus the mind, although it consists of phenomena and not of permanent realities, is highly active, and its activities may be studied and predicted in accordance with mathematical and almost with physical principles. From the Herbartian standpoint the mind has no freedom. If really or transcendentally free, how can it be influenced or educated? 'Not the smallest breath of transcendental freedom', writes Herbart, 'must be allowed to blow through ever so small a chink into the teacher's domain!' The skilful teacher, by first studying his pupil's mind and then applying the necessary presentations or ideas in such a way that they will be combined into suitable complexes with pre-existing ideas, can gradually build up that mind according to his own design.

Herbart's assumption that the human will is not free has important consequences for morality as well as for education. If he has ultimately no freedom, a person cannot be responsible for his action. Herbart meets this difficulty by pointing out that although people are not in reality free agents, yet for practical purposes they must be treated as if they were. Good character consists in a certain balance and proportion of the ideas; and morality is a kind of aesthetic revelation of the world. Good character arises from good actions, which in turn arise from well-balanced ideas. This theory invests the teacher with almost unlimited importance, and education with unlimited possibilities. Given sufficient insight into the pupil's mind, sufficient control of the pupil's environment, and sufficient skill in respect of methods, the teacher is able to fashion the pupil's mind and character in whatever mould he may desire.

At the present time, few psychologists and few teachers are prepared to go all the way with Herbart. It is evident that the great German philosopher makes insufficient allowance for differences of hereditary equipment. He is content with an apparent but unreal freedom. He assumes that the mind is swayed by forces as purely mechanical as those to which the modern behaviourists confine their attention. Teachers find themselves unable to do what they like with their pupils' minds. The human intellect appears to be not merely plastic, but highly elastic. No teacher, even though his pupil be constantly by his side, can do all the good, or all the harm, which the theories of Herbart assume to lie in his power.

Yet, with all these and similar defects, both the psychology and the educational theory of Herbart have done yeoman service. In some of its aspects the mind works mechanically, in some of its aspects it shows little or no freedom; and in such aspects the Herbartian system of thought works efficiently and smoothly. Once ideas have been objectified and erected into what are virtually independent existences, they become subject to the Herbartian methods of analysis and synthesis. Under such conditions, they may be formed into complexes with almost mathematical precision. In the field of apperception or association, Herbart has shown better than any previous thinker how desirable complexes may be erected, fixed, and applied to educational uses.

Like his contemporary Froebel, Herbart visited and was influenced by the famous Swiss teacher Pestalozzi. He wrote critical and constructive reviews of two of Pestalozzi's books, *How Gertrude*

Teaches her Children, and an *Idea of an A.B.C. of Sense-perception.* In 1809 he was appointed to the chair of philosophy at Königsberg, which had previously been adorned by the genius of Immanuel Kant. At Königsberg Herbart founded a pedagogical seminary in which numbers of teachers were trained. In 1833, however, he accepted a chair in the University of Göttingen, where he remained until his death in 1841.

Herbart was satisfied neither with the naturalistic education of Rousseau nor with the conventional education of Locke. These two principles, he perceived, must be joined together. Boys at school should read of ideal types such as they themselves would wish to resemble. For this purpose there is no material equal to the *Odyssey.* It is essential that a many-sided interest should be cultivated. But if all minds are to be made many-sided and well balanced, what is to become of individual personality? The answer is that it may still be secured in the act of reflective thought. In order to produce reflective thought a scientific process of instruction will be advisable. The essential steps in such a process will be clearness, association, system, and method. As is well known, the Herbartian school of educational theory has elaborated these processes into five formal steps of developmental instruction—clarifying the pupil's ideas, presenting new information, associating the new with the old ideas in the child's mind, reducing the result to a systematic form, and finally applying it to new uses. Such steps of procedure are not inappropriate to a lesson in which the object is to convey information to the pupil. In many cases, however, the five steps may be applied to the teaching of a single item, rather than to that of a complete lesson unit.

It will be seen that the typical Herbartian method is instruction. Fill the mind with true and right ideas, and appropriate action will ensue. As a method of education, instruction is quicker than experience, and more systematic than intercourse. The content of the mind is emphasized more than its formal training. Nevertheless the instruction must be so applied as to lead to the formation of 'a sober, clear, firm and determinate judgement'. The circle of thought is of fundamental importance. It develops interests which tend to regulate the desires, which in turn produce actions and so lead to the development of character. Thus character is regarded as arising out of the circle of thought, which in turn has been fashioned by instruction. It should be noted that Herbart does not eliminate all direct disciplinary training from education, but his emphasis is upon the indirect method of character-formation through knowledge. In this as in many other directions his methods may be contrasted with those of Froebel.

In the psychology of Herbart, the unit of mental activity is the idea. Realizing that instincts, impulses, and inborn tendencies are more fundamental than ideas, modern critics have tended to react against a theory which would endeavour to found all feeling, interest, desire, and will upon a strictly intellectual base. These great phases of mental life are certainly more than the mere resultant of an interplay of ideas. Yet some of the developments of modern psychology, such as psycho-analysis, the theory of hypnotism, and the psychology of insanity, seem to take us back directly to Herbart. In all fields where the fixed idea is fundamental, the Herbartian psychology affords a valuable clue to the interpretation of many baffling mental phenomena. For, while ideas are not altogether independent entities, they not infrequently take on such a complexion, for all practical purposes acting as forces which attract or repel one another in accordance with ascertainable laws.

VII

PRINCIPLES UNDERLYING KINDERGARTEN EDUCATION

FRIEDRICH FROEBEL, the founder of the kindergarten, who anticipated all that is best in modern theories of 'education by doing', was born at Oberweissbach in Thuringia in 1782. Having lost his mother in early infancy, he was educated by his father and subsequently by an uncle of more genial type, both of them ministers. The young Friedrich was apprenticed to forestry, and afterwards practised accountancy and studied architecture; but began his career as a teacher in a Pestalozzian school at Frankfurt. He seized opportunities of attending university lectures and of observing the work of Pestalozzi closely at first hand. In 1813 he joined in the war of liberation, but without seeing service at the front. Soon after the conclusion of the war Froebel opened his Universal German Educational Institute at Griesheim, transferring it in 1817 to Keilhau. It was a struggling school with ambitious title and aims. With the help of Langethal, Middendorf, and his first wife, he was enabled to maintain the institution until the theories expressed in his writings led gradually to a demand for the establishment of similar schools.

Of Froebel's written works the most significant are the *Education of Man* (1826) and the *Autobiographical Letter to the Duke of Meiningen* (1827). The school which Froebel founded at Blankenburg in 1837 was in all essentials the first kindergarten, although this name, which came to him with the joy of a new symbolic revelation, was not applied until 1840. After a devoted career as chequered by triumphs and disappointments as that of Pestalozzi himself, Froebel died in 1852.

The following is an analysis of the main concepts which, with high vision and inspiration, though not always with perfect clarity or consistency, he wove into the complex fabric of educational philosophy. To many who are interested in Froebel, the vague terms nature, self-activity, unity, development, freedom, continuity, play, symbolism, romanticism, idealism, and humanity are more familiar than the definite concepts which he intended to convey.

Nature is an ambiguous term which may connote many meanings, the principal being internal or human nature and external nature or the objects about us. Should human nature be a guide? Probably in three senses it should guide the teacher: (1) Our instincts are the material upon which the teacher works, and the process must to some extent be regulated by the material—as when the artist works in one substance or another; thus the fact that one person's instinct is stronger in one direction than another person's, influences the teacher's action. (2) It is not improbable that human nature includes an original or innate sense of right and wrong; if this be so, then to that extent nature must be our guide. (3) It is probable that instincts have been selected and modified during a long period of past social evolution, that they have a survival value, and are in general helpful to the human race; if this be so, there is a positive ground for respecting and following our inborn nature.

The ancient Stoics taught the maxim: 'Follow nature.' A wise man would school himself to bear things not dependent upon the will without displaying feeling. Only things that depend on will should exercise our minds. The Stoic view of nature identified it with reason. The Christian thought of the Middle Ages, however, mistrusted human nature as corrupt and unworthy, notwithstanding that in the lives of the Saints considerable sympathy with external nature is manifest. In these writings we first find thought for animals. Naturalism, however, only reached its zenith in the eighteenth century with Rousseau. Rousseau made human nature a guide in education. Naturalism also led to the conception that plants, minerals, and animals furnish a guide or lesson to man. In the past this view has led to the extensive use of animal fables, most of which gave animals the characters of men, and failed to represent animals as such. The naturalism of the eighteenth century, however, looked carefully into the mirror of nature in the hope of discovering a real clue to the understanding of man and of God. 'Let nature be your teacher,' wrote Froebel. He described nature as 'a manifest, a revelation of God'; and again as 'the image, the work of God'. He held that the spirit of God dwells in nature and develops it. Froebel argued further that nature in all its diversity should be seen as a unity (the spirit in nature). The child, he maintained, belongs out of doors. Nature not only forms a bond between teacher and children; but also leads up to the Author of all things. Therefore, children should be led to nature as to the house of God. The eighteenth century emphasized harmony; the nineteenth century strife, evolution; but surely harmony should be secured in the end.

Froebel regarded the mind as essentially original and active. We are born with the natural tendency to do things. We are already endowed at birth with a number of possibilities of power which are not yet realized, but which must be regarded as dependent, not upon experience, but upon some divine or spiritual gift. Our minds are not blank sheets upon which anything may be written. They are not empty. They are not passive. They bring something to experience and do not receive everything from experience. There are two educational consequences: (1) No teacher, even if he controlled the entire environment of a child, can make his pupil's mind exactly what he pleases; the mind is not so much plastic as elastic. (2) It follows that the soul of the child, being to some extent transcendental, or given apart from experience, must be respected, and should be allowed a high degree of freedom.

Froebel's contemporary, Herbart, expressed a very different view of the nature of the mind and of education. Herbart was a distinguished realist, just as Froebel was an idealist. Herbart pointed out that things are not what they appear, arguing that there is no connexion between the character of reality and the character of appearances. The world as we know it consists of appearances which are certainly not realities, because they continually change, and there is no permanence in them. Realities or reals are not known to us, and cannot be known. They have no parts, numbers, or qualities, but when they come into contact something appears. The soul is such a real, and when it comes into contact with other reals something appears which may be called a a presentation or an idea. On the next occasion when a presentation or an idea comes to the mind, the idea already present combines with or at least reacts upon the new idea. It is clear that from this point of view our ideas are simply the product of experience. They are not in any respect free, and the mind brings no activity of its own to experience. It is simply empirical; and there seems no reason why a teacher, if he knew what ideas were already in a pupil's mind, and if he could completely control all the new ideas to be presented to the pupil, should not construct the pupil's mind exactly as he pleased. It is evident that from the standpoint of Froebel education should be a process of development; from the standpoint of Herbart it should be a process of instruction.

Again, Froebel's view of the *will*, namely, that it develops from an original self-activity which is given before experience, differs from that of Herbart, which regards the will as a disposition of certain masses of ideas to prevail. Herbart's concept of the mind is on the whole true as regards the realm of habit, but the mind is more than habit.

Its reactions are not purely mechanical, and it sometimes manifests powers and tendencies so suddenly and spontaneously that they cannot be the result of the mechanical interaction of ideas. In short, the mind at birth is not destitute of all faculties, powers, or categories; but has a certain original self-activity which reaches out in all directions seeking for material to work upon. Herbart's theory is fairly true as regards the normal mental process, that is the association of ideas—similar ideas assist one another, and the mind passes from one state to another because of some common element. The mind, however, sometimes acts or works, not by association (common element), but by response to stimulus, and this phenomenon (response to a stimulus) is better accounted for by the theory of Froebel, according to which the mind is self-active, than according to Herbart's analysis.

Herbartian education implies the presentation of continuous streams of ideas, which are associated and correlated as much as possible so that they may become a permanent part of the mental structure. Consequently the principal Herbartian method is *instruction*. From the point of view of Froebel, however, since the mind naturally reaches out by virtue of its self-activity in search of material upon which it may realize itself, there is little need of direct instruction. What is necessary is the provision of the right environment and the right material to enable the mind to develop freely. The Herbartian mind has no freedom, and Herbart was compelled in accordance with his principles to deny the freedom of the will. Yet if the will is not free, no person can be responsible for his actions. Herbart suggested that we feel as if we were free, and that society cannot avoid treating people as if they were free; yet they are not so. The position seems unsatisfactory compared with the Kindergarten idea of freedom. According to Froebel, the mind is transcendental. Freedom—a power of real choice which does not necessarily follow the course of the strongest stimulus—consequently appealed to Froebel. Freedom is a thing to be respected as a divine gift, and not to be checked or crushed lightly. Freedom in the moral sense does not consist in the mere absence of restriction. Freedom is enjoyed whenever the laws and regulations which we obey are such as we should make for ourselves. The child's mind can develop freely whenever the laws of the school and home are such as it can appreciate and identify with its own will. So obvious was the insistence of Froebel on freedom that for a number of years the Prussian Government suppressed kindergartens.

Herbart relied upon external influences to mould the mind, Froebel upon inner impulse. Thus, for Herbart, the chief educational agencies are experience, intercourse, and instruction, but Froebel would add a more vital than any of these—*growth* or *development.*

The term *Unity*, as used by Froebel, does not imply mere absence of difference. Indeed, apart from difference, unity scarcely has any meaning. If it means anything, it must imply a certain oneness among differences. Unity in this sense may mean oneness of substance. As an idealist, Froebel believed that the only ultimate reality is spirit, so that in this sense there is a oneness of substance as between nature, man, and God. But unity may not imply oneness of substance, but only oneness of origin. From the evolutionary standpoint this is what unity means. Again, unity may be neither of substance nor of origin, but of end. Froebel assumed and believed in three kinds of unity—(1) unity of substance, since all things are spirit; (2) unity of origin, since all things originate from the divine mind; (3) unity of purpose, since all things strive towards a divinely ordained perfection. Never, on the other hand, did Froebel make the mistake of assuming a complete absence of difference. Everything, he held, is separated as a part, yet united in the universal whole. In fact, Froebel regarded the universe as an organism. An organism may be contrasted with a mere aggregate—a living body is an organism—a pile of stones is an aggregate. In an organism, each part contributes towards the life of the whole, while in turn the whole contributes towards the well-being of each part. The parts have necessary functions, and are described as organs, but the essential characteristic of an organism is that it grows, not as an aggregate might grow by additions superimposed from without; but rather from within by virtue of the innate laws of its own being. Froebel insisted that not only living things, but the whole of nature, constitute an organic whole, even inanimate nature standing in a necessary relation to man and to God. From this point of view life is seen to be, not a mechanical construction, but a development, and a development according to certain laws which Froebel held to be essentially the same in nature and in man. Education, then, is not a mere process of adding ideas, as if one were adding stones to a heap, or of filling the mind; but it is the provision of ways and means which will assist the mind to develop according to the laws of its own being.

In the development of an organism it is noticeable that the simplest bodies—those which have fewest parts—have, as a rule, the least unity. Thus the amoeba may be said to have no parts, and may be divided without injury, which means that it has practically no unity.

The higher the organization of a living body, the closer is the unity and the greater are the differences between the parts. Froebel understood this law. Thus he pointed out that individuality should be encouraged, because it tends to promote unity. In describing the curriculum, Froebel speaks of the principle of *Continuity*. This conception implies both sameness and difference. There can only be continuity between ideas which have some elements in common and other elements not in common; just as the continuity of a chain depends upon the fact that part of each link overlaps part of the next, but part does not overlap. It is true that the mind ordinarily moves from one idea to the next by virtue of a common element. Thus an idea composed of the parts A B C may naturally be followed by an idea composed of the parts A D E, owing to a common element tending to reinstate in the mind any idea of which it forms a part. Continuity is the fundamental principle which underlies the association of ideas.

In one sense, play is a reaction from work, and is a satisfaction of the desire of pleasure. To the credit of Froebel, he perceived that in another sense play is the highest phase of the development of the child. It is, he writes, 'A self-active representation of the inner life from inner necessity and impulse'. 'Play is the purest, most spiritual activity of man at this stage, and at the same time typical of human life as a whole.' Play, indeed, reaches the spiritual height of freedom, completeness, and creativeness. As Plato remarked, 'The plays of children affect their obedience to law.' It has been suggested that 'Man is man only when he plays.' Play and work may be justly regarded as expressions of the same creative activity. Between the two lie games. The striking characteristic of the play of infants is that it seeks no end outside itself. The satisfaction is in the process of playing. The games of older children still reveal this quality, but in addition, some end outside the occupation of the moment is sought—usually the winning of the game. What distinguishes work is that the process is performed chiefly for the sake of its result, not for its own sake. The highest kind of work, however, is that in which the worker loses sight of the fact that he is labouring for an external end, and in which he gains satisfaction from the work itself. The problem of the teacher, therefore, is to preserve the spirit of play even in work. The kindergarten offers the means by which work itself may be conducted in the play spirit, which is practically what we call among adults the professional spirit. If there is a distinction, not social, but psychological, between the professional man and the tradesman, it is that the former derives his satisfaction from the actual performance of his work, whereas the latter derives satisfaction from payment or from some other result outside the actual process of his labour. In this sense the term professional may be applied to all such workers, whether manual or intellectual, as discharge their proper functions in a spirit of play and with the abandon of childhood.

The function of the teacher with reference to *free play*, that is to say, play which is not being directed towards any end outside itself, is threefold. The teacher may help the children to realize their own impulses by inciting or encouraging them to play; or, secondly, may encourage those elements in the children's own plays which are good and useful; or, thirdly, may discourage elements which are injurious or improper. Among the moral qualities which play should develop are justice, moderation, endurance, self-control, truth, loyalty, seriousness and concentration, wisdom and circumspection, freedom, consideration for others, determination, perseverance, co-operation.

The origin of play lies in instinct, but the instinct seems to take three more or less distinct forms. Some play appears to be little more than the expression of superfluous energy, as when a colt gambols or a lamb frisks. Some play, however, contains a dramatic element. It is characterized by the spirit of make-believe. Such plays are, of course, closely connected with the imitative instinct. Finally, a third class of play suggests nature's preparation for future life—such as playing with dolls and keeping house, and in general that class of imitations which relate to the future or adult life. The imitative or dramatic or make-believe type of play is instinctive with some of the lower animals; for example, two dogs will pretend to fight. Even the third class of play is suggested by the kitten in stalking and leaping upon a ball. These considerations may account for the origin of play, but the perseverance of children in it is largely due to the desire aroused in them by a pleasant experience to prolong it. In general, Froebel's statement regarding Pestalozzi's system holds good—'Throughout the realm of childhood, play is the mainspring of moral strength.'

Symbolism rests upon the process of the *association* of ideas. Some idea less easily grasped is connected by our mental activity with an object or an idea more easily apprehended. It is well known that the mind apprehends objects present to the senses, especially visible or tangible things, more readily than abstract ideas. Hence symbolism commonly means that abstract ideas are hung upon concrete objects as upon a peg. For this reason religion is full of symbolism. Even philosophy draws its terminology from the physical world. The word spirit, for instance, originally meant breath. Young children are particularly inept for abstract ideas, and are consequently in need of symbolic education. In symbolism the object may not be actually present to the senses, since the image will suffice to arouse trains of association in the mind. Nevertheless, in most cases the actual presence of the *symbol* to the senses makes a more powerful appeal than its mere image. We seldom realize how great is the dependence of our mind upon symbols. All language is symbolic; a word is nothing more than a symbol which may be heard in speech, or seen in writing, and which stands for an idea.

The connexion between the word and the idea which it represents may be conventional or natural; that is to say, people may simply agree that such and such a word shall stand for such and such an idea; or else there may be a natural resemblance between the word and the idea, as in the case of words like hum, buzz, babble, murmur, hiss. This distinction, well known to students of language, may be applied to symbols in general.

Some of Froebel's symbols are arbitrary, depending upon his individual mental associations, and not necessarily shared by other minds; for example, he held that crystals symbolize in a peculiar way the whole life of man. Arbitrary symbols of this kind have little rational value, and appeal little to other minds than that of their originator.

Some of the symbolism of Froebel's gifts is open to objection. It is too individual, too subjective, too romanticist. The symbols most valuable in education are those which do not depend on the arbitrary associations established by an individual mind, but which rest upon general agreement, or convention, or else upon a natural or rational connexion of the symbol with the idea for which it stands. Fortunately, Froebel's symbolism is not wholly, nor perhaps chiefly, an individual or an arbitrary connexion.

Froebel uses the natural symbolism of dolls to represent the ideas of family life, or the actions of the mother-plays to represent various types of occupation. Nor does he neglect conventional symbols, such as those of language, but he constantly strives to find a natural ground of association beneath the thick layers of conventionality. Thus symbolism may be classified as either—firstly, individual or subjective; or secondly, conventional (proceeding from mere agreement that it should be so); or thirdly, natural. Froebel constantly sought natural symbolism, which is the essential characteristic of the highest poetry and art, and which marks the romanticist temperament. Sometimes his natural symbolism is beautiful and helpful, as when he missed the lily in the beautiful garden. Natural symbolism is employed in the best fairy tales. Such symbolism is not subjective, but objective; it is not merely read into a thing, but is suggested by the thing itself. Objective or natural symbolism becomes far more important to the teacher if, like Froebel, he believes that nature is simply visible spirit. The idealistic philosophy saw in natural objects something that suggested spiritual meanings, because the objects themselves were spiritual. For this reason Wordsworth regarded nature as essentially symbolic; for this reason Tennyson held that to know fully the flower in the crannied wall is to 'know what God and man is'. Whatever point of view may be adopted, however, it cannot be doubted that symbolism is a natural activity of the child mind, which sees in the broom-stick a horse, and in the heap of sand a castle. In education we should adapt our symbolism to the child mind. For the child, child symbolism; for the adult, adult symbolism. In focussing their imagination upon the future—in representing the activities of their seniors in simple concrete forms—children are the unconscious vehicles of social ends.

Not only in literature, but also in such arts as painting and sculpture, a distinction may be drawn between the classic and the romantic. Even in philosophy, religion, and other fundamental branches of human interest this distinction to some extent holds good. The classic is that which represents what is familiar, but in such perfection that it is beautiful, permanent, and of universal appeal. A classic poem or statue is distinguished by the harmony of its parts, and by the moderation, control, and sense of repose it expresses. The classic tends to become formal, and its imitation, unless extremely successful, is apt to be tame and monotonous. On the other hand, the romantic represents the desire of individuals to find beauty in novel forms and in strange environments. While the classical tends to orderliness and simplicity, the romantic seeks what is strange and bizarre. The romantic expresses individuality. It appeals strongly to certain individuals, and then perhaps only in certain moods; while the classic appeals to all and for all time. Romanticism is an assertion of individuality, and generally takes the form of a rebellion against classical conventions. When conservatism has dominated a period so that imitation becomes its prevalent characteristic it tends to be followed by a romantic reaction. Again, while clearness of thought is a mark of all classic movement, romanticism is distinguished by intensity of feeling.

The period of Froebel witnessed a strong romanticist revival in Germany. Writers like Tieck, the Schlegels, Krause, Schelling, Schleiermacher, and Goethe and Schiller in their youthful period threw off the shackles of customary thought and conservative art, striking out into new paths, and asserting the rights of the individual as against society. Instead of following the old and tried way of reason they wrote by intuition. They expressed their individual thoughts and sentiments. They used bold figures and symbols and lived the life of feelings and emotions. In many respects Froebel, who was familiar with the works of these writers, came under the romanticist influence. His difficulty in expressing his own thoughts, his confidence in himself, his readiness to break with the past traditions of education, his love of nature, his assertion that human nature is intrinsically good, his desire that children should express themselves freely, especially in play, the value he set upon love, his free use of symbolism, his ready identification of the individual spirit with the spirit of nature, his own impatience under control, his determination to find the career for which he was born—all these are distinctly romanticist traits in the character of Froebel. On the other hand, Froebel's outlook was less rebellious than that of pure romanticists. He could appreciate much that is good in classicism. Unlike his great romanticist predecessor, Rousseau, he appreciated order, harmony, unity, regularity of habit, and the value of social institutions, as well as freedom. Thus the modern kindergarten should endeavour to combine the freshness, originality, love, self-expression, spontaneity, love of nature, and richness of emotion which belong to romanticism, with the peace, self-control, moderation, harmony, orderliness, universality, and respect for worthy elements of institutional life (home, church, state) which appertain to the classical order of education.

No doubt it is possible that the ideas which originate from the rebelliousness of an individual against his environment may ultimately take the perfection of form which denotes the creation of a new classic. Consequently the problem of the kindergarten is to reach classical perfection without destroying the romance of the individual.

Froebel was an *idealist* in two senses—firstly from the metaphysical standpoint, since he believed that reality is essentially rational, that nature is visible spirit, and that matter has no existence apart from mind; secondly, in the ethical sense, since he held that all things move towards divinely-appointed purposes. He considered that the process of all life, of all existence, is determined by the end towards which it moves; that just as the seed exists for the tree, so the present exists for a nobler future. He explains the life of children from ends rather than from origins. The child in his view is not to be accounted for by the past history of humanity so much as by the divine spark in human nature which it is the destiny of man to develop until it transforms and elevates the whole range of human nature. The kindergarten has not lost its teleological characteristics. The teacher looks not so much at what the pupil and his origins have been, as towards what he may become.

Froebel shared in the optimism which is a general trait in the character of idealists who regarded nature and man as expressions of an absolute mind (self-conditioned or divine mind). Leibniz had said that this world is the best of all possible worlds. Froebel's optimism was less easy-going than that of Leibniz, but he believed, like other great educators such as Comenius and Pestalozzi, that the result of human development is not a matter of chance, but of beneficent regulation. Froebel, however, considered that human effort and the attempt of men to discover and to co-operate with the divine will is of vital importance. He maintained that the world will not end until man has achieved human perfection.

Character depends, in Froebel's view, upon the realization of the oneness of all things with God. Character is developed by putting forth the best in our natures, which leads to appropriate return upon ourselves. It is realized only in contact with other people. It is given scope for exercise in the great social institutions; that is to say, in the home, the school, the Church, vocation, and the State. Many of Froebel's plays are directed towards the development of character through these institutions.

Froebel's outlook on life was philanthropic, but his love of his fellow man sprang from somewhat different sources from that of Pestalozzi. The latter represents the philanthropist as we generally imagine him—a man of great heart and ready to sacrifice himself entirely to his life-work, for the betterment of mankind. Pestalozzi was, however, unable to give a clear account of himself or of the principles upon which his love was founded. The philanthropy of Froebel on the other hand was an ordered, systematic, deliberate attitude—the result of carefully-reasoned conviction. Thus, instead of throwing himself immediately into teaching, he delayed his choice of a career until he could accurately determine what manner of life would best enable him to fulfil his duty as a human being. He sought to help children to help themselves. He regarded mankind as essentially productive and creative; rather than as the recipient of easily-won favours. He desired to show others how to win the powers of action and expression which had in a measure been denied to his own boyhood. He was not only philanthropic, but also patriotic and inclined even to cosmopolitanism. In his time there was a somewhat premature feeling that the era of wars and of national prejudices was drawing to an end. Thus he constantly refers to man and to humanity, seldom to the nation or to the province. His conception of duty was lofty and in general agreement with the views of Kant and Fichte. The right is right, and no exceptions are permissible. Man's duty is to discover the inner meaning of life, and to act in accordance therewith.

VIII

WHAT KNOWLEDGE IS OF MOST WORTH?

COMING from a family of teachers, though his own experience in the art was limited, Herbert Spencer (1820–1903) added to his distinguished philosophical works four notable essays on education, in which the classical traditions of the English public schools were boldly challenged. While Spencer's preference for scientific studies led him sometimes to unjustifiable extremes, there can be no doubt that his influence upon educational thought was both broadening and beneficial. As Leslie Stephen indicated in his *Life of Sir James Stephen, Bart.*, the traditional humanism of the schools at which the leaders of English society were educated had tended to degenerate into an inexcusably trite verbalism. 'Balston, our tutor,' wrote Stephen, 'was a good scholar after the fashion of the day, and famous for Latin verse; but he was essentially a commonplace don. "Stephen major," he once said to my brother, "if you do not take more pains, how can you ever expect to write good longs and shorts? If you do not write good longs and shorts, how can you ever be a man of taste? If you are not a man of taste, how can you ever be of use in the world?" '

This passage, prefixed to one edition of Spencer's four essays, which first appeared as magazine articles, expresses admirably the pitiful degeneration of those humanistic ideas of education which Europe had inherited in a more worthy form from the pioneers of the Italian Renaissance. It was the sweep and grandeur of Spencer's concepts that exercised so profound an influence upon the course of social philosophy, and to a mind of such a mould the pedantry of the Balstons of the day was unendurable. Spencer raised the question of the school curriculum in a striking and definite form in his famous essay, *What knowledge is of most worth?*

The contention of Herbert Spencer was that learning had come to be regarded as a decoration, an ornament, comparable to the useless trinkets beloved of savages, rather than as a philosopher's stone to be applied to the practical problems of life. 'We are guilty of something like a platitude when we say that throughout his after-career, a boy, in nine cases out of ten, applies his Latin and Greek to no practical purposes.' But people feel that they must conform to public opinion. A boy must have 'the education of a gentleman'. A girl must have 'accomplishments', dancing, deportment, the piano, singing, drawing and it is thought ladylike to have a knowledge of French and German. Deference is paid to the opinion of others, rather than to the intrinsic value of knowledge.

It is evident that many of these generalizations may be effectively answered. Latin and Greek originally dominated the curriculum for their usefulness, since all literature of value once was confined to those tongues. Nor are women's accomplishments to be lightly undervalued, even from a practical standpoint. But Spencer realized that it was something almost new even to raise the question of relative values in connexion with the subjects of the curriculum. Yet obviously the question must be raised. The individual has but a limited time in which to acquire knowledge, how may it best be employed? This is a problem not to be solved without a standard. The standard proposed by Spencer is the bearing of the subjects upon life, how they conduce to human welfare and happiness, in short, how far they may be useful. 'To prepare us for complete living is the function which education has to discharge; and the only rational mode of judging of an educational course is to judge in what degree it discharges such function.'

Proceeding in this way Spencer finds it expedient to classify the principal activities of man.

'They may,' he writes, 'be naturally arranged into:

1. Those activities which directly minister to self-preservation;
2. Those activities which, by securing the necessaries of life, indirectly minister to self-preservation.
3. Those activities which have for their end the rearing and discipline of offspring.
4. Those activities which are involved in the maintenance of proper social and political relations.
5. Those miscellaneous activities which fill up the leisure part of life, devoted to the gratification of the tastes and feelings.'

In the opinion of Spencer, the activities indicated above are arranged in something like their true order of importance, so that physiological norms precede psychological, while psychological standards precede literary and artistic values in their significance for human life. It is assumed that on the whole the aim is the good of the individual rather than that of society. Self-preservation, industrial efficiency, parentage, citizenship, and culture represent a scale of activities expressed in descending order of significance. Attention must be paid to all; but not an equal attention. Chief attention should be paid to scientific knowledge such as bears closely upon self-preservation, which may be said to have an intrinsic value; less to quasi-intrinsic knowledge, such as the relation of Latin and Greek to our own language; and least of all to 'the tissue of names and dates and dead unmeaning events' that too often goes by the name of history, and has nothing more than a conventional value.

If then self-preservation be the first essential, it follows that the lessons of hygiene must be properly understood and applied. There must be a knowledge of physical bodies, an indisposition to thwart Nature as stupid schoolmistresses do who deny to girls the privilege of the free physical activities in which they would fain engage, an avoidance of those breaches of physiological law which too frequently entail disease and death. There must be sufficient scientific information to enable the individual to heed Nature's warnings through sensations of fatigue, satiety, and the like. 'We infer that as vigorous health and its accompanying high spirits are larger elements of happiness than any other things whatever, the teaching how to maintain them is a teaching that yields in moment to no other whatever. And therefore we assert that such a course of physiology as is needful for the comprehension of its general truths, and their bearings on daily conduct, is an all-essential part of a rational education.' It seems strange to Spencer that men who would blush to misplace the accent in Iphigenia have not the least shame in admitting that they do not know where are the Eustachian tubes or what are the functions of the spinal cord.

Although this not unmerited reproach is now in a measure removed from education, it remains true that industry, one of the main concerns of every form of civilization, is to a great extent ignored in the curricula of secondary schools, and is not yet firmly established as a primary-school subject. To this great omission in the plan or chart of civilization which a sound course of study should represent, Herbert Spencer was the first to call critical attention. In the main, however, he was content to emphasize the value of mathematics, mechanics, physics, chemistry, astronomy, geology, biology, and social science as sources of prosperity. From a modern point of view the most progressive part of his analysis is the somewhat indirect suggestion that not only these sciences but the forms in which they are practically applied should become the objects of school study. It is not quite clear, for example, whether Spencer fully intended to anticipate the most advanced modern theory by implying that the applications of chemistry, such as bleaching, dyeing, calico-printing, smelting, sugar-refining, gas-making, and soap-boiling should be investigated in their broad industrial aspects by school pupils in the manner desired by Sanderson of Oundle. He certainly foresaw that under modern conditions a degree of scientific knowledge cannot fail to become more and more necessary to every one; and that, in particular, the schools cannot afford to neglect the fundamental principles of physiology and of psychology, so necessary as a preparation for the duties of future parenthood. The school must systematically teach the laws of life.

Without wishing to deprecate their value Spencer felt compelled to relegate the enjoyments of nature, literature, and the fine arts to a position of minor importance. These are regarded as conducive, but not as essential, to human happiness. Architecture, sculpture, painting, music, and poetry are the efflorescence but not the first condition of a civilized life. Our educational system 'neglects the plant for the sake of the flower'. Although modern languages may give refinement, polish, and éclat, although a classical education may conduce to elegance and correctness of style, and to an improved taste, yet these, which are accomplishments of leisure, should be regarded as belonging to the leisure part of education. The aesthetic life is subsidiary to the economic. Moreover, even for purposes of education in the fine arts, there is need of science at all points. Not that science can make artists, but 'Only when Genius is married to Science can the highest results be produced'. Moreover, Science herself is far from unpoetic. 'Sad, indeed, is it to see how men occupy themselves with trivialities, and are indifferent to the grandest phenomena—care not to understand the architecture of the Heavens, but are deeply interested in some contemptible controversy about the intrigues of Mary Queen of Scots!—are learnedly critical over a Greek ode, and pass by without a glance that grand epic written by the finger of God upon the strata of the Earth!'

Spencer's answer to the question, 'What knowledge is of most worth?' is Science. Science not only underlies all that is best worth while in life, but it trains the memory in a causal and not in a mechanical way; it cultivates powers of judgement, constantly exercising the individual reason; it exercises sincerity and perseverance, and encourages true religion and virtue. With Huxley, Spencer fought a hard but winning battle for the place of science in education. If in his eloquent pleading he sometimes overstated his case, or failed to do justice to humanistic traditions and to the fact that it is not the origin but the end of life to which education must direct its most ardent endeavours, yet the modern world has come to realize the force of his contention that Science had been kept too long 'in the background, that her haughty sisters might flaunt their fripperies in the eyes of the world'.

IX

ANATOLE FRANCE ON CHILDHOOD

ANATOLE FRANCE, humanist, academician, littérateur, has drawn a whimsical portrait of his own boyhood. In what he calls *The Book of My Friend* his early years are projected upon an invisible screen and regarded with the eye of the mind. The friend is himself under the pseudonym of Pierre Nozière. The boy is reared in surroundings not unfavourable to the growth of genius. His mother who, indifferent to all questions of scholarship or of higher criticism, was yet a woman of refined taste and sentiment, contents herself in a limited circle of ideas, and refers indifferently to all countries beyond Europe as 'The Islands'. What might have proved a narrowing influence is corrected by the intellectualism of his father. Papa Nozière is a doctor, who, in his zeal for anthropological research, is tempted to leave little Pierre almost exclusively in his mother's care. Yet by conversation at table and on the other occasions, the learned doctor prepares his young son for a philosophic life. The foibles of the parents are indicated only by the lightest touch and serve to make them human; but Papa Nozière appears to have had a moderate susceptibility to female beauty, while Madame failed pitifully to grapple with abstract questions. The father supplied the qualities of the head; the mother those of the heart.

The author claims to remember his early childhood, but in fragments. His earliest recollections include those strange apparitions which often herald the approach of sleep. Entreaties, tears, embraces, and a chase ending in his capture like a rabbit under some piece of furniture, are essential to putting Pierre to bed. Thence he presently beholds a procession of strange monsters, soon to be conquered by the profound sleep of infancy, but vivid enough to be reinstated in the mind of the middle-aged writer. The dreams of children are strange. Some of us can remember the very complicated nocturnal adventures which we had with bears on the house-tops before we were seven. Pierre, like ourselves, was destined to be a child of imagination.

Infants make judgements as well as pictures. Having already begun to dislike a visitor who pays court to a lady in white (Pierre's next-door neighbour), the child resents the man's suggestions that he should be sent home to his mother. A milder exile befalls him; he is told to wait in the next room. For a time he contents himself, but soon begins to peep and to listen, finally opening the door in time to save the lady from very unwelcome advances. Little Pierre comes out well even from his less creditable adventures.

By day, while his mother sat at her work-table, the child would play at her feet with a puppet and a sheep that had three legs, although, unlike the freaks in his father's collection, it had once possessed the full enjoyment of its members. These toys represented the actors in a thousand curious dramas. Whenever anything interesting occurred to one of them, Pierre would call his mother's attention, but she showed far too little interest. It was her great defect. But his mother had a way of calling him *petit bêta*—little ninny—which made amends. Once, lifting him up in her arms, she showed him one of the flowers on the wall-paper, saying: 'I give you this rose.' To recognize it, she marked it with a cross. No present, according to Anatole France, ever made him happier. Is not a sacred niche reserved in every temple of education for love and sympathy?

Most young children feel secure and confident in the omnipotence and benevolence of their parents. On the other hand, their trust in strangers is diminished by many stories which they hear of fact and fiction. Pierre was impressed by the picture and story of the murder of the Princes in the Tower. Having to accompany his mother on a visit to an old friend of the family who lived in what was reputed to to be a tower, although in reality a house, he was seized with emotions of terror. Evidently he was to be murdered. There was some consolation in playing with Finette, a little dog that would surely bark if the murderers approached, just as the dog of Edward IV had given the alarm in the picture. Pierre's thoughts hopped from one thing to another, like birds from twig to twig, until he found himself able to pluck his elderly host by the sleeve and say: 'You know, Monsieur Robin, if Mamma had been in the Tower of London, she would have prevented the wicked uncle from stifling the children of Edward under their pillows.' It appeared to Pierre that Monsier Robin failed to grasp this thought in its full significance; but his mother, when they were alone, called him *monstre* and embraced him.

Another adventure of Pierre is even more typical of childhood. He was prone to envy the washerwoman's son Alphonse, who roamed the streets, paddled in the gutters, and was not constrained to say good-day to people in whose days, good or bad, he felt no interest whatever. Alphonse was at liberty to play freely with the sparrows that he caught, with stray dogs, and even with horses until the driver flicked him away. Pierre went out one day to Alphonse in the courtyard, and was promptly set to carry paving-stones. Snatched up by his nurse and washed, he was informed by his mother that Alphonse had been badly reared; that it was not his fault, but his misfortune. Pierre's attitude towards Alphonse changed rapidly from admiration to pity and terror. The good little Abel pitied the unfortunate Cain. Was there anything he could give him? Suspecting that a flower or a kiss might be unacceptable, he thought of his horse *sans* mane or tail; but such a gift appeared decidedly excessive. Pierre solved the problem by lowering a bunch of grapes to Alphonse by a thread. Abruptly snatching both grapes and thread the washerwoman's son made a derisive gesture and took to his heels. The parents of Pierre, not altogether displeased at his action, commented that one must give one's own property, not what belongs to others.

The lessons of childhood come from many and varied sources, not all of which are controllable. To a certain young lady, a young lady who lifted him up and examined the colour of his eyes, Pierre ascribes the first delicious torments of beauty. With her two arms she opened as it were the infinite world of dreams.

The mother of Pierre used to read to him frequently from the Lives of the Saints. His active young mind dwelt upon martyrdom and to a greater degree upon the practice of austerities. In distant imitation of St. Simeon Stylites he mounted the kitchen sink; but was not permitted to live there as long as Simeon on the top of his column. When he showered his little possessions upon the poor, his father called him an idiot and closed the window. Indignant at so profound an injustice, Pierre found consolation in the thought that his father, not being a saint like himself, would not share with him the glory of the blessed.

Just as St. Jerome and St. Anthony had retired among the lions and the Egyptians, so Pierre also decided to become a hermit. After careful deliberation he selected the Jardin des Plantes as the only desert in which his simple economic necessities might be satisfied. His mother demanded the reason of so strange a resolve. 'I wish to be famous,' replied the child, 'and to put on my visiting-cards: Hermit and Calendar Saint, as papa puts on his: Laureate of the Academy of Medicine and Secretary of the Anthropological Society.' Dropping the comb with which she was doing his hair, his mother declared that he had lost his reason before gaining it. 'At seven he wishes to be famous!' But his father, less perturbed, prophesied that by twenty he would be disillusioned with fame.

As to forsaking the world, Anatole France confesses that he has been daily tempted to this course, but each time Dame Nature takes him by the ear and leads him back to the routine occupations of our humble existence.

To a certain Monsieur Le Beau Pierre owed the awakening of an interest in the things of the mind. M. le Beau was very old when Pierre was very young, conditions which led to a good understanding between them. The old collector, cataloguer, and scholar died when the boy was but twelve. From his example the lad determined that one day he would have proofs of his own to correct, a vow in which he did not fail.

With the death of his grandmother, a crowd of new experiences visited Pierre. Taken to the house of mourning, with which he was already familiar, though he understood nothing of death he felt that it was indeed serious. Everything about him seemed to centre upon this event. For the first time he remarked the beauty of the trees, the mildness of the air and the brightness of the sky. It was a shock to find the well-known little garden and summer-house unchanged. The birds were singing. In the house Pierre saw and embraced the dead. Beside him he heard his mother sob. Then an old servant took him away to a toy-shop and said: 'Choose.' He chose a catapult and spent the rest of the day firing peas into the green leaves. He had forgotten his grandmother. But at a later time the thoughts of the morning returned.

Now all this is education. These are the things that matter in shaping the beginnings of life. The latter part of life depends upon the earlier, although sometimes a character, through the rapid waxing or waning of instinct, may appear to have undergone a reversal. The experience of love and confidence, the habit of benevolence, the soaring flight of imagination, the exercise of taste, the awakening of spiritual yearning—these are of infinitely greater importance in education than the method by which one endeavours to learn subtraction. What shall prevent a Pierre Nozière from becoming an Anatole France?

The most remarkable portent which had attended the birth of Pierre was the simultaneous birth of Puck in the next room. Pierre's father was reluctantly compelled to admit that of the two, the dog grew more rapidly in intelligence than his son. Even after six or seven years, Puck surpassed Pierre in respect of intuitive perception and the knowledge of nature. It seemed almost a reflection upon the faculty of reason, which we like to assume to be the special prerogative of man.

Pierre's father was metaphysically inclined, in theory an optimist, but grave and melancholy in his disposition. Pierre, on the contrary, became a pessimist, but a joyous one. Like the romantic school as a whole, Dr. Nozière loved what is vague and indeterminate. Pierre for his part preferred a refined rationalism and the beautiful symmetry of classical art. In time, without disturbing harmonious relations, these differences tended to make conversation a trifle difficult. As to Pierre's mother, she was endowed with more feeling than strength, tender to a fault, unwilling to let him grown up, happy in the belief that his mind had need of hers, convinced that he was always in danger when not at her side. Pierre endured many reproaches; but gradually built up for himself a rather indulgent code of conduct; a fact for congratulation, if we adopt the view that none but those who are kind to themselves are likely to be kind to others. The suggestion is worthy of our amiable cynic.

While still unable to talk, Pierre found himself picked up and embraced, with transports of emotion, by a little girl, Alphonsine, who was seven years older than himself. Being a domestic animal, like other domestic animals Pierre appreciated the praise which wild creatures disdain. But alas for human nature! The perfidious Alphonsine stuck a pin in his legs. The more Pierre struggled, fought, and cried, the more was he blamed as an unnatural child. His unintelligible babblings explained nothing. The incident, moreover, was repeated on a number of occasions. Alphonsine was ultimately forgiven; had she not advanced Pierre greatly in the knowledge of the world?

Pierre's mother gave him a sweetmeat, the appearance, odour, and taste of which delighted his senses. Some days later, smelling the same odour, he asked for more. When Madame Nozière insisted that there was none in the house, Pierre remained stubborn, reproaching his mother for misleading her little boy. The fact is that the odour which he had recognized was not peculiar to the sweetmeat. But by the reproachful eyes of his mother Pierre was soon convinced of his error. Thus for once did the heart clear up an error of the intellect.

Children long for appreciation. Gradually they learn that it is not invariably forthcoming. Even genius frequently suffers injustice. While engaged in drawing soldiers on paper, Pierre made a momentous discovery. He found that by using two parallel lines instead of one line to make an arm or a leg, an appearance of reality could be produced. He had in fact achieved a revolution in art, without pausing to consider whether it had ever been effected before. Exulting in his triumph, he laid the new drawings before his mother, who failed lamentably to notice the reform. Pierre attempted to snatch away her book; but was forbidden to touch it with his dirty hands. His mother could still see nothing of note; she chided him for a nervous child, and put him to bed. Imagine creating an enormous advance in art, a really marvellous means of expression for the human spirit; and for one's only reward, to be put to bed!

As a little child Pierre venerated animals with an almost religious awe. Whether or not they were the first gods recognized by mankind, they obviously surpassed him in sureness of intelligence. He would have extended his respect to the parrot Navarin, had the latter permitted. But Navarin repelled his advances with beak and claw. Pierre went so far as to offer the bird the largest lump of sugar he could obtain by stealth. Navarin promptly seized Pierre's finger, bringing blood, to the vast discomfiture of his benefactor. Henceforth, there could be only war between the child and the parrot. The boy teased the bird, but reaped a dire retribution when the parrot sprang upon his head and plucked out clawfuls of hair. Pierre was informed that parsley is a deadly poison to parrots. He secreted a supply of the herb, took satisfaction from threatening Navarin with it, and ended by extending his magnanimous clemency to his enemy, whose punishment should not be death, but life. Relations between Navarin and Pierre now ceased to be strained. They became friends.

After he had been taken to a large store, Pierre began to play shop by himself. He set himself to buying, wrapping, and delivering, playing customer and saleswoman in turn. But one difficulty beset him, concerning which he consulted his mother. 'Mamma, in the shop, is it the one who sells or the one who buys that gives the money?' His mother declared this to be not merely a 'howler', but a trait of character Pierre would never know the value of money. He tells us that he never did; or rather, that he learned to know money too well as the source of social evil. He looks forward wistfully with William Morris to a time when craftsmen shall produce their masterpieces not for pay, but for love.

At five years of age Pierre learned to mistrust the gifts of fortune. He wanted a drum. It was not that he wished to be a drummer;

his preference was for being a general. Being no stoic, he made his desire known to those who had the means to satisfy it. But no one would give him a drum; his mother, because Dr. Nozière disliked noise, his aunt, because she was parsimonious, and thought besides that he ought to play with the Noah's Ark which she had given him some time before. But the animals in the Ark had begun to shock his sense of proportion, as the butterflies were bigger than the elephants; and then, most of the animals would not stand on the three legs that were left to them, and Noah's staff was broken. The drum which Pierre made for himself of a butter-dish and a spoon was ruthlessly taken away. At last, however, to his great astonishment and delight, his mother gave him a drum and sent him out with his nurse, and the injunction *Sois sage!* With his drum he marched ahead, proudly leading an imaginary army to certain victory over a discomfited foe. At the same time Pierre began to suspect that the drum had been selected for its lack of sonorous quality. This, however, could be made good by the imagination. Alas, Pierre returned from the walk to find his father and mother both missing. They had gone away for a week, leaving Pierre in the care of the nurse. How he blamed himself for having failed to observe the omens which should have revealed this insidious plot! In his chagrin Pierre deliberately smashed the drum. Later in life, when he would fain have sought the drums and cymbals of public favour and reputation, he has reflected upon the price of fortune's gifts, and desisted from his desire.

Being an only child and playing much by himself, Pierre learned to solace the ennui of lying in bed by the composition of dramas. The Greek tragedy, as Anatole France remarks, sprang from the chariot of Thespis. The drama of Pierre had a humbler origin. His actors were his five fingers. The thumb became a strong, ignorant, violent, brutal sort of fellow, a veritable Caliban. The index was weaker, yet quick and brave; he had no equal for snatching a child from a burning building and restoring him to his mother. The middle finger was the tall, handsome, elegant hero; the fourth a beautiful lady who played all the female parts. The little finger was a boy, or occasionally, if the plot demanded it, as in the story of Red Riding-Hood, a girl.

Both tragedies and comedies were enacted by the united company. Pierre had none of Lamartine's horror of buffoonery; but his comic situations were simple, without irony. At the age of six an improvement was attempted. The actors must be given eyes, nose, and mouth; they should be dressed, and a stage and scenery should be added.

Alas, the attempt to adorn the drama brought about its ruin. The source of inspiration was dried up. All that the drama really needs is greatness of action and fidelity of characterization.

Without following the recollections of Anatole France through a number of minor episodes, let us follow Pierre's chase of a fugitive parrot. Pierre learns from his old nurse that the Countess Michaud's parrot has escaped. Rushing to the window, the child observes a group of people standing below, who gesticulate and point upwards. Soon Pierre's grandfather joins him at the window. 'Where is the bird?' he inquires. 'There,' replies Pierre. His grandfather still fails to see the parrot, as indeed does Pierre, who has affirmed the bird's presence on the authority of others. Pierre repeats with delight in a sort of chant the term *papegai*, which his grandfather has applied to the bird; it was an old form of the word perroquet, found in Rabelais: *Gai camme un papegai*. Pierre was much taken with the name of Rabelais, now heard for the first time, but without any intuition of 'the sublime buffoonery, joyous humour, folly wiser than wisdom' for which it stands. The child's mother questions whether parrots really are gay? The grandfather suggests that we presume the bird's natural gaiety, since *papegai* rhymes with *gai*, and what can be brighter than a parrot's plumage?

Presently Pierre, perceiving the bird on the guttering, raises a wild cry of triumph. Ultimately the family departed, enjoining him to do his lessons. But the powerful demon which governs his thoughts frequently forbids him to learn his lessons, setting in their stead various arduous tasks of surprising diversity. This time the demon keeps him at the window, watching the *papegai*. Of this pastime he was beginning to grow weary when a man entered the room, bearing ropes and a variety of gear. The newcomer, Monsieur Debas, excelled at every kind of business but his own. Pierre knew him as the keeper of a stall. M. Debas specialized in catching stray birds; and regarded the return of the Countess Michaud's parrot as an imperative duty. That elusive bird soon disappeared; and the onlookers below could be heard as they voiced their opinions of his probable course. Would he go into the garden, associated with the forests of Brazil? Would he dart from steeple to steeple, or perish blindly in the Seine? Might he even return to his owner? Acting on the last assumption, M. Debas hastened towards the apartments of the Countess, followed closely by Pierre.

Having arrived, they mounted until there were no more stairs, but merely a ladder leading to a trap-door. With half his body protruding, M. Debas called the bird by name; but this device failing, he proceeded to imitate the parrot's own harsh cry, in case it might be preferred to the human voice. Intermittently he offered civic and moral advice to Pierre, who could see nothing but his legs and gigantic back. The advice ranged from how to blow one's nose in company, to one's duties towards the Supreme Being.

Long hours passed, and evening had begun to descend, when the parrot reappeared. M. Debas held a tit-bit at arm's length, speaking in an ingratiating tone the while. The bird's repartee was simple but effective; he spread his wings and flew away. 'There!' cried M. Debas with Napoleonic brevity. Pierre was entranced. Placing the boy on his back, M. Debas carried him boldly through the streets of Paris in hot but blind pursuit. The recollections of the Homeric incidents which followed became blurred in Pierre's mind; they included a vision of naked figures suspended in every variety of posture in the sky. Probably, through the half open door of the School of Fine Arts, he had obtained a glimpse of a copy of Michelangelo's Last Judgement.

The chase was in vain. Pedestrians whom they accosted advised the hunters to put salt on the bird's tail, or to scratch his head. In dejection they returned at last to the apartment of the Countess Michaud, to find the parrot at home on his perch. The ungrateful creature turned his round eye upon them, opened his beak and hissed savagely. An elderly servant, seated at table with the Countess, remarked: 'He would have returned sooner if you had not frightened him.' The visitors were not detained; the only comment of M. Debas, as they went downstairs, being to the effect that they had not been offered any form of refreshment.

It was night when Pierre returned to find his home in consternation. Vainly did he assure his mother that he had encountered no danger. While desirous of soothing her alarms, Pierre wished also to display his strength and courage. He depicted scenes which included mounting ladders stretched over the void, climbing walls, grasping pointed roofs and running along gutters. Gradually the fears of his mother were appeased; she ended by laughing at him, he had gone too far. And when at last he referred to the naked figures suspended in mid-air, no doubt the truest part of his narration, he was rebuked and sent to bed.

There is a limit to informal education; and the time comes for Pierre Nozière to go to school. The matter is debated by his parents.

According to his father, it is necessary for the child to be apprenticed to social life. Rolling the tooth of a prehistoric *homo* between his thumb and forefinger, Dr. Nozière presently abandons the subject of schooling in order to deliver an eloquent and profound address upon the debt which mankind undoubtedly owes to his primitive ancestors. Although these ancestors responded only to hunger and fear, we owe to them both science and love. 'With science and love the world is made.' By this time, immersed in abstract considerations, Dr. Nozière has forgotten his son altogether. 'Doubtless,' rejoins Madame, 'but the more I reflect, the more I am persuaded that it is to a woman that a small boy of the age of our Pierre must be entrusted.'

Pierre spends his first day at school mainly in looking at his teacher. She appears sad. His next neighbour, the little son of a lawyer, calls him a fool because he cannot see that a lawyer's profession is better than that of a doctor. The children are riotous: they throw things at one another until the teacher enters the mêlée with the air of a somnambulist, and punishes some innocent victim. For six weeks the task of Pierre is to write a meaningless line on a slate. He is touched nevertheless by a little romance which the teacher relates; and which his simplicity believes to be true. Doubtless, Pierre intimates to the teacher, the misfortunes of Jeanne, the heroine of the tale, are the cause of her own sadness. The teacher, irritated, declares the story of Jeanne to have been a fiction. Pierre is no wiser, not knowing the meaning of fiction, until his mother explains that a fiction is a falsehood. Presently his parents decide to remove him, deeming the story of Jeanne, the hamlet, and the bells poor food on which to nourish a young boy's mind. Dr. Nozière has his own system of pedagogy, according to which Pierre should study the habits of the animals which he resembles in appetite and intelligence. His mother prefers a course in hero-worship; Pierre should learn the noble actions of great men.

Together with Fontanet, his intimate chum, Pierre is sent to a large grammar-school, entering with humility the preparatory eighth, if ever there existed so low a class. The imagination of the two boys is fertile, and their ambition gigantic. With these qualities, fortunately, their executive ability is by no means commensurate. They begin by making armour of the wrappings of chocolate. Then they establish a museum. In another moment they have decided to write a history of France from the earliest times, with full details, in fifty volumes. They never get past the legendary King Teutobachus. 'How often', adds Anatole France, 'on the point of beginning some great work or conducting some mighty enterprise, have I been stopped short by a Teutobachus commonly called fate, chance, necessity!'

At school Pierre holds in great awe the master of his form. What a disillusion when at the annual prize-giving he beholds that master crowded into obscurity on the platform, until he is fain to disappear altogether behind a flag in the corner. To think that a man who so excelled in flowers, poetry, and devotion should have been so ignominiously suppressed! Other lessons were gradually learned by the son of Dr. Nozière from his classmates. The fine old portfolio which Pierre carried to school moved his playfellows to ridicule and assault. Its only demerit was unfamiliarity. Whenever Fontanet saw the portfolio he would sit on it; Pierre would retaliate as soon as he was able by jumping on the cap of Fontanet. Both articles were indestructible. But one assault provoked another by inexorable fate, like the crimes of the Atrides.

Pierre, while he hated the grammar of a certain Coquempot, which falsely claimed to teach the mother tongue, profoundly appreciated the classics. One of his masters, who at an earlier stage of his career had been a Franciscan friar, although himself a man of timid nature, revelled amazingly in antiquity and especially in ancient wars. Even when he might pause in his exposition to administer a merited penalty, the tone of the master's voice remained heroic. Anatole France preserves a specimen of his harangue.

The Last Words of Decius Mus: 'About to devote himself to death and already pressing with his spur the flanks of his impetuous charger, Decius Mus turned for the last time towards his comrades in arms and thus addressed them: (If you do not keep silence better, I shall inflict on you a general detention.) I enter for my country's sake on immortality. The gulf awaits me. I shall die for the safety of all. (Monsieur Fontanet, you shall write out six pages of grammar.) Thus has decided, in his wisdom, Jupiter Capitolinus, the eternal guardian of the eternal city. (Monsieur Nozière, if, as it seems, you keep on passing your work to Monsieur Fontanet to copy, as he generally does, I shall write to your father.) It is just and necessary that a citizen should sacrifice himself for the common safety. Envy me, and do not weep. (It is stupid to laugh without reason. Monsieur Nozière, you shall be kept in on Thursday.) My example shall live among you. (Gentlemen, your laughter is an annoyance which I will not tolerate. I shall inform the head master of your conduct.) And I shall behold, from the bosom of heaven, opened to the Manes of heroes, the maidens of the Republic hanging garlands of flowers at the foot of my statue.'

To laugh under a hail of impositions is a pleasure indeed. Yet Pierre was in his way a good little humanist. He loved and appreciated *belles-lettres.* He remained obstinately attached to the classics. 'You may call me an aristocrat and a mandarin; but I think that six or seven years of literary culture give to a mind well prepared to receive it a nobility, an elegant strength, a beauty not to be obtained by other means.' Aided by Livy, his classical master inspired in Pierre the most sublime dreams. Every time that he heard how the remnant of the Roman army gained Canusium under cover of night, he saw that harassed and broken army pass by in silence in the moonlight, and his heart leaped in his breast with admiration and grief.

Being a day pupil, Pierre had certain advantages over boarders. He was not, like them, cut off from public and private life. Nothing, according to Anatole France, makes a child understand the social organization like a street, with its shops and its traders, its dealers and its booths. Moreover, provided the parents be intelligent and good, what an excellent school is the home! If to these influences be added the study of antiquity according to the methods of the old French humanists, what an education is the result! Pierre tasted, in his infant soul, the romantic strength and the grand imagery of the ancient classics. After the dry, meagre fables of Aesop, Pierre revelled in the glories of the *Odyssey*, from which he was unable to tear himself away. Imperfectly as he understood Aeschylus, he owed to Sophocles and to Euripides his initiation into the poetry of misfortune. He suffered many punishments for working outside the course of study. The habit of transcending the prescribed course remained throughout life; is not this the sacrifice which every man of genius makes to the spirit of humanity?

Let us leave the biography of Pierre to be supplemented in other books, and let us turn to a few exiguous chapters about Suzanne. Little Suzanne, who talks to the stars, and who kills the devil, but not for good, when she plays with her black doll, may be supposed to have arrived at an age when her reading must be considered. In a striking and ingenious essay, Anatole France discusses the type of book that should be given to children by way of a present, remembering always that children are poor, and possess nothing at all beyond what is given them.

Should preference be given to books written for children? Experience shows, for the most part, that children exhibit an extreme repugnance for this kind of book. What they want is a revelation of the universe, both real and mystical. Instead of this the writers of children's books force them back upon their narrow circle of knowledge; and weary them by the spectacle of their *enfantillage*. Such writers try to make themselves like children; they become children not according to the precepts of the Scriptures in heart and soul; but in externals only, without innocence and grace. No doubt but they must bring themselves into relation with the juvenile intelligence; but not by playing the fool, or by the clumsy expression of trivialities. The best books for children are the magnanimous, forceful, and meaningful creations of a noble genius, whose well-ordered parts contribute to a luminous whole. Children are enchanted by a good translation of passages of the *Odyssey*, or by suitable portions of *Don Quixote*. Yet these were written for adults. The greatest classic of childhood, *Robinson Crusoe*, was originally intended for grave London merchants and for mariners of the royal fleet. Into it Defoe put all his art, all his experience, nor is this any more than is requisite to satisfy the intelligence of a schoolboy.

In all such works, however, there must be a drama and actors. The best wisdom of the world is wasted on the young when it is expressed in abstract terms. Of some books it may be said that there is no proper age at which to read them. Anatole France endured one such book; a second might have ruined his taste for literature.

Popular science, unfortunately, is identified by our author with vulgarization. Children are being given scientific books for fear that their minds may be spoiled by poesy. The fairy tales of Perrault are reprinted only for artists and booklovers. Illustrated catalogues of children's gifts attempt to beguile them with pictures of crabs, spiders, cocoons, and gas plants. They are discouraged from being children. Beauty of form, nobility of thought, art, taste, humanism, all these ideals are banished. What is left consists of chemical reactions and physiological conditions. Having looked at a book entitled *An Alphabet of the Wonders of Industry*, Anatole France exclaims: 'In ten years we shall all be electricians!'

Accordingly the humblest book, provided it inspires a poetic idea, or suggests a lofty sentiment, or stirs up the soul to emotion, is better for children than volumes crammed with mechanical notions. What children need are beautiful tales in prose and verse, tales that move to laughter or tears. They want enchantment; they want dreams.

Let nobody think that the child is deceived into the view that life consists of a series of charming apparitions; but children are readily deceived into supposing, on the authority of Jules Verne, that people can go from the earth to the moon in a hollow sphere. Such travesties of the noble science of astronomy lack both truth and beauty. Society errs in fearing the imagination, without which nothing is great.

The object of this chapter has been to present, not to criticize, the educational theories of Anatole France. The reader is in the happy position of being able to qualify these views in the light of his own experience. Many books written explicitly for children are undoubtedly educative. What of Ballantyne, Kingston, Talbot Baines Reed, the *Swiss Family Robinson*? Even Jules Verne, although no Perrault, had a magnificent and prophetic vision of future events. But the main argument of our author stands; that children seek to enlarge their experience and resent being driven back within it; and that the best children's books are the *Odyssey*, *Don Quixote*, *Robinson Crusoe*, and the fairy tales of Perrault and others, representing simple, strong, imaginative action enshrined in the pure and noble beauty of classical form.

X

BRITISH AND AMERICAN PATHS TO CULTURE

IT is to be expected that the mental cultivation of the American people should show some differences in kind from that of the parent British stock, that it should be a type evolved in accordance with the needs and ideals of a nation newer in the making and more definitely committed to a doctrine of social equality. The differences may be, in part, evanescent. Yet we should not be blind to them; although the increase of population and the effluxion of time may gradually lead to their partial extinction. The United States are not as under-populated or as free of social distinctions as they were. But they have not, at present, the same problems as Britain, and the national individuality of their problems is reflected in the character of their colleges and schools.

It is dangerous to touch upon the subject of national limitations. One may venture, however, to indicate that every theory of culture is likely to possess the defects of its qualities. The most widely accepted view of culture in Britain is, on the whole, an inheritance of tradition. Yet other views of culture are frequently expressed, even in the most conservative centres. The dominant British view, however, is that knowledge should be sought for its own sake, and not for the sake of some practical end outside itself. Mental cultivation thus achieved is mostly highly honoured. The ideal of a liberal education is an old one; a systematic exposition of it may be found in the last part of Aristotle's *Politics*. Liberal studies are those which would be followed by a man of leisure able to make his own choice. Evidently, such an education would not be governed by considerations of utility. 'God bless the higher mathematics', said a Cambridge don, 'and may they never be of use to anybody.' There is in Britain a tacit assumption that utilitarian studies are unlikely to be as productive of intellectual development as those which are followed purely for their own sake, such as literature and philosophy. Hence a certain pre-eminence is accorded to the classics and to the higher mathematics, which, in reverence and admiration, are held up before the most able minds of the young as the ultimate measure of scholarship.

The British theory of a liberal education further assumes the existence of a large leisured class. The British mind tends to agree with

Aristotle, that leisure is better than occupation. Leisure, however, has nothing to do with idleness; it is, on the contrary, the time which a man is free to devote to the things that seem best worth while. The Briton of leisure maintains high standards of culture. The clergy or landed gentry who waste their leisure time are few. Nay there are thousands of humble scholars possessing just enough to live upon who devote themselves to the attainment or to the increase of knowledge in literature, philosophy, history, archaeology, or the fine arts, and who neither expect nor desire to become wealthy or famous. They follow learning, not because it is expedient or useful, but because it is liberal and noble. In these circumstances there are environmental influences upon the young which lead to higher standards and achievements in taste and in critical insight than are likely to be maintained in countries of relatively utilitarian traditions.

But the gain is fraught with some loss; and in the United States the obverse of the medal is revealed. There the tradition of utility has long been the yard-stick to measure education, although utility is broadly and scientifically interpreted. The American with means to live upon does not, and, from the point of view of his countrymen, should not, forsake the field of trade or industry in which he may be fitted to labour. Young men do, upon occasion, rebel against the tradition of economic productivity, but usually in such cases they encounter the opposition of their families and the criticism of their friends. The American, in general, regards the pursuit of culture for its own sake, apart from practical benefits, as a disingenuous substitute for hard work. He believes less in mental cultivation as such than in practical service. A wealthy young American who would devote himself to poetry, philosophy, or painting is scarcely taken seriously in his own country. Men and women, it is considered, may earn a living by such arts, but should not pursue them for their own sake. Culture is thus regarded as a means rather than an end. It is pursued not in an atmosphere of leisure, but in a competitive spirit. There is much to be said for as well as against this attitude, which seems to contribute directly to social betterment, and to involve a profound as well as a practical philosophy.

What then is the British view? According to the Platonic analysis there are two psychological factors in the progress of civilization, the pure reason and the desires and appetites. The British theory of culture exalts the former factor apart from, and often in opposition to, the latter. The reason should be exercised, if possible, upon materials which do not make for the enrichment of the individual or of society in respect of food, shelter, clothing, or luxuries. Such an enrichment is regarded as the function, not of the highest culture, but of technical education, and of industrial and commercial experience. Thus in Britain, other things being equal, a classical scholar is regarded with higher honour in the intellectual world than an engineer. In the public schools and universities minds of the highest quality are directed as far as possible into those fields of knowledge which are to be explored for their own sake, in order that their natural capacities may develop in the midst of an environment that is pure and undefiled by utilitarian considerations.

The British tradition tends to separate culture from utility. In the United States, on the other hand, there is a strong sentiment in favour of a type of mental cultivation which is likely to help to satisfy the appetites and desires of society. Culture is directly rather than inversely related to the economic life. Work is preferred above leisure, even above leisure well used. The ideal of the scholar is not to be reflective or critical, but to be busy and active. From east to west, the American mind is not so much interested in what people are thinking as in what concrete piece of work they may be doing. In the schools various practical activities are rapidly taking the place of recitations, while the philosophy of pragmatism has almost ousted that of idealism from most of the universities.

Sometimes, however, the British and American theories of culture march hand in hand. Provided that an education has been obtained from pure and unmixed motives, British scholars do not object to its application in everyday life, even to industry or trade. It is sometimes maintained that 'Your classical scholar is your best man of business, if only you can get him to attend to business.' Similarly, the American scholar, however anxious to apply his knowledge to useful ends, does not disdain a laborious preparation in the course of which these ends are but dimly seen. Hence in practice British and American culture, although they may be dominated by divergent ideals, meet in an intimate and friendly way on common ground. They can and do co-operate in many fields of investigation. They learn from one another, exploring the frontiers of knowledge in a spirit of true comradeship. On this rude and unmapped terrain they cease to be conscious of any national or traditional limitations.

It is not to be denied that the dominant British view of culture, according to which it is in general the product of leisure, has a tendency to promote an aristocratic outlook on life. Leisure is on the whole the privilege of the wealthier class, although a generous system of of scholarships makes it possible for many of the talented poor to enter that class. Hence culture, in the older and more traditional sense of a liberal education, becomes in part the privilege of those who are not compelled, at least for the time being, to earn a livelihood. In the *Republic* Plato quotes a saying of Phocylides, to the effect that as soon as a man has enough to live upon he should begin to practise virtue. 'Perhaps sooner', is the obvious comment. But the epigram implied that if a man can leave business and enjoy leisure he should take advantage of the opportunity to study what is worthy of study for its own sake. It is in the same vein that Aristotle in the *Politics* declares leisure to be better than work, since in work we pursue what is necessary, but in leisure what is good. If then, a liberal culture, attained for its own sake, is best, and if it cannot be achieved save through leisure, then the prevailing British theory, which is essentially identical and historically continuous with that of the greatest Greek philosophers, stands amply justified.

And yet it is desirable that the whole position should be reviewed. It is indeed evident that circumstances have changed, and that the environment of modern life differs widely from that of the ancient Greek. Industry is no longer a simple process to be understood without any necessity for the exercise of the higher mental powers; and it is even possible that the study of far-flung and highly-organized commercial or industrial enterprises, under modern conditions, may cultivate the reason as thoroughly as the study of literature or music. Moreover, leisure is only made possible by the success of industry; and perhaps this obvious debt may suggest the possibility of a direct rather than an inverse relation between culture and business. Such a suggestion is borne out by other considerations. For otherwise those communities which have enjoyed the most leisure should have become the most philosophical. The South Sea islander, living easily on his simple crop of taro, coco-nuts, and bananas, being endowed with so much leisure, ought, apparently, to be the superior of both the Briton and the American in the life of reason.

If then the non-utilitarian and leisured scholarship of Britain may convey many valuable suggestions to the United States, so also may the practical and progressive culture of the latter country suggest new reflections to British scientists and teachers. In terms of social psychology America regards the faculty of reason not as the natural enemy of the desires and appetites, but as the means of finding satisfaction for them. Culture may sometimes be subordinated to utility, but utility may in her turn promote culture. From the traditional point of view, time devoted to the economic life is lost to a liberal education; from the American standpoint, a liberal education may be attained through and in the economic life. The Briton attributes cultural value to certain subjects, and to specific types of experience; the American expects to find culture everywhere, in industry as well as in literature, in commerce as well as in logic, in transportation as well as in the fine arts. If food, shelter, and clothing can exercise the reason as well as poetry, music, or painting, then the American view is justified. And who shall say that a great captain of industry is the possessor of less highly developed mental powers than a distinguished philosopher? Many who are educated in the knowledge of the world as well as of books entertain the opinion that the intricate industrial enterprises of modern times make the greatest possible demands upon the powers of the intellect, whether to initiate or to comprehend. This may be said for American scholarship, that it has never made the mistake of deprecating the educational value of practical problems in any field of inquiry whatsoever.

It will readily be seen that the partial limitation of culture in England to people of a certain degree of wealth and leisure, although that degree may be far from high, bears a direct relation to the traditional function of the English universities. That function is to provide leaders for the community. From Oxford and Cambridge there has proceeded an honourable and endless line of statesmen, clergy, warriors, poets, philosophers, and artists. Even in modern and democratic days, when the ranks of society from which leaders are selected have been so widely extended, these universities and most of those that are scattered throughout the British dominions aim chiefly at preparation for leadership. The Rhodes scholarships, for example, have no other aim. Now, as the careers of men like Mr. Lloyd George and Mr. Ramsay MacDonald prove, in England the time has gone by when leadership could be restricted to a particular social class, or even to a particular type of education. But it remains as true as ever that certain social circumstances and a certain type of culture are highly favourable to the achievement of leadership in British communities, and more particularly in England herself. The majority of English leaders spring from the middle and upper classes, which possess the conditions of wealth and leisure to a degree sufficient to enable them to pursue the tradition of a liberal education.

Differing as they do in their concepts of culture, Britain and the United States have provided diverse paths to its attainment. In England there are two school systems, or rather, perhaps, the English schools fall into two main types. The public schools are those which educate most of the leaders of the community. There is nothing to prevent some of the leaders who achieve eminence in the political, the commercial, or the industrial world, from rising by sheer force of ability from the schools of the masses. But their path is relatively difficult. For most of her leaders England looks to the public schools. In England, contrary to American usage, this term implies private foundations, open to the public, but not maintained by public bodies, and not subject to the local education authorities erected by the national government. Public schools to a great extent are boarding institutions; they have their head masters and their governors, their houses and their housemasters, their fees and their traditions, their prefects and their modified fagging, their emphasis on the classics and on the playing-fields. At best they produce cultured English gentlemen; at worst, the 'games and grammar prigs' scorned of Mr. H. G. Wells. Their pupils are recruited in the main from the middle and upper classes; but the attendance of poor pupils of talent is facilitated by a liberal provision of scholarships. They rejoice in an old and honourable history, beginning from the foundation of Winchester school by Bishop Wykeham in the days of Richard II. In many cases the founders originally intended such schools primarily for the sons of the poor; and however this tradition may have been reversed the public schools have never lost their democratic tone. Within the public school rank is equalized; duke's son and cook's son hobnob together. 'What is your name?' asked a tall pupil of a new comer to Eton. 'I am the Duke of Newcastle,' was the somewhat haughty reply. 'Hurrah! Here is one kick for being a new boy, and two for being a duke.' Naturally the lesson was not lost on the distinguished member of the House of Lords, who, in later life described the incident in order to vindicate the training value of the public school.

The older countries of Europe, indeed, are almost unanimous in maintaining a dual system of education. A considerable body of opinion in England, France, and Germany, however, favours an attempt at greater unity, such as, on the whole, Scotland has long since achieved. The United States are generally content with one and the same system of schools for leaders and for followers. They have their private schools, they have schools corresponding to the English public schools; but in the main all classes are satisfied to send their children to the common school system of the city or the district. Not only are class-distinctions kept in the background, but it is not considered necessary to equate leisure with culture, or to create a special non-utilitarian atmosphere in which alone true culture may be achieved. It is held that mental power may be cultivated by the study of any subject and amid almost unselected associations. Any loss of unity and continuity is more or less atoned by a gain in the extensity and variety of education and of experience. The same schools prepare for every kind of social intercourse, occupation, and outlook.

Both the British and the American systems of schools have proved successful. The English public schools produce a type that is the envy and despair of others. There is a freemasonry among English public-school men that is irresistible and apparently inimitable, unless it be among the members of American fraternities. But the English public-school man is not as fully at ease among those who have been differently trained. Educated in an atmosphere remote from practical life, he confronts the competition of business and industry somewhat as a stranger confronts a city new to him; but he knows how to live, and he possesses an adaptability that probably springs more from his life in a 'house' and from his experience on the playing-fields than from the curriculum to which his attention has been directed during the period of his schooling. Most of the Americans, on the other hand, are more like one another than an English public-school boy and an English elementary school boy can possibly be; one educated American 'belongs' in society as much as another, however widely the content of their school studies may have diverged from a common standard.

A contemporary English novelist recently explained, in conversation, the theory of the dual system of schools. 'We do not expect,' he said, 'that you, coming from the colonies, or an American, coming from the United States, will have the same school system as ourselves. You have your own system, and we accept you, a product of it, on terms of perfect equality. We should indeed be surprised and almost disappointed if we found that you had precisely the same system of education as ourselves. But for an Englishman it is different. He knows, and his parents know, what is expected of him. He is well aware that if he aspires to be a leader, it is his business to go to a public school, not necessarily to a great or expensive institution like Eton, Harrow, Rugby, or Winchester, but to some school modelled on the type such as is to be found in every part of England. The choice of his school is the choice of his mode of life and intercourse.'

Naturally, in a community with the keen intellectual life of England, such a definite and typical standpoint as this cannot remain unchallenged. It involves an obvious danger of what the Greeks called *stasis*, the setting of class against class, notwithstanding the provision of many scholarships for able pupils of small family means to the public schools as well as to the universities. The challenge is expressed in two ways. Firstly, there are many who criticize and desire to reform the nature of the English public schools themselves. Gollancz and Somervell vainly attempted to enrich their curriculum and to widen their outlook by the introduction of a course in political, social, and economic problems. Waugh, in *The Loom of Youth*, expressed dissatisfaction with the moral training and experience which are, perhaps, their fondest boast. Mr. H. G. Wells, in *Joan and Peter* and elsewhere, found their atmosphere too secluded and too remote from the practical and useful pursuits of everyday life, and especially from applied science. Mr. Bertrand Russell has declared that although the Battle of Waterloo may have been won on the playing-fields of Eton, the British Empire is being lost there. Secondly, the challenge has been expressed in a practical way by the institution of municipal high schools and of modern universities in which conservative attitudes towards culture have been successfully defied.

The critics of the public schools, however, try to prove too much. In the desire to promote reforms, they overreach themselves. They tend to forget two obvious facts: firstly, that these schools have provided admirable social leaders in all walks of life; and, secondly, that the great majority of those who have been trained in them believe that they run on right lines. The best criticism of the public schools will be the development of schools of another type, perhaps the municipal high schools, provided that the latter can be made to produce equal if not superior results in respect of physical, mental, aesthetic, and moral development.

In both the United States and Britain the most obvious paths to culture lie through the schools and the universities. These institutions are used by Britain primarily for the selection and training of her leaders. A special type of school, however, is expected to provide most of the leaders for the community. This is the English public school, the prototype, be it remembered, of what is known in Australia as the Great Public school. In England the call of the public school is imperative. Rarely does the son of a doctor, a lawyer, a clergyman, or a business man of standing attend the schools of the education authorities, formerly known as board-schools, which correspond to what are termed public schools in Australia or in the United States. The board-schools are not for leaders, but for followers.

By contrast, in the United States a very small proportion of pupils, especially of boys, will be found to attend private schools of a type resembling the English public schools or the Australian Great Public schools. The sons and generally the daughters of all, rich and poor, attend the same kind of school, the rural or city school conducted by the local authorities and subsidized by the State. Leader and follower are educated together, and no one can tell which is likely to become which. A certain degree of wealth cannot fail to be an advantage to education, but not such an advantage as in England. The schools and a few of the universities are free to all, without fees, but also in general without scholarship-allowances. It is considered that if elementary or high schools be provided free, the means of attending them for the necessary period can be found, even by the poorest. Poor students of ability frequently support themselves or receive private local aid in order to earn their way through the high school or the college.

It is an experiment which no other country makes, except Scotland and some other parts of the British dominions, this of educating leaders and followers in and through the same set of schools. But, although England may still hold to the universal European plan of maintaining one type of school for leaders and another for followers, yet it must not be inferred that the English public schools and the universities are open only to the well-to-do. The fact that golden intellects may be found among the children of the masses is recognized and allowed for by the provision of an extensive system of scholarships, not so generous as, for example, the Australian system, but sufficient to supplement the body of educated leaders drawn from the classes by another body of educated leaders drawn from the masses. The scholarships provide the means for exceptionally bright pupils to attend both public schools and universities. It remains true, however, that the British system of higher education is essentially selective rather than democratic.

The aim of American education, on the other hand, is not to produce leaders, but to offer to every individual as much education as he is able to profit by, whether his intellectual powers may be above the average or not. The 'over-education' bogy is laughed to scorn. There are very few and often no scholarships to assist students of high ability; but places in free high schools are found for all comers, and State universities may be attended for the low fee of 50 dollars a year. It is no uncommon thing in an American city to find that 70 per cent. of elementary school 'graduates' proceed to a high school of some kind. Many of these high schools would scarcely be recognizable as such in a British community; in rural districts they frequently have but one teacher. Except in the case of older and more conservative institutions like Yale, Harvard, and Columbia, the mere completion of a full high-school course of practically any kind is generally sufficient to admit a pupil to a university. The object is to make higher education as widespread as possible.

It will be at once apparent that the American system is highly democratic. The States spend enormous sums on the higher education not only of leaders but of the masses; and the cost of education per head in such a State as California is fully double that in New South Wales. The cost per head of higher education is moreover far greater in proportion. In fact, in the United States public education is an attempt to give the people everything they want; whereas in British communities it is an attempt to give what is considered good for them. What are the respective results? Exactly what might be expected, that whereas the average cultured Briton may be even more thoroughly educated than the average cultured American, yet the proportion of fairly well educated people tends to be higher in America than anywhere else in the world. Thus the United States seek a well-educated proletariat, and are getting it, whereas Britain seeks a percentage of highly-trained leaders, and is getting them.

It is not surprising to find that as they ascend, the British and the American paths to culture tend to coalesce. At the top, in the ranks of genius, there is no discernible difference between British and American scientists and scholars. On that lonely summit they face the same enchanted forest in a spirit of *camaraderie*. Even at the lower stages of the climb there is a tendency for the United States system to draw upon the English, and vice versa. An increasing number of American pupils is beginning to attend private schools resembling the English public schools in most of their features. Some Americans even send their sons to Canadian boarding-schools conducted on the English system. Universities like Princeton, Harvard, and Yale are veering towards the tutorial system of Oxford. On the other hand the English public school is beginning to be influenced by the wider choice of studies and by other salient features of the American high school; and English democratic sentiment is knocking harder and harder at the door. Nor should it be forgotten that on many matters British and American schools preserve a common outlook, since what is eternal and universal does not need to be acclimatized.

There can be little doubt, however, of the truth of one generalization more. British higher education continues to be very largely a process of discipline, whereas American is mainly a process of instruction. The greatest value of the English public school is considered to be not what it teaches, but how it trains. The 'house', the playing-fields, the team, the minor responsibilities which fall to the lot of the English schoolboy, these things are regarded as of greater significance than the classics and mathematics in which brighter boys are generally encouraged to specialize. It is assumed that the trained mind of the public-school boy will be capable of adaptation to all the needs of life, however remote his school environment may have been from the scene of his adult activities. His classics and his cricket, his prefecture and his school spirit should suffice to enable him to discharge with distinction the duties of a responsible administrative position in India or in the Cameroons.

This disciplinary theory, which underlies so much of the practice of the English Public school, opens, however, too large a subject to be examined fully at the present time. The American high schools attempt much less than the English in the way of disciplinary training. Being day schools, co-educational, and comprehensive in their range of studies, they do not remove boys and girls from life to educate them. They tend to offer whatever pupils or parents want; they give instruction by interesting and sometimes by 'soft' methods of pedagogy; but they let training as far as possible take care of itself. At the same time, one of the chief lessons of modern psychology is that the older disciplinary theory must be radically modified; that it is unsafe to assume, for example, that neatness achieved in writing will entail neatness in dress, or that ability to lead a cricket team is the same quality as ability to govern an empire. Thus, if it be true that the American schools underestimate training and overestimate instruction, it is equally true that the English schools sometimes fall into precisely the opposite error. Thus the future will provide ample scope for new applications of educational thought.

A SELECT BIBLIOGRAPHY

EDUCATION IN EUROPE DURING THE SEVENTEENTH AND EIGHTEENTH CENTURIES

A

Adamson: *Pioneers of Modern Education.*
Archer: (Editor of *Rousseau on Education*).
Barnard: *French Tradition in Education.*
Boyd: *Educational Theory of J. J. Rousseau.*
—— *From Locke to Montessori.*
Davidson: *Rousseau and Education According to Nature.*
Fitch: *Educational Aims and Methods of Pestalozzi.*
Hodgson: *Studies in French Education from Rabelais to Rousseau.*
Keatinge: *The Great Didactic of Comenius.*
Laurie: *Development of Educational Opinion Since the Renaissance.*
—— *John Amos Comenius.*
Morley: *Rousseau.*
Paulsen: *German Education, Past and Present.*
Pestalozzi: *Educational Writings* (edited Green).
—— *How Gertrude Teaches Her Children.*
—— *Leonard and Gertrude.*
—— *Letters on Early Education.*
Pinloche: *Pestalozzi and the Founding of the Modern Elementary School.*
Quick: *Educational Reformers.*
Rousseau: *Émile.*
—— *Minor Educational Writings* (edited Boyd).

B

Andrews: *Institutes of Modern History.*
Bachman: 'Social Factors in Pestalozzi's Theory of Education' (in *Education*, xxii).
Bardeen: 'Text Books of Comenius' (in *Educational Review*, vol. iii).
Barnard, F.A.: *German Pedagogy.*
—— *German Teachers and Educators.*
—— 'John Amos Comenius' (in *Barnard's Journal*, vol. v).
—— *Pestalozzi.*
Barnard, H.C.: *The French Tradition in Education.*
—— *The Little Schools of Port Royal. The Port Royalists on Education.*
Blackwood: *Genius and Character of Rousseau.*
Bradley: 'Pestalozzi, the Teacher of Children' (in *Education*, vol. xi).
Browning: *Educational Theories.*
Buchner: *Kant's Educational Theory.*
Cole: *A Neglected Educator, Johann Heinrich Alsted.*
Comenius: *Orbis Pictus.*
Compayré: *J. J. Rousseau and Education for Nature.*
De Guimps: *Pestalozzi.*
Dobbs: *Educational and Social Movements (1700–1850).*

Duruy: *French Revolution.*
Dyer: *Modern Europe.*
Emerson: *Evolution of the Educational Ideal.*
Everett: 'Life of Rousseau' (in *North American Review*, vol. xv).
Fénelon: *Education of a Daughter.*
Francke: *Social Forces in German Literature.*
Graham: *Rousseau.*
Green: *Life and Work of Pestalozzi.*
Hamilton: 'Henri Pestalozzi' (in *Educational Review*, vol. iii).
Haney: *Lessing's Education of the Human Race.*
Hanus: *Educational Aims.*
—— 'Permanent Influence of Comenius', (in *Educational Review*, vol. iii).
Harris: *Herbart and Pestalozzi.*
Hegel: *Philosophy of History* (Section III, Chap. 3).
Holman: *Life and Work of Pestalozzi.*
Hoyt: *Studies in the History of Modern Education.*
Hudson: *Rousseau and Naturalism in Life and Thought.*
Hughes: *Loyola and the Educational System of the Jesuits.*
Kellogg: *Life of Pestalozzi.*
Laurie: 'Place of Comenius' (in *Educational Review*, vol. iii).
Leitch: *Practical Educationalists.*
MacDonald: *Studies in the France of Voltaire and Rousseau.*
Monroe, W.: *Comenius and the Beginnings of Educational Reform; Comenius' School of Infancy.*
—— 'Comenius, the Evangel of Modern Pedagogy', (in *Education*, vol. xiii).
Munroe, J.: *The Educational Ideal.*
Nohle: *History of the German School System.*
Painter: *Great Pedagogical Essays* (Comenius, Rollin, Kant, Fénelon, Rousseau, Pestalozzi).
Parker: *History of Modern Elementary Education.*
Paterson: *Comenius.*
Payne: *Rousseau's 'Émile'.*
Rabenort: *Spinoza as Educator.*
Richmond: *Permanent Values in Education.*
Rusk: *Doctrines of the Great Educators.*
Russell: *German Higher Schools.*
Schlosser: *History of the Eighteenth Century.*
Taylor: *History of Germany.*
Texte: *Rousseau and the Cosmopolitan Influence in Literature.*
Vostrovsky: 'A European School at the Time of Comenius' (in *Education*, vol. 17).
Weir: 'Key to "Émile"' (in *Educational Review*, vol. xvi).
Williams: *History of Modern Education.*
—— *Rousseau, Bentham, and Kant.*
Wood: *Richter's Levana.*
Wordsworth: *Scholae Academiae.*

ENGLISH EDUCATION DURING THE SEVENTEENTH AND EIGHTEENTH CENTURIES

A

Adamson: *Educational Writings of Locke.*
—— *Pioneers of Modern Education.*
Bacon, F.: *Advancement of Learning.*
—— *Essays.*
—— *The New Atlantis.*
Browning: *Educational Theories.*
Hoole: *Art of Teaching Schoole* (ed. Campagnac).
Kerr: *Scottish Education.*
Knox, V.: *Liberal Education* (1781).
Leach: *Educational Charters.*
Locke: *Thoughts concerning Education.*
——*The Conduct of the Understanding.*
Lyte: *History of the University of Oxford.*
Milton: *Tractate on Education.*
De Montmorency: *State Intervention in English Education.*
Mullinger: *History of Cambridge University.*
Paterson: *The Edgeworths, a Study of Later Eighteenth Century Education.*
Pattison: *Milton.*
Peacham: *The Compleat Gentleman.*
Quick: *Educational Reformers* (English writers before Locke, Locke, Basedow).
Rusk: *Doctrines of Great Educators.*
Watson: *Beginnings of the Teaching of Modern Subjects in England.*

B

Barnard: *English Pedagogy.*
Boyd: *From Locke to Montessori.*
Daniel: *Locke's Thoughts on Education.*
Dobbs: *Educational and Social Movements (1700–1850).*
Edgeworth: *Practical Education.*
Fowler: *John Locke.*
Gibson: *Education in Scotland.*
—— *Locke's Theory of Knowledge.*
Gill: *Systems of Education.*
Hanus: *Educational Aims.*
Hodge: *Locke and Formal Discipline.*
Hodgson: *Rationalist English Educators.*
Johnson: *Old-time Schools and School Books* (U.S.A.).
Laurie: *Development of Educational Opinion Since the Renaissance.*
Lee: *Great Englishmen of the Sixteenth Century.*
Leitch: *Practical Educationalists.*
Macaulay: *Essays.*
Mark: *Educational Theories in England.*
Moncrieff: *A Book About Schools.*

Munroe, J.: *The Educational Ideal* (Bacon, Locke).
Painter: *Great Pedagogical Essays* (Milton, Locke).
Parker: *History of Modern Elementary Education.*
Quick: *Locke on Education.*
Reynolds, Sir J.: *Discourses.*
Richmond: *Permanent Values in Education.*
Steeves: *Life and Writings of Bacon.*
The Schoolmaster: Essays Selected from Ascham, Milton, Locke, Butler, &c.
Williams: *History of Modern Education.*

EDUCATION IN THE NINETEENTH AND TWENTIETH CENTURIES

No bibliography need be offered for this period; but, above all, the works of Herbart and Froebel on Education should be read; and for English education those of James and John Stuart Mill, Thomas and Matthew Arnold, Robert Owen, Newman (especially *The Idea of a University*), Huxley, Herbert Spencer, Ruskin. See also Farrar: *Essays on a Liberal Education* (1867). (The series 'Landmarks in the History of Education' (Cambridge Univ. Press) will be found useful.)

For English education in the nineteenth century, see

Adamson: *English Education, 1789–1902.*
Archer: *Secondary Education in the Nineteenth Century.*
Birchenough: *History of Elementary Education.*
Halévy: *Histoire du Peuple anglais au XIX siècle.*
F. Smith: *A History of English Elementary Education, 1760–1902.*

Twentieth Century (England):

Selby-Bigge: *The Board of Education.*
Dover Wilson (edited): *The Schools of England.*
Board of Education. *The Education of the Adolescent* ('Hadow Report').

Europe:

Roman: *The New Education in Europe.*
Alexander and Parker: *The New Education in the German Republic.*
Hans and Hessen: *Educational Policy in Soviet Russia.*

INDEX

ꞌUE